William Mitchell Acworth

The Railways and the Traders

A Sketch of the Railway Rates Question in Theory and Practice. Second Edition

William Mitchell Acworth

The Railways and the Traders
A Sketch of the Railway Rates Question in Theory and Practice. Second Edition

ISBN/EAN: 9783744727440

Printed in Europe, USA, Canada, Australia, Japan

Cover: Foto ©ninafisch / pixelio.de

More available books at **www.hansebooks.com**

THE RAILWAYS

AND THE TRADERS

A SKETCH OF THE

RAILWAY RATES QUESTION

IN THEORY AND PRACTICE

BY

W. M. ACWORTH

M.A. OXON. AND OF THE INNER TEMPLE, BARRISTER-AT-LAW

SECOND EDITION

LONDON
JOHN MURRAY, ALBEMARLE STREET
1891

PREFACE

"OF the many ways in which common-sense inferences about social affairs"— so writes Mr. Herbert Spencer in his most recent essay—"are flatly contradicted by events, one of the most curious is the way in which, the more things improve, the louder become the exclamations about their badness." Of this tendency of human nature Mr. Spencer gives not a few striking examples. He might, however have found another at least equally striking in the attitude of the English public to the Railway Companies. A generation back the companies did pretty much what was right in their own eyes, and let their will avouch the deed. Speaking even of a time as recent as twenty years back, the most competent of American observers—Professor Hadley—expresses his unbounded astonishment at the "impudence" with which they "openly defied a regularly constituted public authority." And in those days Parliament and the public made a few timorous protests, one or two half-hearted attempts at legislation, and submitted. And now, to-day, when the Railway Companies have learnt the lesson of triumphant democracy, when in every direction they are showing their anxiety to meet and even to forestall the demands of public opinion, popular feeling is running strongly in the direction of substituting for the old English system of legal redress for proved injuries, of Government inspection and publicity, a new system of direct State regulation, of constant and minute interference by a Government department.

The attempt to substitute the one system for the other, not as part of a well-thought-out and deliberately adopted course of policy, but by a series of hap-hazard and piecemeal decisions, can, I am persuaded, only lead to failure and disappointment. It will before long, in my judgment—and an author has a traditional right to be egotistical in a preface—land the country quite unexpectedly in a logical *impasse*, from which there can be no outlet except by State purchase of the entire railway system. Now, I am no foe of Government railways. On the contrary, I believe that in countries with a population less self-reliant than our own such a policy is necessary. In a country with a bureaucracy as well-trained and as well-organised as that of Prussia, it may even be desirable. Nay more, I am not concerned to deny that even here State-purchase might do something to bring up the worst railway services more nearly to the level of the best. But a careful study of the evidence has convinced me that in the long run State control ends in keeping down the best to the level of the worst, and that, taking them for all in all, the private railway companies of England and the United States have served the public better than the Government railways of the Continent or of our Australian Colonies, and—which is still more to the point—are likely to serve it better in the future.

When, therefore, it was suggested to me some months back, on behalf of the Railway Companies' Association, that I should attempt a sketch of the Railway Rates question from the Railway point of view, I gladly complied. The case for the opponents of the existing system has been publicly stated again and again. The Railway Companies have hitherto—unwisely as I think—been content that their defence should be entombed in Blue-books; and the pages which follow — the responsibility for which is of course entirely my own—are almost the first attempt to make it generally accessible to the public. Needless to say, I am not vain enough to imagine that any words of mine can produce an appreciable effect on the decision of the momentous question with which Parliament will be called on to deal within the next few months. Still, if they enable any member, whether of Parliament or of the public, who desires to approach the question in a judicial frame of mind, to see that the Railways have something to say for themselves as well as the Traders, to realise that some of the problems presented for solution are not as simple as they appear at the first glance, my purpose in writing them will have been accomplished.

February, 1891.

CONTENTS

INTRODUCTION

Private ownership and management of railways practically confined to Great Britain and the United States—Possibility of change to system of State ownership—Need for competent criticism of the issues involved—Absence of such criticism here—Contrast offered in this respect by the Continent and the United States—Value of American experience to us—Self-contradictory accusations made against our railways—The complaint of Cardiff that the foreigner is not favoured—Greenock *versus* Liverpool, and Wick *versus* Grimsby—Professor Hunter, M.P., on losing rates 1

PART I

RAILWAY PRINCIPLES

CHAPTER I

COST OF CARRIAGE

Mr. Jeans and the 'exact Cost of Working'—Why precise Figures are unattainable—The demand for Rates based on cost of service—An expert opinion on the point—The items which make up cost of service—Movement expenses—What is a train-load—Station expenses—Fixed charges—American statistics—Interest on capital—Cost of service, if it could be ascertained, no guide in fixing a rate 17

CHAPTER II

EQUAL MILEAGE RATES

Want of logic in the critics—A railway not a carrier's cart—Tolls for the use of the road—The way to put an end to railway competition—The Liverpool traders' demands in theory and practice—Sea competition—Long and short haul—A typical instance—The German 'reform' tariff 35

CHAPTER III

WHAT THE TRAFFIC WILL BEAR

No evidence that the traffic cannot bear the rates—The exorbitant profits of the railway companies—The margin of viability—A principle leading, not to high, but to low rates—Report of the Inter-State Commerce Commission—The consumer more important than the trader—Analysis of train-mile expenditure—How rates, fixed according to what the traffic can bear, first originated—When competitive with sea-carriage—When article carried is of small value—The Delaware oyster growers—How special rates are really fixed—'Group' rates—Exceptional import rates—Using railways as instruments of Protection—A case for the Cobden Club—All loss and no gain—Export rates—A Turkish atrocity 49

CHAPTER IV

WHAT THE TRAFFIC WILL NOT BEAR

Charging what the traffic will bear, a principle widely adopted in other transactions of daily life—Analogies from turnpike tolls, from taxation, from local rates, from professional charges, from brokers' commissions—Whether one portion of the traffic is done at the expense of the rest—Utilisation of bye-products—Joint cost—The extreme difficulty of rate fixing—Experiment the only practical guide—Reductions mainly in low-class traffic—Depriving places of their natural geographical advantages—Some applications of this theory—The Traffic Act of 1888 and special import rates 78

CHAPTER V

WHO SHALL FIX THE RATE?

PAGE

The railway manager as a special providence—Mr. Jeans and the Lancashire and Cheshire Conference on secret rebates—Transportation experts—From the carrier's point of view—Rate fixing not an exact science—A task requiring the constant employment of a large staff—French and American experience on this point—Taxation must be fair all round—Arbitration between rival interests—Irresponsible monopolists—The power of public opinion—Reduction of passenger fares—Competition actual and potential—Two companies may starve where one can grow fat—The West Shore and the 'Nickel Plate' Railroads—The restraining influence of laws and law-courts—Can a more satisfactory substitute be found?—The price at which the French nation has purchased its rights of control—Too late in the day to set up the French half-way house here—Political influences, real or suspected—State interference certain to lead to keeping rates high—Professor Hadley's opinion —Fetching back the age of gold 96

PART II

RAILWAY PRACTICE

CHAPTER VI

SOME EXTORTIONATE RATES

The meaning of the word—The typical trader's attitude—Rates may stop traffic without being extortionate—Indefensible inequalities—Nature's discriminations—Traffic not worth carrying—Actual working expenses—A testimonial from Sheffield—Cost of carriage in case of tea, Bradford woollens, and cotton—The extent of the consumer's interest—Fish Traders' Associations—Where does the money go?—An exceptionally expensive traffic—A labourer's annual budget—The railways, the middlemen, and the public—The traders' dilemma 120

CHAPTER VII

COMPETITION AND COMBINATION

PAGE

Robert Stephenson's aphorism—Practical experience on the question—English rate wars—All loss and no gain—American rate wars—Sir Bernhard Samuelson's ideal as seen in actual operation—The value of fixity of charge—What the American public thinks—What the Inter-State Commerce Commission thinks—What railway experts say—The argument that the advantages of competition in facilities may be bought too dear—The alternative, stagnation—The deliberate conclusion of the Italian Commission—Does the public in fact pay the bill?—Railway business must be looked at as a whole—The paramount importance of speed—The price the foreigner is ready to pay for it—A railway only a shop on a gigantic scale . . . 146

CHAPTER VIII

CONTINENTAL RATES

The secrecy of English railway accounts—The need for ton-mile statistics—Two English amateurs and one Continental expert—Some detailed comparisons of rates, here and on the Continent—Continental facilities compared with English—Time of delivery—Compensation for damage—Station accommodation—Miscellaneous points—Where the Continental stations are—The German *Spediteur*—Is he to be acclimatized here?—A glance at the tariffs of other countries—The Cape, Ceylon, Argentina, Australia—Indian traffic conditions—Where paper comparisons would land us 176

CHAPTER IX

AMERICAN RATES

Magnificent, but mythical, presents—The average American rate—On the basis of Chicago—The result to the American shareholder—The British capitalist and the Farmers' Alliance—Averages meaningless—Extreme instances—Professor Hadley's estimate—American hotel-keeping—The great wholesale secret—American plasticity—The car-load the real American unit—The economy thereby effected—The price paid—Neglect of local traffic—Ruining the American farmer—The action of

CONTENTS

PAGE

Parliament and the Courts here in keeping rates up—Contrast with the American legal decisions—The individual *versus* the public—The cost of terminals in New York and Philadelphia—Carrying capacity of English and American lines—Manufactures and raw produce—Comparative cost of car-load and less-than-car-load traffic—The price paid for safety—The public attitude towards new lines here and in America—Two companion pictures—The tubular-frame car fad—The real question for decision—Some specimen American rates—Rates in the Southern States—A summary of results 204

NOTE ON THE AMERICAN 'EXPRESS' SYSTEM 245

CHAPTER X

WHY ENGLISH RATES ARE HIGH

Some prevalent misconceptions—Rates fixed at the point where the largest *net* revenue can be obtained—Where capital cost does come in—What traffic a line can hold—The Barry Railway and Dock Company—Agricultural branches—Their extravagant cost—The need for further capital expenditure—Full train-loads in theory and practice—Sweeping reductions in passenger fares—Some Great Western figures—Neglected recommendations—Sir Rowland Hill and the Royal Commission of 1865—Canal competition here and elsewhere—Competition by sea—The Liverpool 'plate-way' scheme—The prospect before the American railroads—Rapid rise of expenses—Competition in facilities—A public benefactor 249

PART III

THE PROBLEM FOR PARLIAMENT

CHAPTER XI

THE TRADERS' DEMANDS

The Lancashire and Cheshire version of the Parliamentary history—The report of Mr. Gladstone's Committee of 1844—The Committee of 1846—The Committee of 1853—The Royal Commission of 1867—The Joint Committee of 1872—The

Committees of 1881-2—The history of terminals—In Parliament—In the Courts—The principle now admitted—Its proposed application—Two mutually inconsistent policies—The balance of advantage—Killing the golden goose—The traders' real protection—Terminal charges on a cost-of-service basis—A gigantic mare's nest—Classification—The brand-new 40-class classification—The 'cast-iron' classification—The English and American classifications compared 282

CHAPTER XII

THE BOARD OF TRADE PROVISIONAL ORDERS

Train-load rates—Providence on the side of the big battalions—A judgment of the Inter-State Commerce Commission—Practical American experience—Uselessness of fixed maxima—Professor Hadley's account of the Granger attempt—Extortion not absolute but relative—Maxima fixed by nature better than by Parliament—An illogical position—Mr. Hudson's opinion—Sir Henry Tyler and Sir Thomas Farrer on the question—Other witnesses on the point—The recommendations of the Committee of 1882—The Railway Companies' Consolidation Bills—The Traffic Act of 1888—The untenable position of the Board of Trade—Mr. Facing-both-ways—Wanted, a principle—Existing rates may be justified, but must be reduced—The new truck-hire schedule—The official after his kind—Are the Board of Trade proposals in the interest of the British public?—New railway capital urgently needed—Where is it to come from?—Amateur critics on extravagance of working expenses—Curtailment of facilities—Crippling the smaller companies—Pettifogging reductions—The logic of the Board of Trade position—Symmetry on paper—A solemn warning to all English railways, 'Never reduce rates'—The treatment of the Great Eastern—The outlook for the future 326

APPENDIX A

RAILWAY RATES FOR PROVISIONS TO BIRMINGHAM . . 369

APPENDIX B

DETAILED COMPARISON OF ANALOGOUS RATES IN ENGLAND AND AMERICA 371

THE RAILWAYS AND THE TRADERS

INTRODUCTION

FROM China to Peru—the statement is made in all literalness—the nations of the world have, after somewhat more than half a century's experience, finally decided either that their governments shall own and work their railways, or at least that in return for a generous measure of State support their railways shall accept an equally ample measure of State control. Two countries only are to be excepted—important exceptions without doubt, seeing that between them they contain half the railway mileage and half the railway capital of the world—the United Kingdom and the United States.

Whether or no these two great nations will in the end follow the example of the rest and nationalise their railways, is one of the serious problems of the future. Probably in neither country is there at the present moment any considerable body of opinion convinced in favour of the step, though large numbers, in America more especially—for discontent with private management is much more acute there than here—are prepared to listen to arguments in favour

B

of State ownership, or, if not ownership, supervision and responsibility, with at least benevolent neutrality. But if a step so grave, a step which at one stroke would double the annual budget of either country and add to its permanent civil service five per cent. of the adult male population, is to be taken at all, it evidently ought not to be taken except after full consideration of all the facts involved. And it is in the belief that these facts are less familiar to the public in England than elsewhere that the following pages are written.

No one can be so well aware as the writer of his lack of qualification for the task. "Who then"—said Rasselas, when his guide explained to him what was meant by philosophy—"who then can be a philosopher?" So too one might ask, "Who is qualified to discuss the problem of railway charges from the double point of view of railway profits and public interest?" The man, it may be answered, who can unite in his own person the following characteristics. He must have a thorough training in the abstract principles of political economy; he must have a close practical familiarity with the conditions under which the different industries of the country are carried on; must know for each trade the amount of raw material used, its sources, its cost, the amount of the finished product, its destination, the quantities in which it is consigned, the proportion of bulk to value, the severity of the competition to which the manufacturer is exposed, and fifty things more. For all these matters enter, or should enter, into the consideration of a railway manager in fixing a rate, and the justice or injustice of the rate when fixed can therefore only be properly appreciated by one who is similarly qualified. Then, further, the railway manager must know, as far as it can be known, the cost of working different descriptions of traffic, what allowance to make in each case, according as the distances are long or short, the gradients are easy or difficult, the traffic is all in one direction or fairly balanced inwards and outwards, speed is essential or unimportant, the goods are easy or difficult to handle, and so forth—and on all these matters his critic must be able to follow him intelligently. Last but not least among the necessary items of the *apparatus criticus*, may be mentioned sufficient legal training to appreciate the bearing of the rules as to discrimination and undue preference as laid down by Parliament and interpreted by legal decisions.

Such would be the qualifications of the ideal critic. But in Great Britain, strange as it may seem for a country which gave birth, not only to George Stephenson, but to Adam Smith, one result of our system of private management and consequent lack of publicity is that criticism falls even further short of this ideal than elsewhere. In France or in Germany, where the change of each railway rate is as much an act of State as the imposition of a new or the discontinuance of an old excise or customs duty, railway questions necessarily arouse considerable public attention. The subject is one as to which each citizen may be called on from time to time for his opinion Where a reduction of rates has to be made up, not by reduced dividends at the expense of individual shareholders, but through taxation at the expense of the public at large, the matter is evidently one of practical politics. So, again, if the construction of a new branch line depends upon the political pressure which a local member of the legislature can bring to bear upon the government, his constituency may be trusted to keep their attention fixed on the point. Consequently, in Continental countries, we find that an unceasing and intelligent interest is taken in all railway questions. Professors lecture on the subject of railway transportation to their pupils at the universities, and publish exhaustive treatises which are accepted as classics. A particular railway policy is identified with the name of some prominent statesman—a Depretis, a Freycinet, a Bismarck—and is fought for by his followers with all the science and knowledge which they can enlist in his support.

With us railway literature of a serious kind is, with the single exception of Mr. Grierson's admirably temperate but necessarily partisan work on " Railway Rates," absolutely non-existent. Two illustrations may perhaps be given. In Professor Hadley's well-known work on " Railroad Transportation "—a professor of political economy at Oxford or Cambridge would as soon think of publishing a treatise on grocers' shops as on railways—there is a rough bibliography of the subject.[1] For English railway history readers are referred to the works of Gustav Cohn.[2] Only

[1] *Railroad Transportation, its History and its Laws.* By Arthur T. Hadley, Professor in Yale College, Connecticut. Putnam's Sons, New York, 1886.

[2] *Untersuchungen über die Englische Eisenbahnpolitik.* By Gustav Cohn. 3 vols. Leipzig, 1874, 1875, 1883.

three English authors are named: Professors Sidgwick and Jevons and Sir Thomas Farrer, each of whom, in works dealing with other subjects, incidentally devotes a few pages to railway questions. Take again Mr. Jeans's oft-quoted work on "Railway Problems." Everyone must admire the patience and ingenuity with which Mr. Jeans has collected and elaborated his very interesting statistics; but in discussing problems of such difficulty an author who occupies the position of a pioneer labours under almost insuperable difficulties. And, apart from mere statistics, Mr. Jeans appears only to have been able to find two predecessors in the field from whom to borrow—Nicholas Wood, the last edition of whose work was published in 1831, and Mr. Dorsey, the author of a prize essay, which obtained, as it assuredly deserved, a gold medal from the American Society of Civil Engineers, for a paper demonstrating conclusively that in every single item, from baggage-checks to bogie-trucks, American railways differ from English much as cheese does from chalk.

Continental railway literature is unfortunately of but little use to English students. Not only is it in a foreign language—and the prose of your German professor or Regierungsrath is not as a rule as limpid as that of Lessing or Heine—but also it deals with conditions so different from our own that it is almost impossible to argue from one to the other. Military reasons, which are almost without weight here, are all-important there. Private capital, which is scanty and timorous in the one case, is superabundant and over venturesome in the other. Trade in England is much further developed, more highly organized, more sensitive, more flexible; between all important points there are two if not three competing routes; further, the competition of that great free-trader, the sea, if not actually *in esse*, is always in the background; our government, from the administrative side at least, has much less authority, less prestige, than the governments of France or Germany. It may well be that conclusions which are correct on Continental data would be incorrect if it were sought to apply them here.

There is, however, one country from which we in England can obtain information of the utmost value. That country, needless to say, is the United States. It is true that, there as here, railways are private enterprises; but in the States they are something more. They are enterprises that for a generation past have been managed full in the public view. The reasons for the difference are not far to seek. In the first place railways in this country came merely as an improvement of existing means of conveyance. In America they have been from the outset almost the only means. In the West railways went first, and highways, if they came at all, only followed after. London Road is to this day a main street, not only in Manchester, but in Edinburgh; but it is impossible to imagine a New York Road in St. Louis or Cincinnati. Then, again, America has forty legislatures, while we have but one. The very number of railway bills which are presented to our Parliament every spring prevents any considerable amount of public interest being directed to any one of them. Half a dozen committees are engaged simultaneously in the consideration of as many different bills. Their decisions are announced, but their reasons are never given, and it is not impossible that, if they were, it would be found that committees A, B, and C had rejected bills for the very reasons which had induced committees D, E, and F to pass analogous schemes in the adjacent rooms.

For our English method of dealing with each case *per se* on its merits, whatever may be its advantages, has, especially when the judges are laymen with no general scientific knowledge of the subject under discussion, at least this disadvantage, that the broad principles involved need never be brought out at all, unless it be, which it often is not, the interest of either applicant or opponent to do so. Whatever may be the decision of the committee, only in the rarest instances is it reviewed in the House downstairs. Contrast this system with the American one. The passage of a railway Act, the modification of the railway charter, may be the most important event of the legislative session at Springfield or at Hartford. The matter is dealt with by the ordinary procedure to which public bills are subjected. The newspapers discuss it at length, railway officials and prominent public men are interviewed on the subject. Even the pernicious system of "lobbying" has this advantage, that suggestions are made and opinions expressed to legislators privately which could not or would not be expressed publicly.

But there is much more than this. The railway question in America is tenfold more important than with us. The carriage of goods, except of the commonest and cheapest kinds, amounts with our short distances to such a very small percentage of the total price, that it is only in times when trade is bad that the charges made are scrutinised. In America the rate is a question of life and death. The farmer in Iowa or Missouri may, as happened a few years back, be burning his grain for fuel while his rivals further east in Illinois and Wisconsin are selling it at profitable rates in the Liverpool market. However cheap be the American rate per mile, and however extortionate the English one—let us here assume, for the sake of argument, that the one is four times as much as the other for the same service—it is evident that a thousand half-pence are more important to the man who pays them than fifty two-pences.

There is another reason: the French private, as we know, carries a field-marshal's bâton in his knapsack; in a country where there are no foreign affairs, and no army or navy to speak of, the *carrière ouverte aux talents*, the career which attracts the best intellect of the country, is the railway service. Not only the great fortunes, but the great reputations of the country have been and are made in it. The Presidents of the Pennsylvania Railroad and of the New York Central—the latter of whom is commonly spoken of as a possible President of the United States—are much more important personages than mere Cabinet Ministers. Their movements are chronicled, their utterances are recorded from day to day by the newspapers, most of which print, it may be added, a column or two of railway intelligence in every issue. For all these reasons, and many more which might be given, railway questions have been much more scientifically studied and discussed in America than here, and the public at large is much more familiar with the main principles involved. I offer no apology, therefore, for the fact that in what follows large use is made of American railway literature, which in fulness and value far surpasses anything existing on this side of the Atlantic.

One advantage the American railways owe to the fierce light of publicity in which they live and the consequent enlightenment of the American people on railway questions. With all their faults, and they are neither few nor small—one might carry the famous quotation further and add that hatred itself can deny to American railway management no title to glory except virtue—American railways are seldom pilloried for crimes which they have not committed. The English railways are often tried and convicted on each of two mutually inconsistent counts at the same moment. Here is an instance. If there is one charge whose heinousness has impressed the public mind more than another, it is that our railways have " favoured the foreigner," that, in the words of the report of the House of Commons Committee of 1882, " imported produce is given a bounty over home produce by being carried at a lower rate. . . . That the export trade enjoys rates which are preferential as compared with those for the home consumption trade." The most commonly quoted instance has been the rate of 25s. per ton for meat from Liverpool to London, as against 45s. to London from intermediate stations. The fact that such are the rates is undeniable. Let us assume for the moment that they are absolutely unjustifiable. The company which imposes them, let us admit, is simply levying blackmail upon the necessities of the struggling English farmer. But what then shall we say to the following, culled within the last few months from the leading columns of a London daily paper?

"Railway rates are seriously affecting an industry recently established in Cardiff, for the supply to London amongst other places of meat from New Zealand and the South American ports. The rate for dead meat from Cardiff to London, a distance of 162 miles, is 35s. per ton, or $2\tfrac{6}{10}d$. per ton per mile. From Liverpool, which is 201 miles, the rate is only 25s. per ton, or $1\tfrac{5}{10}d$. per ton per mile. From Bristol to London, a distance of 118 miles, the rate is 20s. per ton, or 2d. per ton per mile. Thus it will be seen that the Cardiff rates are something like 30 per cent. more than those of Bristol and Liverpool. It is satisfactory to know that the Cardiff Chamber of Commerce is taking vigorous action in the matter; but as the trunk lines are in agreement, they will find it difficult to remove the grievance of which they justly complain."

It is evident that the writer can have no sympathy with the struggling British farmer when he quotes with approval these "preferential" rates for foreign produce which are given at Liverpool and Bristol. Perhaps he has come to the conclusion that the consumer in London has also an interest, that, namely, of getting his meat as cheap as possible; possibly he even sympathises with the traders and "dockers" at Cardiff who are trying to make a livelihood out of the establishment of a new industry.

But when the Cardiff Chamber of Commerce takes the vigorous action which it promises, it is not difficult to know what will be the reply of the Great Western Railway. "Gentlemen," the Company will answer, "what would you have? You can't both have import rates and not have them simultaneously. You say that the Cardiff import rate is higher in proportion than that given to Liverpool and Bristol. Quite true; but these are old-established rates, and yours is a new one. We are by no means sure, if we were taken before the Railway Commission under Section 27 of the Traffic Act of 1888, whether we should be able to justify either the Liverpool or the Bristol rate. Still we are prepared to run the risk sooner than disturb an old-established trade. But when you come and ask us to make a new rate, it is a different matter. In view of the wording of the Act—and you must remember that it was passed at the instance of the Chambers of Commerce and Agriculture—we must be very careful not to make any difference in the charges for home and foreign merchandise in respect to the same or similar circumstances. Some concession we can make to you, because your meat comes in wholesale quantity, and because it is worth less per pound than ordinary Welsh mutton. That we have done. Further we cannot go, except by deliberately defying the Act of Parliament. No doubt you would be able to satisfy the Commissioners that with a 35*s.* rate the trade will never make much progress at Cardiff, that the meat will continue to go all the way to London by water, that a 25*s.* rate would be better for you, and better for us, for we would rather take 500 tons at a profit of 5*s.* than 100 tons at a profit of 15*s.* But all that would be of no avail, for, as you of course remember, the Act specially provides that the Commissioners shall not have the power to sanction any difference in the rate for home and foreign produce unless it corresponds to a difference in cost of service, and that difference, as you must admit, is fully allowed for.

"You suggest that we might reduce our rate for local meat. But, if we did that, we should have to reduce the rate proportionately all along the line from here to London. And then would come in the question whether we were not giving the farmers on the South Wales line an undue preference compared with those on our main line to Cornwall or in North Wales and Cheshire. Even supposing we were to face this loss, that would only be the beginning, for we should be at once called upon to adjust all our other rates in conformity. You see all our rates hang together. We have always had to be very careful not to favour one class of traffic at the expense of another, and we have to be tenfold more careful nowadays. According to Professor Hunter, M.P., 'The existing law is' —and we are not inclined to risk a law-suit to prove him mistaken—'that railways are not to reduce their rates merely upon one particular part of the line without giving the benefit of that reduction all round.' We are very sorry, gentlemen, to be able to make no other answer. Nobody can be more anxious to develop the trade of Cardiff than we are, but you must see it is impossible."

It is easy to imagine the railway company making some such reply as this; it is not so easy, however, to see what the Chamber of Commerce would say in rejoinder. But let us leave the question of special import rates for the present. We shall return to them later on, when the time comes for discussing the basis on which rates ought to be fixed. Here is another instance of the way in which inconsistent charges are brought against the English railways. Witness after witness before the Committees of 1881 and 1882 protested against the railway companies, in the words of Mr. Barclay, M.P., "neutralising the natural advantages of any locality by giving cheaper rates to a locality not so favourably situated." According to Mr. (now Sir William) Forwood, its mayor, Liverpool is "deprived of the advantages of its natural geographical position" by the low rates given to Barrow and Fleetwood. Mr. Grotrian, an ex-president of the Hull Chamber of Commerce, declared that the rates charged in the north-eastern district were all "based upon a system of preference to the northern ports of Hartlepool and the Tyne over the port of Hull."

More typical still was the complaint of the London sugar refiners, which is thus summarised in the Committee's report: "Thirty-nine towns in England to which sugar is sent are at an average distance of 292 miles from Greenock, and the same towns are at an average distance from London of only 156 miles. The rates for these distances from London and Greenock, respectively, are about the same, representing in the case of the Greenock rate 1·09d., but in the case of the London rate 2·13d. per ton per mile. In other words, sugar from Greenock is for the same sum carried double the distance as sugar from London. This enables Greenock to compete at these thirty-nine towns, and this is what the refiners of London object to. The demand from London, therefore, is that either the rates for the longer distance should be raised or those for the shorter distance reduced. The effect of compliance with this demand would be to close some of these markets against Greenock sugar, to deprive the northern lines of a considerable portion of their trade, handing it over to the southern lines, and to give a practical monopoly to the London sugar refiners, who would be real gainers by the transaction."

Such is the Committee's account of an instance in which the railways have certainly gone further than usual in depriving a place of its natural advantage of geographical position, in which they seem fairly open to the charge brought against them by one witness of claiming a right to interfere as a special providence. It is only right to add that the verdict of the Committee on this evidence is given in the words following the passage already cited: "It does not appear to your Committee that such a result" (as the closing, namely, of southern markets to Greenock sugar for the benefit of London refiners) "would be either just or reasonable. . . . This competition cannot but be advantageous to the public. That Greenock sugar refiners should be in the same market as the sugar refiners of London, while it may be a grievance to London refiners, must be an advantage to Greenock refiners, and cannot be a disadvantage to buyers of sugar."

This is plain speaking, and would seem to imply that the Committee had scant sympathy with the wrong of Liverpool and Hull. The Committee, however, was not infallible. Instances undoubtedly do occur where railways have given certain towns undue preferences over others. Let us suspend our judgment for the present. Meanwhile, we may notice at once that, if the companies have sinned by too much levelling-up the distant places, it is at least hard that they should be charged simultaneously with keeping distant places out of the market by extortionate rates. And yet the charge is constantly made. Take the fish rate for instance. The Scotch fishing ports average from three to four times as far from London as Grimsby. The rate is about double, and yet an influential witness from Scotland declares that his trade is strangled by high rates. In other words, if the rate were less he would be better off. One may admit the fact without accepting his deduction as to the iniquity of the railway companies. There is, or was in the days of the Pharaohs, much good brickearth in Egypt, yet there is no need to credit the Peninsular and Oriental Company with extortion as a reason why Egyptian bricks cannot compete with Kent stocks in the London market. "Witnesses from Forfarshire and Cornwall," says the Committee's report, "contend that with the lower rates the traffic in fish and vegetables would develop enormously and prove more advantageous to the railway companies than the present limited traffic at high rates, while not only those engaged in fishing and farming would greatly benefit, but also the consumers in the large centres of population."

The benefit to producer and consumer may be taken for granted, but the gain to the companies must surely depend on what is the cost of the service they render. On this point the evidence of the critics is somewhat conflicting. Professor Hunter, M.P., says: "From Wolverhampton to London the railway companies charge 45*s.* a ton for English meat, and for American meat to London they charge 25*s.* from Liverpool, so that in that case I should strongly suspect that they are charging the people about Wolverhampton in order to make up the loss from Liverpool." One must hope that the Professor's suspicions are unfounded. The 25*s.* rate, for roughly 200 miles, is equal to $1\frac{1}{2}d$. per ton per mile, which is about three times the average charge made for transporting one ton one mile on the American railways. If this be a losing rate, what shall we say for the critics who tell us that English railways can, or at least ought to be able to, carry as cheaply as their American rivals? The truth is, we may safely take it for granted that no English railway carries any regular goods traffic at a loss—it may of course carry at a loss an individual load of fish or other perishables under exceptional circumstances—though the profit in some cases is very much larger than the profit in others. But it is time to see what is meant by the expression, "cost of carriage."

PART I

RAILWAY PRINCIPLES

CHAPTER I

COST OF CARRIAGE

"THE railway managers of this country," says Mr. Jeans[1] in the work to which we have already referred, voicing a complaint which has been made scores of times by critics of English railway management, "profess that they are unable to furnish the exact cost of working any particular description of traffic. It would be extremely ungracious to suggest that it probably does not suit their purpose to know too much on this subject. But it is beyond all question that, if this item is not known on English lines, it is well enough known on foreign ones. It has been proved, for example, in the United States that the cost of working goods traffic within the last few years has been reduced by one-half, and in some cases even more." It will not need any very exhaustive consideration of the question to convince any ordinary reader that the charge against

[1] *Railway Problems*, p. 304.

English railway managers, that they profess themselves unable to furnish "the exact cost of working any particular description of traffic," simply because it does not suit their purpose to give the information, is not so much extremely ungracious as extremely foolish. English railway managers do not furnish the information, for the very sufficient reason that they cannot, and that in the nature of things it is impossible that they should be able to do so.

Take an illustration from a case a thousand-fold more simple than railway traffic. A doctor keeps a carriage. Sometimes he drives one horse, sometimes a pair. Some of his patients live close round the corner, others several miles off. At one time an epidemic brings on his hands half a dozen cases in adjoining houses. At another the sickness is distributed equally in all directions throughout his district. Once or twice a week his wife borrows the carriage to visit her friends. At the end of the year the doctor, after making an estimate—and it can only be an estimate—of the depreciation of horses and carriage, finds that his stable has cost him, say, 250*l.* So far so good, but supposing he is asked what percentage of a particular patient's bill is due to what we may call, in American phrase, "transportation" expenses, will he not reply that the question is unanswerable? He can divide the 250*l.* by the total number of visits he has paid in the twelvemonth, and say that the result is the cost of each visit, though even then he has neglected his wife's use of the carriage—which, however, as she never would have expected to have it, if there had not been a carriage already provided for professional purposes, he is probably quite justified in doing—but further than this he cannot go. If he attempts to give the actual, instead of the average, cost of every single visit, his answer is so largely made up of conjectures and estimates as to be absolutely valueless.

Take another instance. An omnibus starts from Hammersmith and runs right across London to Bow. In the course of its journey it carries a hundred different passengers. Some of them travel a few hundred yards, others for several miles. Some get in when the omnibus is nearly full; at another time a single passenger has the whole vehicle and the services of the horses and two men all to himself. Add the fact that, before the particular journey commences and after it was finished, men and horses were engaged, some for a longer and some for a shorter time, in earning money on other routes, so that the one single run can only be debited with a part, more or less indeterminate, of their cost *per diem*, and it will be sufficiently evident that, with the best intentions in the world, the omnibus proprietor is not in a position to state what is the cost to him of the conveyance of any particular passenger. And if this be so in such simple matters as single carriages or single omnibuses, what shall we say in the case of an organism as vast and as complicated as that of a railway company?

The cost of the brougham or the omnibus includes no item for the provision of a roadway over which to run, or a staff to open gates and let down drawbridges. But to bring a ton of goods up from Liverpool implies not merely 5,000*l.* worth of engine and trucks and guard's van, and the services of driver, guard, and fireman, and of the men who load and unload at the two ends—that is the smallest matter—it implies also a share of the services of, say, two hundred signalmen, and twice as many permanent-way inspectors and platelayers, and the use of the 20,000,000*l.* sterling of capital which is invested in the North Western line between Edgehill and Broad Street. Not of course that the single ton of goods ought to be debited with a large share of the charges under these two latter heads. Still, it should bear its share, and if that share must be, as I think it can be shown to be, matter of computation incapable of accurate ascertainment, it is evident that on this ground alone "the exact cost of working any particular description of traffic" is and must remain a figure about as conveniently vague as the size of the traditional lump of chalk.

Here is how Mr. Alexander[2] puts the case. "Railroads, in common with authors, doctors, inventors, labourers, lawyers, manufacturers, and most other people who have anything to sell, base their prices upon the value of what they offer, rather than upon its cost. The case of a railroad's estimating the cost of doing a particular piece of business is not unlike that of a lawyer estimating the cost of giving an opinion. He has fitted himself for that particular business, and, as it were, invested his life in the

---

[2] *Railway Practice.* By E. P. Alexander. Putnam's Sons, New York, 1887. An admirable little book, which might with advantage have contained a good deal more than sixty pages.

education and experience necessary to transact it. His time is good for nothing else, and if he is not called upon for opinions, will be worthless to him. He can therefore render opinions up to a certain limit almost without cost, except for stationery. So a railroad is a large fixed investment capable of furnishing transportation and nothing else. Up to certain limits it can always take additional business without cost, except for a very small amount of fuel. The money it receives for the new business above the small *additional cost*, is all clear profit. It adds that much to the ability of the road to serve other patrons at low rates."

"But," says Mr. Jeans, "if this item is not known on English lines, it is well enough known on foreign ones. It has been proved, for example, in the United States that the cost of working goods traffic has been reduced by one-half." This latter fact is no doubt true, but it is beside the point. Mr. Jeans asks, if his words mean anything, for the exact cost of working, not goods traffic or passenger traffic as a whole on the average, but particular descriptions of traffic—passengers, say, first, second or third class, coal or pig iron, vegetables or leather, tea or Manchester goods, each independently.

Nor is Mr. Jeans alone in his demands by any means. Witness after witness before the House of Commons Committee of 1881 and 1882 made the same claim. Mr. Muspratt, for instance, ex-President of the Liverpool Chamber of Commerce, expressed the opinion that, except in the case of raw materials, the rate of conveyance should be fixed " upon the basis of the cost of conveyance." And when asked, "There is no exception to that rule which you would lay down?" he replied, "No." Professor Hunter, M.P., author of a well-known work on railway law, repeated again and again the statement that the true principle of railway management was to charge everybody " a rate according to the cost of conveyance to the company." Mr. Simons, who appeared as representing the colliery owners of South Wales, in answer to the question, " Are you prepared to say that the railway companies should be compelled to make the same percentage of profit on every portion of their line?" said, "I am prepared to say that is what I hope for as the result of this and future discussions." In answer to a member of the Committee, Mr. Barclay, M.P., whose own views are apparently formulated in a leading question put to another witness in these words: " You would advocate that the railway companies should charge in proportion to the cost of conveyance, and not upon some arbitrary terms that they themselves adjust," Sir William Forwood expressed the opinion that "the cost to the railway company of performing the service ought to be adopted as a fundamental principle in adjusting the rates for carriage." It is evident, therefore, that when the views of these gentlemen prevail, it will be necessary to determine the cost of the carriage of each article.

Let us see how it is to be done. No one doubts that the American reports—and it is impossible not to admire their exhaustive statistics—give separately the cost of working goods traffic as a whole and passenger traffic as a whole, or, as the report of the New York Central more accurately puts it, the "expenses *allotted* to transportation of freight," and the "expenses *allotted* to transportation of passengers"; but American railway men are much too clear-headed not to know that these expenses, as far as certainly fully one-fourth of the whole is concerned, are not actual facts, but simply estimates; while the most self-possessed and courteous amongst them would probably find it difficult to suppress a smile if he were asked to give, as it is stated he does give, "the exact cost of transporting each particular kind of traffic." But on this point it is perhaps worth while to call a witness whose capacity no one is likely to dispute, Mr. Albert Fink—probably, when experience of practical management, grasp of abstract principle, and power of literary expression, are all taken into account, the first railway authority in the world.

Here is what Mr. Fink says:[3] "A careful investigation shows that, under the ordinary conditions under which transportation service is generally performed, the cost per ton-mile in some instances may not exceed one-seventh of a cent, and in others will be as high as 7⅗ cents per ton-mile on the same road.... It is impossible to predetermine the cost of carrying freight on any one road, unless the conditions under which it is to be carried, as far

[3] Mr. Fink has unfortunately never published any connected work on railway rates. His luminous writings on the subject are scattered amongst a multitude of pamphlets and reports of evidence before legislative committees. The quotations in the text are from a reprint of the Annual Report of the Louisville and Nashville Railway Company for 1874, contained in a volume of *collectanea*, which is not, however, published, entitled *Railroad Transportation*.

as they affect the cost of transportation, be previously known. . . . A mere knowledge of the average cost per ton-mile of all the expenditures during a whole year's operation is of no value whatever in determining the cost of transporting any particular class of freight, as *no freight is ever transported under the average condition under which the whole year's business is transacted.*" Or, in other words, Mr. Jeans's "exact cost of working any particular description of traffic" is as far removed from the facts of real life, and as much a figment of the imagination, as Plato's ideal table.

It will not need any very lengthy consideration to see why this must be so. Broadly speaking, the cost of carriage, whether of passengers or of goods, is made up of four items: locomotive or movement expenses, terminals or station expenses, maintenance of way and works, interest on capital. Let us consider them separately. In round figures, an English locomotive costs on the average 1,000*l*. a year, for wages, fuel, repairs, and depreciation. It runs in that period, say, 20,000 miles. In other words, it costs 1*s*. per mile. If it runs with a load of 50 tons behind it, it will perhaps burn 20 lbs. of coal per mile; when it is hauling 600 tons it will perhaps burn 60 lbs. So that between, practically, no load at all and a long and heavily loaded train the variation in locomotive cost is hardly more than the price of 40 lbs. of coal, or say from 11*d*. to 1*s*. 1*d*. But the 11*d*. may have to be charged upon perhaps 20 tons of paying load, and the 1*s*. 1*d*. perhaps on 400 tons. Anyone practically familiar with the conditions under which our English goods service has to be carried on will know that this immense discrepancy represents not simply theoretical possibilities, but actual facts.

An engine, for instance, may run between London and Rugby with forty fully loaded waggons behind it, while the branch that diverges from Weedon may only be able to supply loading for two or three trucks. Yet an engine must go down the branch at least once a day, and collect what traffic there may be. The few hundred-weights of meat, of butter, or of vegetables, or the small consignments for the local grocer or draper, cannot be kept back for a month or two till a train-load has been collected. Now for another point. On one line the traffic in opposite directions is fairly balanced, on another it is all in one direction. A train-load of coal into London, for instance, must evidently be debited with the cost of sending back the train of empty trucks. At Hull, or at Liverpool, imports and exports are not so very disproportionate to one another. Or, again, on a line some hundreds of miles in length, a locomotive can run straight forward for the whole of the time it is supposed to be at work. On a short branch the time lost at the two ends is often much more than the time during which it is actually in motion.

One factor more. There are lines in this country on which 45 trucks is the recognised engine load. There is one line, at least, on which the gradients limit the load to a single truck, and loads of 10 and 12 trucks are by no means uncommon. The traffic on the line from Birmingham to Bristol, for instance, has to pay in perpetuity a tax of 5,000*l.* a year, because the best way that could be found through the Lickey Hills implied a gradient of 1 in $37\frac{1}{2}$ for two miles, and the working of this gradient involves the constant maintenance on the spot of five assistant or " banking " engines. Mr. Fink, in the paper already referred to, brought all the considerations which have been summarised above to the test of actual figures. He analysed the movement expenses on his own line, and this is what he found: that on the main line they amounted to ·7365 of a cent per ton per mile; on the Glasgow branch they reached 5·4928 cents, or more than seven times as much No wonder he protests against the crude notions according to which " the ton-mile, without further inquiry as to its adaptability, is made the measure of cost." " If," he continues, " by comparing the tariffs of different roads, or the tariff for different services on the same road, a difference be discovered, the road charging the higher rates stands convicted of practising extortion and undue discrimination."

Here is an English instance to show how difficult it is to apportion even actual movement expenses to particular portions of traffic. One of our great lines used at one time to compete by a very circuitous route for the carriage of coal to London. The chairman went very carefully into the matter, calculated the receipts per ton per mile, and finally came to the conclusion that the traffic did not pay. Accordingly, by his orders, the competition for this traffic was abandoned. At the end of the year the gross receipts were reduced by its absence to the extent of 20 000*l.*

"But where," said the chairman, "is the economy in locomotive expenses?" It could not be traced. Presumably there had been a saving; evidently 40,000 or 50,000 tons of coal had not been hauled for nothing; but the cost, whatever it was, had been so inextricably mixed up with the rest of the expenses, that it was impossible to disentangle it, and say precisely where the saving had come in. An analogy between railways and hotels suggests itself. Every new guest who enters an hotel undoubtedly costs something for food actually eaten; yet in an hotel with 500 or 600 persons to feed every day, the addition of an extra half-dozen would make no perceptible alteration in the manager's bills. All it could do would be to reduce the theoretical cost per head per diem from, say, 3s. to 2s. 11¾d.

Perhaps after this it will seem somewhat of a paradox to add that of the four classes of expenditure, for which the rates charged have got to furnish the recompense, the expenses of movement are unquestionably those which can be most easily ascertained and allocated to each different description of traffic. But such is the fact, as will be seen when we come to deal with the other three classes. Take station or "terminal" expenses, as they are commonly called here, including under this head, not what are in future to be known as "station terminals" (allowance, that is, for the cost of providing the permanent accommodation), but merely the expenses of handling the traffic. Now, it is obvious that, if there are two similar consignments alongside in the Great Northern goods shed at Farringdon Street, and the one is loaded into a truck to go to Hornsey or Southgate, and the other to go to Aberdeen, the cost of loading and unloading, weighing, invoicing, shunting, &c., will be identical. But in the case of the short distance this cost will be perhaps three-quarters of the whole charge made to the sender, in the other it will not be more than a fifth part.

Further, the consignments are by no means similar. Tea and furniture stand side by side in the fifth, or highest class of the classification, but to load a ton of tea is one thing, to load a ton of furniture is quite another. Then, again, in a London station or at Aberdeen there is a separate goods-staff, and it is quite certain that the whole of their wages must be debited against the consignors of the goods taken as a whole; but at a small station, where the station-master and the porters are responsible both for goods and passenger work, no line can be drawn. The trader may say, as he said again and again by the mouth of his representatives at the Board of Trade inquiry last year, "These people are here in any case, and have to be paid to attend to the passengers; it costs you nothing to employ them between whiles to load and unload our goods." But the passenger can with equal justice reply, "These men are retained to deal with the goods, it is preposterous to add anything to the price of our tickets because every hour or two they come out of the goods sheds and open the carriage doors for us." And the one contention would be just as reasonable as the other.

Yet it is out of an equation with this indefinite number of unknowns that the railway companies are assured they ought to have no difficulty in extracting the precise proportion of the total rate which can properly be allocated to the payment of station expenses. If the railway companies are unable, however, perhaps Mr. Fink's figures will be useful to those who are anxious to formulate their own scale. He found that the percentage of the total rate due to this one item varied from 4·3 on the Knoxville branch to 18·1 per cent. on the main line. Putting it another way round, as the cost per ton-mile, his figures show that on the Knoxville branch station expenses cost ·1823 of a cent per mile; on the main line they reached ·3233; while on the short Glasgow branch they were no less than ·9563.

Now we come to the third head, or maintenance of road, under which we may, for convenience' sake, include signalling. Two things here are obvious. In the first place, every road, and every mile of that road, has different cost of maintenance. The maintenance of the Forth Bridge or the Severn Tunnel is one thing, the maintenance of the landward approaches on either side is quite another. Even on an ordinary line there must be taken into consideration the contour of the country, whether tunnels and viaducts are few or many, whether the soil is light or heavy, whether stone for ballast is readily accessible, and fifty things more. The lay-reader, for instance, might be startled to know what some of the Lancashire railways have had to spend to prevent their trains descending into the mine-workings beneath them—it having pleased a beneficent legislature, doubtless for good and sufficient reason, to provide that the conveyance of land to a company, under the Railway

Clauses Consolidation Act, shall not, like an ordinary conveyance, avail to pass all the rights which the vendor has in the property, but that, unless the company, after buying the land, not as a rule at too modest a price, goes on to make a separate bargain for the minerals, the landowner, on giving a month's notice, may proceed to dig, not only coal, but brick-earth lying within six feet of the railway sleepers. Here is one item of the total cost of maintenance which it would puzzle the most accomplished statistician to divide proportionately among the different descriptions of traffic passing over the London and North Western, or the Lancashire and Yorkshire.

Or, again, when the Llanddulas Viaduct between Chester and Holyhead was washed away by a storm some ten years ago, and the company had first to divert the traffic by another route, then to erect a temporary wooden bridge, and then to replace the permanent structure—ought the accountant of the North Western to have been able to furnish the exact cost of working the Irish traffic under all these different conditions? Let no one answer that these things are accidents; that it is only normal conditions which must be regarded. There are no normal conditions applying to any single individual consignment. "*No freight is ever transported under the average condition.*"

But the difficulty is not merely in deciding what expenses are to be reckoned in calculating the cost of carriage. The difficulty of settling what traffic is to bear them is at least equally great. Much the larger part of the permanent-way expenditure remains constant, whether ten or two hundred trains a day pass over the line. Ballast washes away, sleepers rot and rails rust, bridges and station-buildings need repointing and repainting, ditches must be cleaned out and hedges trimmed, signals must be maintained, and signalmen paid their wages, whether the traffic be great or small. What could be the practical value of a North Western table which should show that, say, ·15*d.* was the average cost per ton-mile of the maintenance of the road, if a little further investigation showed that this average was made up, as of course it would be, of figures as wildly discrepant as those which Mr. Fink worked out on the Louisville and Nashville? On that company's system, the maintenance of road on the main line, with numerous bridges and heavy works, cost for one year 1,134 dollars per mile. On the Glasgow branch it cost 84 dollars, say one-fourteenth. But, on the other hand, the main line had over 400,000 tons of freight over each mile of it; the branch had about 6,000, or, say, one sixty-seventh. Consequently, the charge against each ton of goods on the branch comes out to 1·78 of a cent, as against ·26 on the main line. In other words, on cost-of-carriage principles, the charge under the head of maintenance of road for the use of the cheap line would have to be seven times as much as for the use of the dear one.

The fourth and last of the items which go to make up the cost of carriage is interest on capital.[1] If it

---

[1] We shall see later on that interest on capital never enters into the consideration of a manager in fixing a rate. He gets the best price he can. If it pays interest, well; if not, providing it pays working expenses, it is better than nothing. But though cost of capital does not affect individual rates, it does affect the rates as a

was difficult under the three previous heads to settle what share of the total cost was to be borne by each particular kind of traffic, the difficulty here is enhanced tenfold. In the other cases it was possible to ignore, or at least to keep in the background, the question of the value of the article transported. But it is impossible to do so any longer, for the practice of the civilised world is agreed in this, that, though possibly all classes of traffic ought to be called on to pay their share of the working expenses, the cheaper kinds ought to be largely relieved of the obligation to pay interest on construction capital. Even in Germany, where more than anywhere else the so-called "natural" system of basing the tariff on cost of service has been adopted—a system, in fact, about as natural as the old English legal system of paying a solicitor in accordance with the length of the deed he drew—even in Germany the attempt to make coal pay as large a share towards interest on capital as drapery goods would be a revolution.

Here, in London, to take one obvious instance, such a system would render it impossible to continue bringing in bricks, or carrying out street refuse, over railways which have cost hundreds of thousands of pounds per mile. But, leaving this point

whole. For, if the total earnings do not give a reasonable interest, no new capital will come into the business, and improvements and new construction will be brought to a standstill, till either rates are raised or the volume of traffic increases so as to give a sufficient margin of interest. To the capitalist who invests 10,000*l.* in building a mile of line it is evidently indifferent whether that line carries 1,000*l.* worth of traffic, worked at 50 per cent. of the gross receipts, or 2,000*l.* worth of traffic worked at 75 per cent. Either one-half of 1,000*l.* or one-quarter of 2,000*l.* gives him his income of 500*l.* a year.

to which we shall have to refer more at length later on, it is evident that, if interest on capital has to be taken into consideration, the proportion of the rate attributable to this cause must of necessity be ten times as high on a line which can only afford traffic for six trains a day as on one where sixty can be profitably employed. Further, the rate must rise and fall in different parts of the system according as construction is rendered, by the natural features of the country, expensive or cheap. Again, is the company to claim the interest on all the capital that stands in its books as expended, regardless of the fact that the capital was wastefully spent on a badly planned line, or a line that never was wanted at all; or even that the contractor was paid in shares issued at a discount of sixty or seventy per cent.? Is such a scheme as this in the public interest? One question more. Who is to determine what rate of interest the railway capital is to bear? And supposing a competing company to open a rival line, say from London to Bristol, is an Act of Parliament to be passed forthwith to enable the Great Western to raise its charges, so that its diminished traffic may still permit the proprietors to receive their old return?

But perhaps enough has been said, not, indeed, to prove—where the details are so bewilderingly numerous that only the outline of a case can imperfectly be sketched, it would be too much to claim that anything has been proved—perhaps enough has been said to show two things. In the first place that "to furnish the exact cost of working any particular description of traffic" is a problem which the railway manager has some slight justification for declaring insoluble: and in the second place, that, if any such figures could in fact be furnished—unless, indeed, customers could be found who would be ready to pay two or three shillings per ton per mile in certain instances for the carriage of their coal or ironstone—they would be of about as much value for fixing a work-a-day schedule of rates as would be a computation of the united ages of the board of directors multiplied by the amount of the general manager's salary.

CHAPTER II

EQUAL MILEAGE RATES

COST of service, however, is not the only principle on which it is asserted that rates ought to be fixed. Another principle, that of equal mileage, has also its devotees. Indeed there are some railway critics who find it possible to worship at both shrines at once. Sir William Forwood, for instance, Mayor of Liverpool and ex-President of the Liverpool Chamber of Commerce, told the House of Commons' Committee of 1881, as we have seen a few pages back, that "the fundamental principle in adjusting the rates" ought to be the difference of "the cost to the railway company of performing the service."—yet half an hour before the same witness is reported to have expressed himself as follows:

Q. You are perfectly satisfied that the principle of equal mileage rates ought to be applied, having regard to distance?

A. I think so in any general system of railway rates.

Q. There can be no doubt about the clearness of that principle?

A. I am quite sure of it.

At the intervening quarter, Sir William amalgamates the two principles together in the following remarkable confession of faith :

"I think that if we had general legislation on the subject it should lead to equal mileage rates for equal distances, and that the cost of conveyance would be a consideration that would enter into the fixing of those rates."

Bearing in mind the facts and figures as to cost of conveyance which have been given in the last chapter, we can hardly be wrong in concluding that the most striking feature of Mr. Forwood's system of equal mileage rates, fixed after consideration of the cost of service, would be their inequality.

Professor Hunter, M.P., likewise lays down that "equal mileage rates should be the rule, but that any railway company desiring to depart in any respect from equality should prepare a scale and obtain the sanction of the Railway Commissioners to that scale," though, as we have seen already, he also lays it down that the railways ought to charge everybody "a rate according to the cost of conveyance to the company," and we have also seen that the cost of conveyance to the company bears no fixed relation whatever to the distance the traffic is carried.

If such be the logic of mayors and professors, it would be waste of time to cite the opinions of the smaller fry. But a glance at the Indexes to the Reports of the House of Commons' Committee in both 1881 and 1882 will be sufficient to show that numerous other witnesses asked for equal mileage rates subject to one or more specified exceptions. The Committee's report, it is only fair to say, declares that equal mileage rates, strictly so called, "have not been advocated on this occasion as before former Committees," and that no doubt is the fact. The schoolmaster—experience, the best of all his tribe—has been abroad since 1853, and even since 1867 or 1873 has had time to teach something. And experience has taught even the least observant critic that equal mileage rates, pure and simple, are an absolute impossibility. In truth, equal mileage rates are only cost-of-carriage rates in their crudest form.

The earliest critics judged by the analogy which to them was most familiar—the carrier's waggon. The carrier had nothing to do with the maintenance of the turnpike. He had no stations to provide; instead of maintaining an expensive staff at fixed points, whether there was work for them to do or not, he picked up his consignments here and there along the road. He paid a toll of so much a mile, proportioned roughly to the weight of his vehicle, and beyond this his chief expenditure was for actual haulage. For services such as these a mileage tariff, coupled with a rough-and-ready classification of goods, not so much perhaps according to their value—for the commoner and cheaper kinds of goods simply stopped at home—as according to the space they occupied, was an equitable method of remuneration enough. It needed, however, no very exhaustive study of the question to show that at least three circumstances must largely modify the cost of railway working. A carrier's waggon was usually, no doubt, pretty full; if more goods were offered than he could take they had to wait till the next time he came along the road. But a railway company on one line may be able to spread the cost of its locomotive over a full train-load, on another it can only secure traffic to fill half a dozen trucks. Or again, it may be limited to the same load, not by the impossibility of obtaining more, but by the exceptional severity of the gradients. Once more, it is obviously cheaper to carry one ton of goods one hundred miles than to carry a hundred separate consignments of one ton each for one mile. These three considerations therefore must, it is admitted, affect the cost of working, and Professor Hunter accordingly is willing that they and they only should be allowed for, as modifying what, except for these accidents, ought to be an equal mileage rate.

But the only reason which can be given why these considerations should be regarded, and fifty others, some of them certainly at least equally important, should be disregarded, is because they are obvious, while the others are not equally patent at first sight. There is no need to repeat again what these latter considerations are. They have been enumerated in sufficient detail already, and one of the most important amongst them, the cost of terminal accommodation and handling, which is the same whether the goods be carried five miles or five hundred, is not likely to be overlooked nowadays by any who has ever come within hearing distance of a Chamber of Commerce. But we may well emphasize at this point the fact that, as was shown in the last chapter, cost of conveyance or equal mileage rates can at best only be applied to one portion of a railway company's business. For an English railway company, it must always be remembered, carries on as a rule two separate and not infrequently separated businesses. Its most conspicuous business is that of a carrier, but it is also a capitalist owner of a road. In Italy, and also to some extent in Holland, the State owns the line and private companies work the traffic. Not a few instances where the two functions of carrier and road proprietors are dissociated can be found here too. The East London Railway Company, for example, and the City of Glasgow Union have never carried a passenger or a ton of goods. The former of these companies leases its line to its larger neighbours for a fixed money rent, the latter employs two other companies as its agents to work the line and receives in payment an agreed proportion of their receipts. The Metropolitan and Metropolitan District Companies are carriers of passengers but not of goods. The North London, on the other hand, only owns 17 miles, but it works over nearly five times that length of line.

Now, admitting for the moment, for the sake of argument, that mileage distance, as modified by allowance for gradients, &c., is a reasonable basis for calculating the proper remuneration of the carrier, it has obviously nothing in the world to do with the charges for the use of the line. These latter must depend upon two main considerations, the cost of making and maintaining the road, and the amount of the traffic which passes over it. Everybody, in days when turnpike tolls existed, admitted the justice of imposing an extra toll for passing over an expensive bridge. And, on the other hand, every one can see that, though Waterloo Bridge may have cost as much as the

Menai Suspension Bridge, a toll of 2*d.* in the one case was as fair and gave as good a remuneration to the proprietors as 1*s.* in the other, for the reason that the London traffic was sixfold denser than that of Anglesea.

There is one argument against equal mileage rates, which seems tolerably obvious to anyone who reflects on the subject, which, however, as I have never seen it more than mentioned by English writers, is perhaps worth bringing forward at this point. Our English railway system, unlike that of the Continent, has grown up on the basis of competition. It is true there are some people who believe that English railways have ceased to compete, because nowadays they agree to maintain identical rates, as though, forsooth, there could be no competition between the Grand and the Langham Hotels as long as the charge for bed and breakfast, for attendance and dinner, is the same at both establishments. Those, however, who know how railway work is really carried on are well enough aware that the competition is as intense as ever, only that it takes the form, not of decreasing the charge but of increasing the accommodation provided. Traders, moreover, have not ceased to put their trust in competition as their best protection.

When, for instance, there was the great fight in the Parliamentary Committee rooms last session, to decide whether the North British should be permitted to absorb the Glasgow and South Western, the mercantile witnesses on the one side supported the proposal on the express ground that the North British would be a stronger competitor with the

Caledonian in the West of Scotland than ever the South Western had been; on the other hand, traders who opposed the scheme declared that they did so because it was more difficult for three competitors to agree to cease fighting than when there were only two.

Now it is evident that Professor Hunter's system of equal mileage rates, modified by allowances for gradients, average length of haul, and volume of traffic, would, equally with his alternate system of rates based on cost of conveyance, put an absolute embargo on the competition between different railway companies. At the present moment, for instance, the Midland, the Great Northern, the Great Western, and the Great Eastern, all compete with the North Western for the traffic between Liverpool and London. The mileage is in no two cases the same; the distance being $193\frac{1}{2}$, $220\frac{1}{4}$, 229, $237\frac{1}{2}$, and 261 miles by the five lines respectively. It is safe to say that the cost of carriage by the North Western must be less than by any of the rival routes, three of which have, in addition to extra distance, to contend with exceptionally heavy gradients, while the Great Western has to "lighter" its traffic across the Mersey from Birkenhead. Now the theorists who would fix railway rates on what they term a natural basis are face to face with this alternative. Either the rates by the different routes must be different, in which case, of course, all competition is at an end, and the North Western takes the whole of the traffic, or else, the rates remaining the same by all the lines, and being in practice fixed by the shortest mileage, the Midland, the Great Northern, the Great Western, and the Great Eastern must be content to add to the cost of carriage less than their theoretically proper percentage of profit.

Now there is no question that the Liverpool trader, whatever may be his abstract ideas, in a committee-room at Westminster, on the ethics of railway management, will prefer the second horn of the dilemma when he gets back to his counting-house in Dale Street. He is quite clear that he gains by the maintenance of competition between the different railway companies in Liverpool, and he means to maintain it, even though in so doing he makes himself an accomplice in the crime of charging the traffic, not according to cost, but according to "what it will bear." Probably he will hold to this opinion even though he be assured by the traders in Stockport and Warrington that he is getting this benefit at their expense, as it is evident that, if the Midland can afford to carry all the way to Liverpool for, say 35*s*., it must be able, if the officials choose, to carry at a lower price to a place thirty miles nearer London.

But unfortunately the Liverpool trader has made a dangerous admission. He has acknowledged that a railway may be justified in taking half a loaf when the alternative is that it gets no bread, even if by such conduct it deprives another railway company of "the advantages of its geographical position." The Midland thereupon turns round and says: "Now you will understand why we have made our rate from Leeds to Barrow the same as the rate from Leeds to Liverpool. It was not because we wanted to reduce our own percentage of profit, but because we knew that, if we attempted to put the rate any higher, the Lancashire and Yorkshire or the North Western would get hold of the traffic and take it to Liverpool. You see the principle cuts both ways and Liverpool can't always expect to benefit by it." But at this point the trader is suddenly called back to Westminster to explain the theory of the application of railway rates in a perfect vacuum, so his answer to the Midland goods agent cannot be recorded.

In his absence, however, we must be allowed to carry the discussion one stage further. Once admit competition between two companies, and the whole theory of equal mileage or cost-of-service rates vanishes into air. For if two railway companies may compete on land, why not a railway company on land with a steamship company on sea? Is the Great Eastern, for instance, to stand aside and leave the traffic between London and Yarmouth to go by water? Is it not better that it should make what profit it can on a low rate—the steamer rate *plus* a small addition for speed and certainty of delivery—even though it seems to be acting unfairly by charging no more for the 120 miles to Yarmouth than it does to Ely and Thetford, which are not much more than half way? But the matter does not end here. Norwich, let us say, which is a dozen miles on the London side of Yarmouth, gets the benefit of the cheap rate induced by the steamer competition to Yarmouth. But to Norwich the Great Eastern has a competitor, the Eastern and Midland, which comes in by a longer route round by Peterborough and Lynn, but is of course obliged to adopt the Great Eastern rate. Now this line to get to Norwich passes through

Melton Constable, a market town of some importance, at which it has no competition. Melton Constable is distant 120 miles from London, and has no access to the sea, so the Eastern and Midlands can charge between London and this town an ordinary local rate. The result is that a ton of goods may pay from

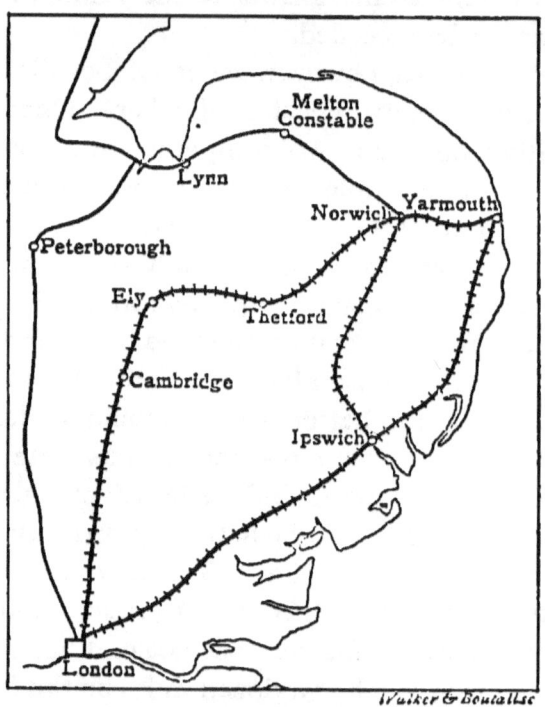

London to Melton Constable, say 25*s.*, and another ton may be carried in the same truck 20 miles further at a total charge of 15*s.* Now it would be easy to represent this as simply gross extortion without a shadow of justification. On the other hand, it is equally easy for the manager of the Eastern and

Midlands to reply—and in his case there is no question of bloated dividends, for the debenture interest is long in arrear, and it is only by very hard work that the line is made to pay its working expenses at all—that he cannot get more from the people of Norwich, and he cannot afford to take less from the inhabitants of Melton Constable. The Norwich rate pays actual movement expenses, and a small part of its share of the fixed charges. Unless Melton Constable and its neighbours are prepared to pay, not only the working expenses of their own traffic in full, but also a part of the working expenses of the Norwich traffic, the line will have to be closed altogether. And that, though it would matter comparatively little to the people at Norwich, who have the Great Eastern to fall back upon, would be a fatal blow to the prosperity of Melton Constable.

But this point is of such fundamental importance that we must come back to it in the next chapter. Meanwhile let us notice that in America, a country which, if low rates mean happiness, should surely be the paradise of the farmer and the trader, not only is it a habitual practice, where water competition comes in, to make the rates for the portion of the distance higher than for the whole;[1] but in several instances

---

[1] The famous "long and short haul clause" of the Inter-State Commerce Act is very far from being the drastic provision it is commonly supposed to be. Indeed it is safe to say that it does not go at all as far in the direction of equal mileage as the English statutes and English decisions have gone. Moreover, the Commission has exercised its dispensing power with considerable freedom. The wording of the clause is as follows:

"It shall be unlawful for any common carrier subject to the provisions of this Act" (*i.e.* engaged in commerce beyond the limits of a single state) "to charge or receive any greater compensation in the aggregate for the transportation of

where two lines compete, the one being direct and level, and the other hilly and roundabout, it has been recognised as fair that the longer and more expensive line should charge a lower rate, as if it charged the same as the direct route it would be unable to secure any share of the business at all. At the opposite pole from the United States stands the German Empire.

The nearest approach to equal mileage rates that can be found anywhere is probably the so-called "reform tariff" which has been in force for about a dozen years on the German railways. The German Government occupied an exceptionally strong position for trying an experiment of this kind. It could ignore the complaints of its customers whose established position was affected, in a way no private English railway company would venture to do for an instant. The whole of the railways of the country were under Government control. Their territory was mainly inland and comparatively little exposed to sea competition. The German traders were secured in their own markets by a strong protective tariff, while their external trade was but a small percentage of the

passengers, or of like kind of property, under substantially similar circumstances or conditions, for a shorter, than for a longer distance over the same line in the same direction, the shorter being included within the longer distance, but this shall not be construed as authorising any common carrier within the terms of this Act to charge or receive as great compensation for a shorter as for a longer distance; provided, however, that upon application to the Commission appointed under the provisions of this Act, such common carrier may, in special cases after investigation by the Commission, be authorised to charge less for longer than for shorter distances, for the transportation of passengers or property, and the Commission may from time to time prescribe the extent to which such designated common carrier may be relieved from the operation of this section of this Act."

whole. Further, the political history of the country had prevented the aggregation of particular trades in particular districts in anything like the measure to which we are accustomed here.

But even with all these advantages, nature was too strong for the German Government. In theory the reform tariff is based upon an equal charge per ton per mile, *plus* a fixed terminal charge for station services. At the outset it was found that the terminal, if charged in full, would be so heavy as to kill the short-distance trade. It therefore was deliberately fixed at less than its real amount, and the loss of revenue thence accruing was balanced by an increase of the mileage charge. But then came the further difficulty. The short-distance traffic had been relieved at the expense of the long (or at least longer) distance traffic, and the mileage rate had consequently been made so heavy that German goods could not bear the cost of transit from the interior to the frontier. So an elaborate series of special export rates had to be introduced—it was no part of Prince Bismarck's policy to encourage imports—to redress the balance. Finally, after the scales have been pushed and pulled, first to the one side and then to the other, the *Archiv für Eisenbahnwesen*,[2] the official organ of the Ministry of Public Works, is able triumphantly to proclaim that only 50 per cent. of the tonnage returning 39 per cent. of the revenue is now carried at special rates—rates, that is, fixed, not according to mileage, but according to an arbitrary determination of what the

---

[2] P. 279 in the volume for 1890.

traffic will bear. If it needs all this calculation to know whether the principle will apply or not, and if, when all is said and done, it will only apply to fifty cases out of every hundred, is it not very questionable whether the principle is fit for active service at all? But if cost of service and equal mileage fail us, there is nothing to fall back upon but the principle of charging what the traffic will bear.

CHAPTER III

WHAT THE TRAFFIC WILL BEAR

"CHARGING what the traffic will bear" is a principle which has unquestionably got a bad name. "Bleeding the traffic to death" is pretty much the interpretation which has been put upon it by indignant traders from time to time. It is, however, satisfactory to learn, from Board of Trade reports, income tax returns, and similar documents, that the trade of the country is not yet moribund. Like Dryden's milk-white hind, it is "still doomed to death but fated not to die." This, however, may be wholly due to the native vigour of the patient. The charges of the companies may be extortionate and exorbitant, even though the trade of the country has prospered under them. Probably, indeed, some of the rates do actually deserve this condemnation. Unless the management of the lines were wholly in the hands of beings, angelic not only in virtue but in intelligence, it would be unduly sanguine to expect anything else.

But, in dealing with a question as large as that of English railway management, we must claim a right to neglect individual cases and to look at the working of the system as a whole. The assertion that English rates are extortionate might be fairly held to be established if either of two things could be proved: that English railway companies avail themselves of their position as monopolists or semi-monopolists to exact from the public markedly more than the normal rate of return for their capital, or else that they charge the public markedly more than is charged elsewhere under the same conditions *for the same services*. On this second head we shall have something to say later on; meanwhile, let us deal briefly with the first point.

In 1889, the most prosperous year the English railways have ever known, the return on the 876,000,000*l.* sterling which they have cost averaged, according to the official Board of Trade figures, a little under 4¼ per cent. Less than one two-hundredth part of the whole received more than 8 per cent., and even this was quite exceptional, as in the previous year the proportion earning this rate of interest was less than one three-hundredth of the whole. About one-tenth of the total capital is returned as having earned in 1889 more than 6 per cent., but this over-represents the actual success, for the bulk of the stock returning this high rate of interest belongs to two great companies, the North Western and the North Eastern, whose shares have for many years past commanded a high premium, and who have taken advantage of this circumstance to put 6*l.*, 7*l.* or 8*l.* worth of new work and new materials into their line for every 5*l.* they have added to the nominal amount of their ordinary capital. In the last half-yearly report of the London and North Western, under the head of "receipts on capital account," stands this entry: "Premiums on issue of stock and shares, 5,142,874*l.* 4*s.* 5*d.*"

At the other end of the scale we find no less than one-fifteenth of the capital receiving no dividend whatever, a good deal of it never likely to receive any.

Without labouring the point further, we may then take it as proved that, if by "extortionate" we are to understand "producing an excessive or unfairly large return to the companies," it is only by an abuse of language that our English goods rates as a whole can be called extortionate. Perhaps, however, we shall not be far wrong if we assume that persons who bring the charge of extortion refer not so much to the rates as a whole as to individual rates and to the apparent disproportion between them. Further, and this point is of the very greatest importance, they may be ready to admit that their own rate *per se* is reasonable enough; yet they say the company proves it to be extortionate by the fact that it is ready to treat a competitor so much more favourably. "Often," says the report of the Committee of 1882, they "really mean, not that the rates they pay themselves are too high, but that the rates that others pay are too low." The Mayor of Blackburn, for instance, is compelled to admit that, after all said and done, the total sum charged him for the carriage of his cotton is so fractional a part of its value that it cannot seriously be supposed to cripple his trade; still nothing can shake his conviction that, if the company can afford to carry coal at 4s. 8d., it must be an abuse of strength to compel him to pay over the same distance 10s. 10d. for the carriage of cotton.[1]

[1] See Mr. Harrison's evidence before the Committee of 1881, Questions 2525-2976.

Mr. Harrison's contention—and I quote Mr. Harrison because he brings forward categorically what is the underlying gravamen of scores of other traders' complaints—raises the whole question of the basis on which railway rates ought to be fixed. We have seen that they cannot be fixed on a mere mileage basis, or even on the less crude basis of the cost of conveyance *plus* a fixed percentage of profit. And this, in brief, for the following reasons :

1. The cost of conveyance cannot practically be ascertained ; the cost of an average consignment for an average distance is of no use as a guide to the cost of an individual consignment under its own special circumstances.

2. If it could be ascertained, the standard could not be applied : (*a*) because it would absolutely prohibit all competition, it being inconceivable that the cost of conveyance by two competing routes would be identical ; (*b*) because the full cost of conveyance, *plus* a full share of profit, would produce so high an average rate of charge that goods of little value could not afford to pay it. They, therefore, would not go at all ; the railway would lose the profit, whatever it was, which it formerly made by carrying them, and, in order to maintain its financial position, would be compelled to raise its rates on the remainder. Thereupon the process would again be repeated. Other goods, hitherto just above the " margin of viability "[2] —if one may coin a phrase, in order to show how

---

[2] The doctors have attempted to introduce the word "viable," importing it apparently *via* Paris, to mean "capable of living." I venture to think that the word ought to mean "capable of travelling."

Ricardo's famous doctrine of rent applies—would fall below it. They, too, would cease to travel, the railway would raise its tariff once more, and so on *da capo*, till finally the line was left empty, save perhaps for occasional consignments of Brussels lace and bullion. There was, says Mr. Alexander, in his "Railway Practice," a "hotel in Arkansas, whose proprietor charged each guest the expenses of the house since the last one left, and collected with a shot gun."

But if cost of conveyance be abandoned as the basis of a tariff, the only other basis is that of charging what the tariff will bear, subject, however, to this limitation, that the carrier shall always make some profit, however small, out of the carriage—that the railway, that is (for the profit may in certain cases be indirect), shall be on the whole better off if the traffic goes than if it does not go. The phrase, let it be confessed at the outset, is an unfortunate one. "*Not* charging what the traffic will *not* bear," would be more logically accurate. No company could ever attempt to attain the maximum of charge which the most expensive class of goods could support. The price of a seat, for instance, in a first-class carriage is, as Sir Bernhard Samuelson once remarked, precisely the same whether the occupant be a Rothschild or one of his clerks. So, again, there is not a little traffic in bullion between London and Liverpool. The rate is 10*l.* per ton, and as the value of gold is something like 100,000*l.* per ton, it is safe to say that the rate would need to be a good deal higher before it induced the Bank of England to withdraw its bullion shipments from the "Etruria" or the "Majestic" and send them to New York by a cattle boat from the London Docks. Here, at least, Mr. Jeans will probably admit that his strictures on English management are not justified by the facts. "The railway companies" (so we are told in "Railway Problems") "make no secret of the fact that, in cases where there is little or no competition compelling a different course, the guiding principle is that of imposing on the traffic *just as much* as it will bear." The words which I have italicised are, of course, simply a parody of the real principle.

It should not, I think, be difficult to demonstrate that the principle of charging what the traffic will bear is one which leads not to high rates but to low rates. Two facts at least will not be denied by anyone acquainted with the rudiments of the question. The United States have pushed the principle further than any other country in the world, and the United States have the lowest freight rates in the world. Later on I hope to show that the one fact is the logical consequence of the other.

Here is the account of the matter given in their first annual report by the Inter-State Commerce Commission, a body whose reason for existence, it is worth remembering, was mainly the efforts of American railroad managers to charge the non-competitive portion of their traffic rates which it could not bear. This fact, however, has not blinded the Commission to the value of the principle when properly applied. "It was," they say, "very early in the history of railroads perceived that, if these agencies of commerce were to accomplish the greatest practicable good, the charges for the transportation of different articles of freight could not be apportioned among such articles by reference to the cost of transporting them severally; for this, if the apportionment of cost were possible, would restrict within very narrow limits the commerce in articles whose bulk or weight was large as compared with their value. On the system of apportioning the charges strictly to the cost, some kinds of commerce, which have been very useful to the country, and have tended greatly to bring its different sections into more intimate business and social relations, could never have grown to any considerable magnitude, and in some cases could not have existed at all, for the simple reason that the value at the place of delivery would not equal the purchase price with the transportation added.

"The traffic would thus be precluded, because the charge for carriage would be greater than it could bear. On the other hand, the rates for the carriage of articles which within small bulk or weight concentrate great value would on that system of making them be absurdly low; low when compared to the value of the articles, and perhaps not less so when the comparison was with the value of the service in transporting them. It was, therefore, seen not to be unjust to apportion the whole cost of service among all articles transported, upon a basis that should *consider the relative value of the service more than the relative cost of carriage.* Such method of apportionment would be best for the country, because it would enlarge commerce and extend communication; it would be best for the railroads, because it would build up a large business ; and it would not be unjust to property owners, who would thus be made to pay in some proportion to benefit received. Such a system of rate making would in principle approximate taxation ; the value of the article carried being the most important element in determining what shall be paid upon it."

Later on in the same report they recur to this subject in the following words : " To take each class of freight by itself and measure the reasonableness of charges by reference to the cost of transporting that particular class, though it might seem abstractly just, would neither be practicable for the carriers nor consistent with the public interest. The public interest is best served when the rates are so apportioned as to encourage the largest practicable exchange of products between different sections of our country and with foreign countries, and this can only be done by making value an important consideration, and by placing upon the higher classes of freight some share of the burden that on a relatively equal apportionment, if service alone were considered, would fall upon those of less value. With this method of arranging tariffs little fault is found, and *perhaps none at all by persons who consider the subject from the standpoint of public interest.*"

In these concluding words the Commissioners hit square on the head one of the most important points in the whole question. A producer or a trader may object to a system which makes his trade pay a portion of his neighbour's charges ; may object even where a portion of his expense of transport is charged on his neighbours, because some one else has managed to shuffle off a still larger share; but while only a section of the nation are either producers or traders, all are consumers, and the interest of the consumer must therefore be paramount. And that the system of charging what the traffic can bear is in the interest of the consumer there can be no doubt whatever. But it is time to see what the expression really means when stripped of glosses improperly put upon it.

To understand what the phrase does mean, and how the principle which it embodies is applied in practice, let us analyse in outline the receipts and expenditure of the English companies. As the figures we shall use are only for purposes of illustration, there can be no harm if we keep them as round as possible. A train, then, earns roughly 5s. a mile. One-half of this sum, 2s. 6d. a mile, is absorbed in working expenses, the other half goes to pay interest on capital. But the 2s. 6d. for working expenses can be divided once more into two parts: one-half of the expenditure is on fixed charges, maintenance of road and stations, signalling and telegraphs, office expenses, and so forth, which are only slightly affected by the addition of new business; the remaining 1s. 3d. is the actual out-of-pocket expense of working that particular train. Unless therefore a train can be got to pay 1s. 3d. per mile it will not be run at all, except—and in practice in England the exception is doubtless an important one—that a branch train, earning even less than this, may be run to act as a feeder for the main line. Rates on the whole must be fixed to give a return of 5s.; but if in the case of a particular traffic they produce 2s. 6d. the traffic pays its way, though there is no profit left for capital. Even at 1s. 3d. the company is not actually out of pocket. At any point above 1s. 3d. the company is better off if the traffic goes than if it does not go.

For 1s. 6d., say, pays working expenses and leaves a contribution of 3d. towards the fixed charges which are equally incurred whether this particular train is run or not. Now let us apply these facts. A railway is built to connect, say, Birmingham with London. The two places have hitherto had no connection except by canal-boat or by coach. The railway naturally fixes its rates on what we may call the 5s. scale. Even then they are so much below the rates previously exacted by the canal that the completion of the line is hailed with pæans of acclamation, and the shareholders, whose capital has built the railway, are looked upon as national benefactors. Then, in a year or two, another company, the Grand Junction, gives Birmingham access to the sea at Liverpool also. It likewise invests its money in the belief that the Birmingham-Liverpool traffic will be ready and willing to pay on the 5s. a mile scale. Nor is it disappointed: the traders show their gratitude to the new-comer in the most practical manner by abandoning the canals and using the railway almost exclusively. But then the London and Birmingham and the Grand Junction unite their undertaking, and with the advent of the London and North Western, with its through route all the way from sea to sea, from London to Liverpool, commences a new order of things. Liverpool and London have been accustomed to communicate with one another by ship. Their traders show none of the alacrity to make use of the new method of communication which was displayed by Birmingham. It may be better, say they, than the old, but it is certainly not cheaper. Thereupon, the North Western directors take counsel and say, "What shall we do? Birmingham and its neighbours evidently cannot furnish traffic sufficient to fill our line, which half the day stands empty, earning nothing, while the cost of maintenance and the interest of our shareholders' capital runs on all the same." And thereupon they resolve to make an attempt to induce the Liverpool men to send their London traffic by the railway instead of by sea, and they go to them and offer a 4s. rate, which the Liverpool men accept.

And this was how the directors reasoned: "The 4s.," said they, "will pay not only the cost of moving the Liverpool traffic, but also its full share of the establishment charges. Further, it will contribute 1s. 6d. per mile towards paying our dividend. A small sum certainly, but it is better than the alternative—nothing, which is what the Liverpool traffic pays us as long as it continues to go by water. Probably Birmingham will complain at the outset that our through rate per ton for the whole distance is 40s., while the sum of the two local rates would be 50s.; but when the matter is explained to them they cannot fail to see that the mere fact that goods passing through Birmingham pay a lower rate per mile than goods starting from there is no injury to them. They will believe us when we say that we should be only too happy for our own sake to charge the Liverpool people more, if we could persuade them to pay it, and when we point out to them also that, in so far as the Liverpool traffic helps to give us a reasonable rate of interest for our money, there is a smaller balance which we are likely to ask Birmingham to make up."

It was, we may assume, in some such way as this that railway managers reasoned in the early days when first competitive rates had to be established. And if the principle involved had always stood out as clearly as it does in the ideally simple condition of things which we have imagined here, no doubt the Birmingham traders would have frankly admitted the cogency of the argument. At least such traders have been known to exist in America, if not in England. Here is a story of actual fact told by Professor Hadley in his "Railroad Transportation:"

"On the coast of Delaware, a few years ago, there was a place which we shall call X——, well suited for oyster growing, but which sent very few oysters to market, because the railroad rates were so high as to leave no margin of profit. The local oyster growers represented to the railroad that if the rates were brought down to one dollar per hundred pounds the business would become profitable, and the railroad could be sure of regular shipments at the price. The railroad men looked into the matter. They found that the price of oysters in the Philadelphia market was such that the local oyster-man could pay one dollar per 100 lbs. to the railroad and still have a fair profit left. If the road tried to charge more, it would so cut down the profit as to leave men no inducement to enter the business. That is, those oysters would bear a rate of one dollar per hundred pounds and no more.

Further, the railroad men found that if they could get every day a car-load, or nearly a car-load, at this rate, it would more than cover the expense of hauling an extra car by quick train back and forth every day, with the incidental expenses of interest and repairs. So they put the car on, and were disappointed to find that the local oyster growers could only furnish oysters enough to fill the car about half full. The

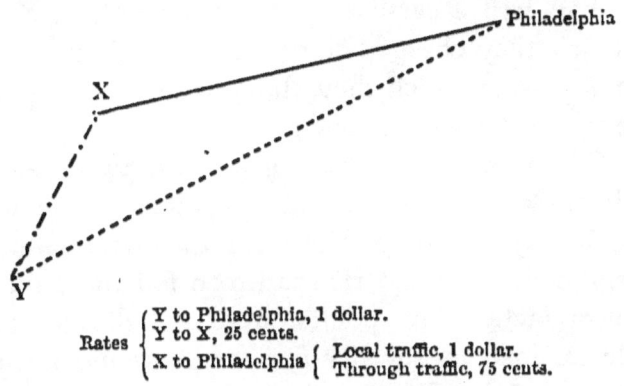

Rates { Y to Philadelphia, 1 dollar. Y to X, 25 cents. X to Philadelphia { Local traffic, 1 dollar. Through traffic, 75 cents.

expense to the road of running it half full was almost as great as of running it full ; the income was reduced one-half. They could not make up by raising the rates, for these were as high as the traffic would bear. They could not increase their business much by lowering rates. The difficulty was not with the price charged, but with the capacity of the local business. It seemed as if this special service must be abandoned.

"One possibility suggested itself. At some distance beyond X———, the terminus of this railroad, was another oyster-growing place, Y———, which sent its oysters to market by another route. The supply at Y—— was very much greater than at X——; the people at Y—— were paying a dollar a hundred pounds to send their oysters to market. It would hardly cost twenty-five cents to send them from Y—— to X——. If, then, the railroad from X—— to Philadelphia charged but seventy-five cents a hundred pounds on oysters which came from Y——, it could easily fill its car full. This was what they did. They then had half a car-load of oysters grown at X——, on which they charged a dollar, and half a car-load from Y——, on which they charged seventy-five cents for exactly the same service.

"Of course there was a grand outcry at X——. Their trade was discriminated against in the worst possible way—so they said—and they complained to the railroad. But the railroad men fell back on the logic of facts. The points were as follows: (1) a whole car-load at seventy-five cents would not pay expenses of handling and moving; (2) at higher rates than seventy-five cents they could not get a whole car-load, but only half a car-load; half a car-load at a dollar rate (the highest charge the article would bear) would not pay expenses. Therefore: (3) on any uniform rate for everybody the road must lose money; and (4) they would either be compelled to take the oyster-car away altogether, or else get what they could at a dollar, and fill up at seventy-five cents. There was no escape from this reasoning; and the oyster men of X—— chose to pay the higher rate rather than lose the service altogether.

"This is a typical case. The business of a railroad is of two kinds. Some of its business, like the oysters of X——, must be done over this railroad, or not at all. Of such business it is sure, even at high rates; the only limit is the value of the service—the excess of the selling price at market above cost of production at X——. But a railroad may also do business like that of the oysters from Y——, which can be sent to market by other routes. To do this it must make special concessions at lower rates."

Unfortunately railway rate problems refuse as a rule to present themselves in a form dissected out and separated from surrounding circumstances like an anatomist's specimens. They are complicated with questions of classification, of the allowance which should be made for exceptional conditions, gradients, or what not; of the amount of increased traffic which reduced tariffs would bring; of the method in which the existing traffic ought to be worked so as to produce the best economic results, and fifty things more. Further, the trader, who in ordinary times never gives these subjects a thought, brings to their consideration, in periods of bad trade, a mind in which philosophical calm is not induced by the knowledge that, while he is losing money, the railway shareholder who sits at home at ease is still receiving a six per cent. dividend. No wonder the result of his consideration is for the most part unscientific. No wonder if he is anxious to run with the hare and hunt with the hounds: if at one moment he declares, as the Liverpool witnesses did before the Committees in 1881 and 1882, that railway companies ought not to be allowed to deprive a place of the advantages of its geographical situation—in other words, that equal mileage rates ought to be put into force in order to handicap Fleetwood and Barrow out of the race—and then the next moment he goes on to assume as self-evident that the North Western Railway has no corresponding rights to its advantages of geographical position, and that he has a natural right to the benefit of the differential tariff which is secured to him by the fact that the different companies competing to Liverpool, and therefore compelled to charge the same rates, arrive there by routes of varying length.

Let us leave therefore for a time the heated air of contemporary controversy and come back to a consideration of another problem which had to be solved in the early days. The story of the Mr. B., who, when it was suggested that the London and Birmingham Railway should commence the carriage of coal, exclaimed, "Coal! Why they will be asking us to carry dung next!" has become classic, and may serve to remind us that there was a time when the through traffic in coal and other low-priced articles—as distinguished from the short distance coal traffic which lines such as the Stockton and Darlington, and the Monkland and Kirkintilloch, and the Leicester and Swannington, were built to serve—was thought to be impossible. Newcastle could put coal into the London market by sea for a price far below that which it would cost—" cost " including movement expenses, fixed charges, and interest on capital—to bring coal to London from Derbyshire or Staffordshire. One can fancy Robert Stephenson and Mr. Glyn discussing the question. The case was not, it will be seen, at all the same as the Liverpool one. The Liverpool traders could pay higher rates if they chose, but, having the sea to fall back upon, they refused to give the railway more than the sea rate *plus* a certain small addition for extra speed and certainty of delivery. For the Staffordshire coal-master there was no such freedom. At the one end the cost of his coal was fixed by the rate of wages and the other expenses of production, at the other end the price he could get for it was also fixed by the competition of the sea-borne article. The railway rate must be less than the difference between these two figures, otherwise his coal would stop at home. Say, for the sake of argument, that the difference between them was 8*s*., a sum which, when worked out at a mileage rate, would evidently give a good deal less than a penny per ton.

To such rates the London and Birmingham Company was in those days unaccustomed, but it wanted the new traffic, and it could get that traffic on no better terms. So down the rate came, and its fall, along with that of the Liverpool rate, taught the lesson that, when a certain locality, from its advantageous geographical position, *will not* pay its full share of fixed expenses and dividend, or when a certain article, from its small value, *cannot* pay its full share, the railway company will be wise, both in its own interest and in that of the public, to accept the traffic on the best terms it can get—always provided, however, that better paying traffic is not thereby crowded off the line, and that the new traffic at least yields some profit. Of the interest of the railway in taking this course we have spoken already. That the Liverpool trader and the Staffordshire coal-master also gain, needs no demonstration. That the senders of more highly charged goods do not suffer is equally clear. They were paying full rates to start with; if anything, the extra profit of the new traffic is likely to reduce their rates. Finally, that the London public gains by the opening of new routes or new sources of supply is unquestionable. Doubtless the Liverpool shipowner complained of the competition with the craft by which he had his wealth. Doubtless the Newcastle coalowner protested that he was being "deprived of the advantage of his geographical position," and with truth, if not with justice. But their right to do anything more than protest could only be recognised on principles which would give every butcher and baker a right to compensation if their neighbours transferred their custom to a shop a couple of miles off.

Here then, in its most simple form, we can see the principle of "charging what the traffic will bear" at work. At the risk of repetition, we must emphasize once more two facts. Its effect has been to raise rates nowhere, to reduce them somewhere, and therefore on the whole to bring down the average. Secondly, to benefit the consumer by widening the area of supply, and so securing that the products he consumes shall reach him charged with no monopoly profits. And, thirdly, to benefit the country at large by opening up fields of profitable industry in districts which previously were handicapped out of the contest by the cost of carriage.

Now let us briefly notice one or two other applications of the same principle. An ironmaster wishes to increase his output, but he cannot get more ore from the mines which at present supply him, and which are situated at an average distance of 20 miles, as they are already being worked to their full capacity. So he casts about and finally meets with some deposits at a distance of 30 miles from his works. Before, however, making up his mind to purchase, he goes to see the manager of the railway and puts the case to him. "At present," he says, "I am paying 1s. 8d. a ton for the carriage of my ore 20 miles. I can't afford to pay you at the same rate for the 30 miles. What can you do for me? If you can make me a substantial reduction it will be worth your while, as if I get my new blast furnaces you will have another 1,000 tons of pig-iron every week to carry."

"Well," replies the manager, "let me think over it, and see how what you ask will affect your neighbours, and I will let you know in a day or two. By-the-by, before you go, just tell me: your present ore, I think, gives about 50 per cent. of metal—what is the grade of the ore at your proposed new mine?" "Not so good, unfortunately," is the answer. "I doubt if it will run to as much as 40 per cent." The manager does think over it, he causes a rate-clerk to tabulate the other ore rates of the district, and to work out accurately what amount of 40 per cent. ore will be needed to produce each ton of "pig"; he considers how often his engine will be able to go backwards and forwards each day, and what profit roughly he may expect from the new pig-iron traffic; and then he makes up his mind as to what he thinks will be a reasonable rate. Then, perhaps, he consults the company's solicitor as to whether the rate he means to offer will be liable to be objected to as affording the applicant an undue or unreasonable preference over his competitors ; and if the answer is, as he expects, that there seems no reason to fear this, he sends off his letter, which runs as follows : " Referring to our conversation of two days since, I have the pleasure to inform you that, on the understanding that you expect to be able to raise about 300 tons of ore a day from your new mine, I shall be ready to recommend my directors to give you a rate of 2$s.$ per ton. I may add, however, that I am recommending this partly in consequence of the low grade of the ore, as the rate is a good deal below our usual scale."

Take another instance, which is given in Mr. Grierson's book on "Railway Rates" as an actual piece of history. " About 30 years ago, when the ironworks at Westbury in Wiltshire were constructed, it was anticipated that fuel would be obtained from the Radstock district, about 14 miles distant. But, after sinking collieries, it was found that the coke was not suitable, so that it has now to be obtained from South Wales, a distance of about 130 miles. The pig-iron is sent to South Wales in the return coke waggons, and also to South Staffordshire, a distance of 140 miles. The coke and pig-iron are carried at special low rates below those in force for traffic to intermediate stations. Without such special rates, or if mileage rates were charged, the works would have to be closed." Now carry this one step further. Suppose that Westbury, instead of being inland, had been on the sea, and that the pig-iron had been usually sent away to South Wales by water. Would not the Great Western have said: "Here are our coke waggons going back empty; any rate for pig-iron which will pay something more than the difference between the cost of hauling an empty and a full waggon will be a profitable rate for us?" And would not the company have been wise to try to undersell the ships which hitherto had done the business, even though the profit to itself was but a very small one, and such as it could not dream of taking as an accepted standard?

Take another instance. The cost of getting house coal in the various collieries of the South Yorkshire district is precisely similar, let us say. So is the value of the coal when brought to bank. The only difference is that some collieries are 20 miles further from London than others. The owner of the nearest colliery is forced by the competition of Newcastle and Derbyshire to be content with an average profit; the owner of the furthest colliery cannot in the long run work for less. Either, therefore, the railway must forego its charge for the extra 20 miles of haulage, or else the nearest colliery monopolises the market. So the railways put in force what is termed a "group" rate, and London consumers and Yorkshire colliers have both good reason to thank them for their action.

One instance more, which raises the most burning question of all, that of special export and import rates. It perhaps may be a sign of audacity rather than of discretion to attempt to defend these latter. The House of Commons Committee of 1882, which laughed equal mileage and cost-of-service theories to scorn, which when invited to curse "grouping" blessed it altogether, which accepted it as self-evident that companies engaged in long distance traffic should be satisfied with what profit they could get, when to get a more satisfactory profit was impossible; the Committee which recommended that "the right of railway companies to charge for station terminals should be recognised by Parliament," and reported that "on the whole of the evidence they acquit the railway companies of any grave dereliction of their duty to the public"—this same Committee did not venture to stand up for exceptional import rates.

But neither, on the other hand, did they condemn them outright. "It must," says the Committee, "be admitted that, when a farmer sees American wheat carried at a lower rate than his own, or when a manufacturer near a market has his profits in that market reduced by a competitor at a distance who is brought into the market by the lower rate given to him, it is not surprising that there should be complaints and that attempts should be made and from time to time repeated, to fix some standard by which rates shall be determined." After which cautious avoidance of the question whether these complaints are or are not justified, the Committee passes on to show conclusively—drawing its illustrations however only from internal traffic—that exceptional long-distance rates may be for the public interest, and further that a fixed standard of charge is both practically unattainable and theoretically undesirable. Now, why at this point the Cobden Club did not step down into the arena it is impossible to imagine. An annual excursion to Greenwich cannot absorb the whole energies of that august society. Yet never was there a clearer case for its intervention.

The Committee justified a low rate for fish from Wick and a comparatively high rate from Grimsby, though the railways made a very different percentage of profit, on the ground that they could not get more; that if the rate were raised the long-distance traffic would either go by sea or cease to go at all; that it was for the benefit of the London consumer that both places should be in the market in competition, and that the starvation or other inconvenience thereby caused to the fishermen at Grimsby was balanced by the advantage to the fishermen at Wick. Now it is absolutely indisputable that precisely the same considerations applied to the American meat from Liverpool and the Belgian hops from Boulogne. The sole difference was that the fishermen were fellow-countrymen, the producers of the meat and the hops were foreigners. Look at the facts. It was not denied that the American meat was at a disadvantage already, that its total rate from Wyoming or Dakota—for American beef does not come into existence at the Liverpool Docks—was twice or thrice that which the English farmer had to pay; that American beef was, when it reached its market, an inferior article, and as such entitled to a lower classification. Still less was it denied that the North Western authorities were ready to take a higher rate, if they only could get it.

It was acknowledged that, if the rate were raised, the beef would either cease to come or would go round to London by sea. Now it must have been in the interest of the Londoner that this meat should continue to come—for meat is even more a necessary of life than fish—that it should come, moreover, by the shortest and quickest route, so as to arrive in as good condition as might be. And if the English farmer, who had retired to the workhouse, and the English landlord, who in lieu of rent was harvesting a fine crop of thistles and ragweed, suffered, did not the farmer in Wyoming gain in equal degree, and was he not also a man and a brother? And yet the Cobden Club never spoke one word in defence of his rights.

Now, it is quite possible to believe that Free Trade is a dogma which ought to be, if it is not, held and acted upon *semper, ubique, ab omnibus*. It is possible also to believe that in this work-a-day world no abstract political principle is of universal application, and that, in the very exceptional conditions of ten or twelve years ago, when a sudden combination of circumstances (which can hardly, one would think, ever again recur simultaneously) crushed the British agricultural interest to the ground, some special assistance ought to have been given to that interest, even though theorists might raise the cry of Protection. But what is surely impossible of belief is that, while the policy of the Government of the country continued to be a Free Trade one, it was the duty of individual citizens who happened to be railway managers to inaugurate a policy of Protection.

Take the second of the two cases of "favouring the foreigner," of which we heard so much a few years back—a case which is still from time to time, though the rate has long ceased to exist, thrown in the teeth of the South Eastern Railway—the charge of 35*s.* per ton for hops from Ashford to London as against 17s. 6d. for foreign hops from Boulogne, *viâ* Folkestone and Ashford. Admit for the sake of argument that the 35s. rate for English hops was a high one,[3] though it was proved to demonstration that the real rate for purposes of comparison was only 26s. 6d., and that the English traffic was exceptionally expensive to work. Still, it could not be denied that it was perfectly legal, and further that it only amounted to from $1\frac{1}{2}$ to 2 per cent. of the value of the article.

It was evident that the foreign hops were much cheaper to carry, were worth less, and therefore had a right to a lower rate, and yet that their total rate from the point of origin must have been at least as high as the rate for the English hops. It was evident also that the South Eastern could not raise the French rate, as there were half a dozen steamers, some of them no doubt heavily subsidised by the French Government, ready and willing to take the hops to London by water at the same price, and in almost the same time. And yet the attempt of the company to earn an honest halfpenny—a penny being absolutely unattainable under the circumstances—was received with a perfect storm of indignation. Once more, the only difference in principle between Boulogne hops and Wick fish was that the hops were Belgian and the fish Scotch. Can the outcry be

[3] The present writer has no wish to go back here from the position which he has publicly maintained more than once of late, that the charges of the South Eastern are too high—that, in other words, the adoption of a more liberal policy would be judicious in the interest not only of the public but of the shareholders. Such a belief, supposing others to share it, might explain, but could not justify, the outcry about the Boulogne hops.

explained, therefore, except as an instance of the natural and corrupt love of Protection implanted in the human breast? And against such a reappearance of the old Adam ought not the Cobden Club to have entered its solemn protest? Have not the foreigners who grow hops as strong a claim to its good offices as those who grow sugar-beet?

One word more about import rates. Public opinion has prevailed, and the Boulogne hops now go by water. By the same way, and for the same reason, went also last summer the German cherries which the Dutch boats brought over from Flushing to Queenborough, and which formerly Chatham and Dover trains brought up from that point. The barge-owners on the Medway and the Thames gained, it may be presumed, the profit which the Chatham and Dover lost; the London doctors, too, perhaps gained something, as the cherries mostly arrived somewhat the worse for their journey. But where the advantage came in, either to the London consumer or to the rival Kent producer, is by no means so apparent.

Why the Kent producer did not gain, may be seen from an illustration borrowed from a pamphlet published a short time back in France, dealing with a precisely similar question.[4] From Bordeaux to Paris the rate for wine is 6 centimes per litre. From the Spanish frontier, 200 miles further, to the same destination, it is 4 centimes, the reason for the difference of course being the water competition *viâ* Havre. But at the 6 centimes rate 3,000,000 tons are carried as against 200,000 tons

[4] *La Concurrence,* Paris, 1886.

at 4 centimes. An agitation being raised against the French railways for "favouring the foreigner"—and very justly, one cannot but think, considering that the French national policy is Protectionist, and the French Government largely subsidises its railways—the demand is made that the Bordeaux rate and the Spanish rate shall be properly readjusted. "No!" replies the author of the pamphlet—writing obviously on behalf of the French companies—"we cannot raise the Spanish rate, and we will not lower the Bordeaux rate. If you like we will cancel the Spanish rate altogether; the total traffic is small and the margin of profit still smaller, but we cannot afford to tamper with a rate which is reasonable in itself and at which 3,000,000 tons are carried." One more instance of the truth of what has been stated already, that the abolition of a so-called "preferential" rate—it has been proved over and over again in the case of judgments of the Railway Commission—means not levelling down, but levelling up.

Export rates need not detain us long. Their chief interest is the evidence they afford in disproof of the oft repeated assertion that man is a reasoning animal. Theoretically we all admit that the political economy primer is correct, when it tells us that exports can only be paid for by imports. But practically we resent special import rates, though they increase the quantity of foreign beef or hops which we can obtain in the English market in exchange for a given quantity of English manufactures, while we approve of special export rates which mean the increase in a foreign market of the amount of our manufactured goods which will need to be given in exchange for a certain quantity of foreign produce. If the consumer pays the carriage, as it is commonly supposed he does, logically we ought to be more anxious to cheapen the rates on imports than on exports. Practically, however, the feeling runs all the other way, and while shippers are entirely conscious of their advantages, the local consignee only complains, if he complains at all, on the ground that if the railway can afford to carry for the shipper at 25*s*. per ton, it ought to carry for him for less than 40*s*. But with this fallacy we have already dealt at quite sufficient length. Export rates, it should perhaps be added, rest on the highest statutory authority. The first Railway Act ever passed, that for the Stockton and Darlington, prescribed as a maximum toll for coal for local use 4*d*. per ton per mile, for coal for export the maximum was ½*d*.

There is one other point which, to those who think that the course of trade can be regulated by Acts of Parliament, should not be without interest. England is not the only country where there has been an agitation against import rates as "favouring the foreigner." A general manager at, let us say, Constantinople, wrote a letter not so long since to the manager of an allied road across the frontier, at, say, Athens, and this is the substance of what he said: "The agitation against our special import tariff is becoming so serious that I expect we shall have to yield to it. Now, it will never do to kill our exchange traffic. What I suggest is this. There is no feeling against special export rates. Therefore I will make a merely nominal rate, say 1s. a ton, on goods exported to Athens, and you can then levy on them as soon as they get on your side of the frontier a rate twice as heavy as you get now. In return you will be content with a nominal rate on what you send to us, and I can cover our existing revenue by doubling the rate from the frontier to Constantinople. The senders will pay just the same as before, and I can report to the Minister that special import rates have been abandoned." With which piece of evidence of the ability which railway managers bring to the decision of the question, what the traffic will bear, we will postpone further consideration of the subject to the next chapter.

CHAPTER IV

WHAT THE TRAFFIC WILL NOT BEAR

THE objections that are taken to the principle of charging what the traffic will bear fall under two main heads: the one theoretical, that the principle itself is wrong; the other practical, that its equitable application is a task so difficult and so delicate, that, even supposing the best and most upright intentions on the part of the railway managers of the country, the power to make rates is larger than can safely be entrusted to any private individual, and that the practical abuses have been so great in the past as to point to the conclusion that, if the principle must be applied at all, its application can only be entrusted to State officials. That the principle must be applied, simply because no other principle can possibly be adopted, has been argued at sufficient length in the previous chapters. But it is worth while here to add to that argument that the objectors perhaps fail to see how common the application of the same principle is in all the affairs of life. Take the turnpike roads themselves for instance. Theoretically, no doubt, a toll calculated on the amount of damage done to the road was an eminently just one. Practically, however, the principle was never enforced. A light dog-cart, weighing only two or three hundred-weight, was charged the same as a ponderous carrier's cart, weighing two or three tons. The dog-cart, it was felt, could bear a heavier rate. Needless to say, the taxation of the country is adjusted on the same principles. A Rothschild receives no more benefit, it may well be argued, from the army and the navy than a clerk on 200*l*. a year. Each is protected in life and limb, and in the possession of his whole property; but the one pays in income tax a thousand-fold more than the other.

Take again the principle of local rates. A man who lives in a house rated at 1,000*l*. a year makes no more use of the roads, or of the street lamps than his neighbour in a 20*l*. cottage. The services rendered to the two men by the local authorities are precisely identical; yet the one, because it is felt that he can afford it, is fairly made to pay fifty times as much as the other. The principle, in fact, is this. The government of the country, the maintenance and cleansing and lighting of the streets, have to be provided for somehow, and the money for so doing must be raised from those who can best afford to pay it. Now, consider the case of the railway. We must, of course, ignore the movement expenses, for they increase or diminish in direct proportion to the volume of traffic which actually goes, and they therefore must in fairness be charged upon that traffic itself; but, as we have seen, out of the 70,000,000*l*. sterling which the railways of Great Britain annually obtain from the public, one-half is required to pay 4¼ per cent. interest to the persons who have provided the road, while half of the remainder goes to maintain that road in a fit condition for the use of the traffic. This fifty odd millions, therefore, may fairly be looked upon in the light of a tax to be levied upon the total traffic, in a manner which, on the whole, is most for the convenience of the public at large.

No analogy will bear being pushed too far, and it is of course open to critics to ask, for instance, why on this principle a first-class passenger gets a ticket at the same price, whether he be an officer on half-pay or a millionaire financier? The reply would be, I conceive, that it is for the same reason which prevents the Government from introducing a graduated income tax, or from imposing an *ad valorem* scale of duties on wine or tea. Theoretically, this might be right; in practice, the difficulties of working it out would be so large, and the cost of collection would be so great, that the whole of the increased receipts would be swallowed up in increased expenditure, and nobody would gain. But, leaving taxation, we shall find that, in every affair almost of life, the principle of charging what the traffic will bear is fully recognised. Water, for instance, is supplied in every town in the kingdom, not at so much a gallon, but in return for a percentage charge on the rent of the house. No one supposes that a bachelor in Piccadilly or St. James's Street uses more water than a dozen poor families in the East End; but water is a necessity of life, just as much as railways, and those who undertake to provide it must be rewarded for their outlay somehow. Take again the professions. A doctor visits a patient, and charges him half a guinea; he then goes into the next room, and prescribes for the patient's cook at the charge of half a crown. It would surely be a slur on an honourable profession to assert that the doctor gave four-fold more attention to the one case than to the other. Take, again, a solicitor who undertakes the conveyance of an estate. The wisdom of Parliament has enacted that his remuneration shall be fixed on an *ad valorem* scale, which allows him to receive ten times as much where the purchase-money is 100,000*l.* as where it is only 5,000*l.* And yet, as every lawyer knows, the larger the estate the more likely the title is to be free from difficulties. In commercial matters, too, the same principle is almost universal. A stockbroker sells Consols for a commission of one-eighth per cent., though the trouble and cost to him is practically the same, whether the amount sold be large or small. But here comes in another point, where also the analogy to railway practice is instructive. The stockbroker, instead of dealing directly with his client, may be employed to make the sale by a banker or a solicitor, and the intermediary, who introduces the business, will claim to be permitted to share the commission. The stockbroker consents, reasoning doubtless somewhat as follows :—

"I am accustomed, as a rule, to charge A. 25*s* for selling 1,000*l.* stock, and B. 12*l.* 10*s.* for selling 10,000*l.*, and this is fair enough, for B. can afford to pay ten times as much as A., and I have got to make a living out of the business somehow. But now, when C.'s banker comes, and claims half the commission on the sale of C.'s 10,000*l.* Consols, I hardly see how I can refuse to give it? I am obviously not hurting B.; he will pay the same commission in any case, and, though somebody declares that I am taking this business at a loss, and recouping myself by overcharging the rest of my clients, who pay me the full commission, this is evidently nonsense, for it costs me nothing to do the business, beyond a few pence for papers and stamps. But if I don't take the half commission, I shall not get the business at all, with the result that I shall be 6*l*. 5*s*. poorer, and have to live and keep my office going just the same as before."

The stockbroker's calculations furnish then two analogies to the case of the railway. He charges what his traffic will bear, subject however to this, that if he attempts to make certain classes of traffic, which occupy an exceptionally strong position for dictating their own terms, pay the full rate, he loses that traffic altogether, and therefore, acting on the principle that half a loaf is better than no bread, he does this exceptional business at less than his ordinary percentage of profit, less than the percentage perhaps at which he could do the whole of his business and live.

The theory that railway companies do one portion of their business at a loss, and recoup themselves by overcharging the rest, is really so unreasonable that it hardly deserves to be met with serious argument. But it is so often met with that one is forced to believe that there are some people who really believe it. So a short consideration of the matter will not be out of place. Railway companies have been constantly told that they carry American meat or French hops at the expense of their English customers; but why they should do so, unless on the supposition that the managers are not only knaves, but fools, which hitherto has not been asserted, no trader has ever condescended to explain. It would be at least as reasonable for a gentleman in the stalls at Drury Lane to declaim against the management of the National Theatre, which, having charged him 10*s.* 6*d.* for his seat, then proceeded to admit the gods at a shilling a head at his expense. Or, take another and a better analogy, that of an hotel. An hotel has this in common with the railway, that a large part of the fixed expenditure runs on just the same whether the house be full or empty. But what should we say for the intelligence of a summer visitor at Ilfracombe, who protested against the hotel proprietor entertaining, at his expense, the few guests who were attracted in December by the offer of special winter boarding terms?

Here, again, is a more elaborate comparison with a condition of affairs which in manufacturing industries is common enough, and is there known as the utilisation of bye-products, for which we are indebted to Professor Hadley.[1]

"A wire manufacturer imports the rods which he intends to draw out into wire. He finds them covered with rust. As the first step in his process he washes off that iron rust with sulphuric acid. The washings are often allowed to run to waste. But if a manufacturer will put up the necessary sheds for collecting them, and boiling them down, he can obtain a quantity of crystallized sulphate of iron, or copperas. The commercial value of this copperas is very small.

[1] *Railroad Transportation*, p. 113.

It is probably not worth as much as the acid which it contains. Certainly no one would think of deliberately dissolving iron in sulphuric acid, and selling the copperas thus made. But the wire manufacturer has the material on his hands in the form of washings. It is better for him to sell for the merest trifle rather than let it run to waste.

"Now suppose a legislator says : 'Here is this man making arbitrary discriminations. He has the only wire-mill in the region, and so makes a large profit on this wire, while he allows the consumer of copperas to have it at prices which hardly pay expenses. In fact, he sells it at a less sum than the materials cost him. Let us enact a law which will prevent him from making more money on one part of his business than another.' What would be the result of such a law? Would he reduce his price on wire so as to make no more profit than on his copperas? Obviously not. Would he reduce his prices for wire, and raise them for copperas? No. He could not sell his copperas at the higher prices, or he would have charged them to begin with. The only result will be that he will stop making copperas. His prices for wire will remain the same. If anything, they will tend to run higher, because one slight source of advantage is cut off, so that competitors are not so likely to be tempted to come into the business. It would be nonsense for the man who buys wire to say that he is 'taxed' to furnish another man with copperas below cost."[2]

---

[2] It is worth notice that if the wire manufacturer had had, not only a monopoly of the wire-trade, but of the copperas trade of his district, he would have been able to charge the same rate of profit on the copperas as on the wire, subject only to this, that he might

In a paper on the "Theory of Railroad Rates," read last December at Washington, before the American Economic Association, Professor Taussig, of Harvard University, dealt with the whole question of the relation between rates and cost in a very lucid manner. Nearly the whole of the expenses of a railway are, as he pointed out, of the class known to economists as "joint cost." The classical instances of this are gas and coke, and mutton and wool. Let us see what this means. Ask the Gas Light and Coke Company what it costs them to produce a hundred-weight of coke; their reply must be that this depends on what the public will pay for the gas. Put the question the other way round, and ask them what it costs to produce a thousand cubic feet of gas, and they will reply that this depends on the price at which the public will purchase their coke. The working expenses of the whole operations of the company are so much. The result of those operations is the output of a certain quantity of gas and a certain quantity of coke. Supposing that they can get for the gas the whole of their outlay *plus* interest on capital, the cost of the coke to them is nothing. Anything they can sell it for is pure profit. Now take, on the other hand, a Durham firm, manufacturing coke for the use of the neighbouring blast furnaces. The firm can use

then have made the copperas so dear that no one would use it. So with a railway. The German Government, for instance, has a monopoly of its railways, and can charge, therefore, the same rate of profit all round, except where foreign competition comes in, or where there are waterways accessible, or where, as in the case of coal, full rates would kill the traffic. But in England there are not only rival railways, but sea competition is said to affect three-fifths of all the station rates in the country. (*See* Report of Committee of 1872.)

a certain quantity of gas, no doubt, to heat its coke ovens, but for the rest it has possibly no market whatever. In this case, evidently, the coke must be looked to for the repayment of the cost of production and the interest on capital, and the most that can be expected of the gas is that it shall help in some slight degree to lighten the burden.

Take, again, the instance of mutton and wool. If the price of mutton at Smithfield is high enough to pay for keeping sheep in Lincolnshire, any price that the farmer can get for his wool, over and above the cost of shearing and packing, is so much to the good. But the squatter in Australia, whose mutton is worth, perhaps, $\frac{1}{2}$d. per pound, practically depends upon the price he can get for his wool. But neither farmer nor squatter can say positively what it costs him to produce either a pound of mutton or a pound of wool. The English farmer can say that, if the price of mutton falls to fourpence, he must either get more for his wool, or else go out of the business; and the Australian squatter can say that if the increasing demand for frozen mutton enables him to sell his meat for a penny a pound, he can afford to reduce the price of his wool; but beyond that neither the one nor the other can go.

The price of what is in each case the main article of production is largely determined by the value which the public puts upon what may be termed the byeproduct—the wool of the English farmer, the mutton of the Australian squatter. Now compare this with the case of the railway. The company invests its capital, provides an extensive plant and a large staff, in order to furnish transportation for passengers of different classes, and for goods, whether these latter be silks and velvets or coal. The railroad and its equipment is provided for passengers and freighters on their joint account. Fix for the company what it will receive for passengers and merchandise, perhaps it may be able to answer what it must charge for moving a ton of coal. Fix again the receipts from the coal and the merchandise, and it may be possible to find the cost of working a passenger train; but as in practice the one side of the equation is always variable, it is impossible to give a positive value to the other.

Broadly, this principle can be laid down. For the service as a whole, the cost of the service must measure the rate, which is, in other words, to say that, if the rate falls below this point, accommodation will be curtailed and new construction will stop; if it rises permanently above this, fresh capital will be attracted into the business. On the other hand, for any single part of the service, the only measure of the rate is the value which the public puts upon that service. If, for example, the Penzance mackerel or the Bradford woollens will not bear the rate charged, the traffic falls off or ceases altogether, and the rate comes down in order to entice it back again. But, whether the rate be high or low, so long as it pays mere movement expenses there is no question of working the traffic at the expense of other traffic. In one sense it is no doubt true that the more the company can get out of Bradford goods the cheaper it can afford to work its coal, but if the Bradford goods decline to pay fourpence a mile it is better for the coal-master that they should be enticed back on to the road by a rate of twopence, rather than that his coal should be left to bear the whole of the railway charges unaided.

If our analysis thus far is correct, it is evident that the position of a railway manager is immeasurably more difficult than that of a gas company or a farmer. Broadly speaking, the relation between gas and coke, between mutton and wool, is constant. To so many cubic feet of gas belongs also, as of course, the production of so many hundredweight of coal. So much mutton, so much wool. And whether coal is dear or cheap, whether sheep be fed on grass or turnips, the result is pretty much the same. And the farmer or the gas company has nothing to do but sell each of the products at the highest price it will fetch. But with a railway it is very different. The produce is infinitely various, and consists of transportation: for passengers, at various speeds, under various conditions of comfort or discomfort, on a contract for a single journey or for a series extending over many months; and for goods, under conditions yet more infinite in their variety. Exactly what each of these forms of transportation costs no man can tell, and therefore no man can tell what in each case is the profit of the company. It is known, however, that an improvement in the transportation at the same price, or a reduction of the price for the same facilities, is almost certain to increase the quantity sold: must, therefore, increase the gross profit, but may or may not increase the net profit, of the sellers.

A manager, therefore, surmises—it is really nothing more than a guess, for two men equally qualified will come to diametrically opposite conclusions on the same evidence, and actual experience alone can settle which of the two has decided correctly—that he will increase his net earnings by reducing such and such a rate, that he cannot afford to reduce such and such another, and he acts accordingly. The result sometimes proves him right, and sometimes wrong. The effect of a reduction may be that, whereas he was carrying 500 tons at 3*s.*, giving a gross profit of 75*l.* and a net profit of 37*l.* 10*s.*, he now carries 1,500 tons at 2*s.* 6*d.*, giving a net profit of 75*l.* It may be that the reduction of the rate only increases the traffic from 500 tons to 750, in which case his profit remains stationary, and while the trader has gained, the railway is where it was. Or, once more, the traffic only increases to 600 tons, and then, though the trader has gained, the railway profit has fallen from 37*l.* 10s. to 30*l.*

And then naturally the railway manager casts about for some new source of income. In this sense, and in this sense only, can it be said that one portion of a railway company's business is done at the expense of the rest; that, if one portion gives a small profit, the rest of the business will have—if capital is to continue to flow into railway enterprises—to redress the balance. In any other sense the phrase is meaningless. A railway is no more likely to increase the rate on fish, in order to be able to carry American meat at a loss, than a gas company is likely to raise the price of gas in order to be able to give away its coke gratis.

There is one leading principle which guides the practical railway manager in reducing rates. He never makes, if he can help it, a reduction which will be inappreciable by those who have to pay it, for he could not hope by so doing to develop fresh traffic. One penny on a local rate of sixpence for coals may possibly make a difference. On a rate of six or seven shillings to London, it could hardly do so. Again, the practical man knows that on valuable articles the railway rate can produce no effect one way or another. The inhabitants of Lancashire will not buy more velvet dresses, even if the stuff were carried all the way from Lyons *gratis*. Reductions, therefore, when made by goods managers, are mainly in considerable percentages on articles of small value, the trade in which is capable of almost indefinite increase. Here, on the other hand, is an instance of rate reduction based not on practical considerations, but on abstract theory. The Great Northern rate for musical instruments from London to Knebworth is 25*s*. The Board of Trade Report proposes to reduce it to 24*s*. 3*d*. Now, it is tolerably safe to say that, if Lord Lytton wished to buy a new grand pianoforte, he would not be deterred by the fact that he would have to pay 12*s*. 6*d*. for carriage. Nor, if he found the charge brought down to 12*s*. 1½*d*., is it likely that the unexpected economy would induce him forthwith to purchase a second. In a word, a pettifogging alteration such as this—and this is only a type of hundreds and thousands—simply means to the railway a dead loss with no prospect of recoupment from increase of traffic, and to the customer a gain so infinitesimal that nine hundred and ninety-nine times out of a thousand he will be utterly unconscious of it.

Take another instance. Almost an entire page of

the Report to the Lancashire and Cheshire Traders' Conference is devoted to an exposure of the crass folly of the railway management which for years retained imitation lace in the same class and charged it at the same rate as the hand-made article. A refusal "to distinguish between lace at 2*d*. per yard and lace at 2*l*. 2*s*. per yard"—could anything be more unreasonable? Let us look at the facts. The writer has taken a piece of Nottingham lace, not a narrow piece worth only 2*d*., but a piece three inches wide and costing 8*d*. per yard. He finds it to weigh per yard 2 drachms. In other words, it is worth 4*l*. 5*s*. 4*d*. per pound, say, in round figures, 9,557*l*. per ton, or more than its weight in silver. Now, it is quite true that if anybody were to spend two millions and a half sterling in collecting a ton of fine Brussels lace, he would be able to send it down from London to Nottingham by goods train for 52*s*. 6*d*. But is this fact sufficient to prove that other lace, worth over 9,000*l*., is unable to bear a similar charge? As has been said, the companies have lately, in order to avoid further irritation, brought down the rate to 47*s*. 6*d*., with a further reduction to 40*s*. on consignments for export. It is, perhaps, unduly sanguine to expect that the change will do much to restore to Nottingham its former prosperity, unless for the reason that the manufacturers will be able in future to devote to the improvement of their designs the time which they have spent to little profit in a barren wrangle.

Another argument which has been largely used is that fixing the rates according to what the traffic will bear, means depriving places of the advantages of their natural geographical position. To this, the only answer is to say that of course it does, and that unless one holds "the monstrous faith of many made for one," we cannot but desire that it should. Put the claim for the advantages of geographical position in its baldest form, and one sees what it means. The railways running into London have established an elaborate system of workmen's trains and cheap fares. Some pressure is now being put upon them to extend that system, even though they should do it at a pecuniary loss. Now, supposing Lord Northampton or Lord Alington, or some other large owner of workmen's property, were to come forward and protest that he was being deprived of the advantages of his geographical position, that the action of the companies was reducing the rental value of his estate—what would be thought of such a claim? Would not anyone who ventured to make it be told with emphasis that his selfish personal interests could not be allowed to stand for a moment in the way of the general good; that it was for the public interest that workmen should have more space for their houses; and further that, from the mere individual point of view, his interests as a landlord in London might be balanced against the interest of the landlord at Neasden or Earlsfield, whose estate was proportionally enhanced in value.

If such be the argument as applied to workmen's dwellings, why should the same considerations be ignored when it is a question of workmen's food or workmen's clothing? The truth is that by nature all men are Protectionists at heart, and that the cry in favour of preserving the advantages of geographical position is one which has been raised again and again, from the first moment when railways began to revolutionise the trade of the world.

At a meeting of the Statistical Society in the year 1843 a paper was read on the "Agricultural Prices of the Parishes of Middlesex." The writer pointed out—the quotation is from a contemporary railway journal—"that the railway had greatly affected prices in the cattle market at Southall, and had occasioned much discontent among the farmers, who complained that in consequence of the facility that it afforded for the rapid transfer of stock from one county to another, they had been deprived of the advantages which they formerly possessed from their proximity to London; 500 head of sheep and 100 head of cattle had upon more than one occasion been suddenly introduced into the market from the West of England, and the prices had been proportionately forced down." The complaint of the Southall farmers was fortunately disregarded. Had it been otherwise, by this time, no doubt, the entire parish would have been turned into one vast series of cattle-fattening sheds, and Southall market might have been a monopoly as lucrative as that of Covent Garden.

For, it should be observed that, in the view of the geographically well-situated farmer or trader, cheap carriage of cattle for him to fatten, or raw materials for him to work up, is apparently open to no objections. However, as we know, the Southall farmer did not get his way, and cattle continued to pour into London from the West of England. Then the railway system extended itself to the furthest corners of Scotland and Ireland. The little red Highlanders and black polled-Angus were seen at Smithfield side by side with the great Hereford and Devon oxen. Then it was the turn of the West of England farmer to complain, and once more his grumblings were met with the answer that London wanted more food and wanted it cheaper.

The railways of Great Britain had now reached the end of their tether, but, thanks to the railways of America and the triple-expansion marine engine, the rapidly rising demand of the British working classes for wholesome animal food was met by the produce of the boundless Western prairies, and then at length, after a long series of years of steady enhancement, the price of meat grew stationary, and finally began to descend. Once more the farmer—the farmer this time throughout the British Islands—and his landlord had been deprived of the advantages of their geographical position—to their loss doubtless, but to the benefit of the immeasurably more numerous consumers.

But here comes in the strange part of the story. The railway companies, which in their humble way had been endeavouring—not, of course, without an eye to their own advantage—to promote the trade of the country by improving communication, and which certainly would never have presumed to attempt to thwart the declared policy of Parliament and the British nation by imposing exceptional taxation on beef because of its foreign origin, suddenly found themselves assailed with a storm of indignation, and, as the upshot of eight years of agitation and strong language, the Railway and Canal Traffic Act of 1888 was passed. By that Act it is provided that "no railway company shall make, nor shall the Court or the Commissioners sanction, any difference in the treatment of home and foreign merchandise in respect of the same or similar services."

The intention of the section is obvious, but any one familiar with the history of the question would naturally have expected the words to be expressed in a precisely opposite sense, for nothing can be more certain than that the railway companies were as innocent of treating or wishing to treat American beef in a way different from that in which they would have treated English beef, if they could have got it under the same circumstances, as Mr. Gladstone was of discriminating in favour of our fellow-citizens in Australia and the Cape Colony, when he reduced the duty on Bordeaux wines. The section of the Act referred to still waits interpretation at the hands of the Railway Commissioners; but the railway companies will perhaps be wise in the interval, if they understand it to mean, as certainly the public understands it, that while producers in Great Britain *inter se* have no absolute right to their advantage of geographical position to the detriment of the consumer, where the producer is a foreigner this rule is reversed.

But let us leave this point and come to another and a more important one.

CHAPTER V

WHO SHALL FIX THE RATE?

THE very fact that railway rates must affect such important interests over so wide an area is not infrequently advanced as a reason why the power to fix rates should not be entrusted to private individuals at all. "We object," said one trader, frankly, before the Committee of 1881, "to a railway manager acting as a special providence to set up one town and pull down another." Other traders press their objection not because they dislike a despotism, but because they look upon the despot as ignorant of the subject with which he attempts to deal. Before the Board of Trade representatives at Westminster last year the point was strongly pressed that only those who were in the trade themselves could judge what classification was just, or what rates the trade could bear. A third objection has been taken. It is expressed as follows by Mr. Jeans:[1]—

"The well-known custom of the railways is to profess to carry out the spirit of the law, which required that they should treat alike all traders in the same description of merchandise in the same localities; but they make differential rates by allowing

[1] *Railway Problems*, pp. 293, 294.

large rebates and discounts, and there is probably no company that has not got secret arrangements of the kind." And again: "There is not a single trader in the country who is not well aware that the railway companies do not, as required by the Traffic Act, avoid undue or unreasonable preference or advantage in favour of particular persons or descriptions of traffic; that they do not, as required by the Railways Clauses Consolidation Act, 'charge the same tolls equally at all times to all persons;' and that they do not, as required by the same Act, exhibit all charges actually made upon one toll-board or more, in distinct black letters on a white ground, in some conspicuous place on the stations."

Let us deal with these points *seriatim*, and though Mr. Jeans's point comes last, we will take it first, because, if the railway managers are, as Mr. Jeans says, dishonest, the fact must largely affect our view of the whole question.[2] No one ever suspects the permanent civil servants of the Crown of dishonesty. And dishonesty is so serious a matter—has produced, for instance, in the United States, such terrible results—that if honest management cannot be got from the

---

[2] On the blackboard count, if Mr. Jeans's law had been correct, the managers would, perhaps, have been wise to plead guilty, and if asked what extenuating circumstances they could allege, to point out that a literal compliance with the Act would have caused a famine in Baltic timber in the Surrey Docks, while exiguous station premises, such as those of St. Pancras or Paddington, would have needed to be enlarged to thrice their size, if they were to afford wall-space for the Parliamentary blackboards. But in fact the clause of the Act to which Mr. Jeans refers does not deal with " charges actually made " at all, but only with tolls. After the discussions of the last few years it may, I think, be assumed that the reader least familiar with the subject knows the distinction between a toll and a rate or a charge.

existing railway managers, most of us would be inclined to advocate, if not State ownership, at least a very stringent measure of State control. Let us see, therefore, what the evidence is. In the old days of railways, there is no question that advantages were given to one trader above another for private reasons. Small blame to the railway men of those days if it was so. A wholesale merchant nowadays does not consider himself a misdemeanant because he allows a personal friend to obtain a retail quantity of goods at wholesale price, and in the early days the public character which distinguishes the trade of railways from the trade of private firms had not been sufficiently appreciated. It was to put a stop to this that the Act of 1854 was passed. If we may judge from exhaustive investigations which have taken place since then, that Act has not failed of its purpose.

The Royal Commission of 1867 reported as follows: "It is due to the railway companies to state that whatever may have been the transactions of the companies at the commencement of railway enterprise, it is now generally regarded by them as impolitic to grant any preference tending to favour individual traders, and some managers disapprove of the transmission of large quantities of goods on more favourable terms than smaller quantities. The witnesses examined before us concur in the expression of belief that there is no disposition on the part of the railway companies to afford personal preference for the special profit of individual traders; but that the distinctions of rates made by railway companies are based upon considerations affecting the profit and interest of the railway companies themselves." Again, in 1872, there was an inquiry by a very strong Joint Committee of both Houses. The only allusion to the matter in the report is in these words: "One railway manager almost admits that all traders are not charged equally." But Sir Thomas Farrer, speaking as the permanent official head of the Board of Trade, and taking on not a few points a position strongly hostile to the companies, gives this evidence: "It seems to me that it really is to the interest of the companies to give this publicity. One sees that there are all sorts of suspicion of unfair favour on the part of the traders, but in almost every case, when it comes to be sifted, it is shown that there is very good reason for what is done; and why should not the companies let the traders know it?" Lastly, the Committee of 1882 dealt with the subject very definitely, and this is what they say: "Your Committee report that on the whole of the evidence they acquit the railway companies of any grave dereliction of their duty to the public. It is remarkable that no witnesses have appeared to complain of 'preferences' given to individuals by railway companies as acts of private favour or partiality, such as were more or less frequent during the years immediately preceding the Act of 1854."

As far as the present writer is aware, no trader brought any charge of this kind before the recent Board of Trade Inquiry at Westminster. This being so, Mr. Jeans's language is, to say the least of it, unfortunate. "Secret arrangements for large rebates and discounts" might naturally be supposed to imply dishonest arrangements. As there is no published evidence in support, it really is Mr. Jeans's duty to produce it. The injured trader need not be deterred by considerations of expense. If he has got a good case, it is quite worth his while to bring his action. A differential rate, not granted dishonestly but in all good faith, is understood to have involved a Scotch Railway Company recently in damages and costs estimated at something like 140,000*l*.

A similar charge is insinuated—it is not made in definite terms—in the Report to the Lancashire and Cheshire Conference. After asserting that "railways have had granted to them the virtual monopoly of the highways of the kingdom,"[3] which is only another way of saying that the members of the Conference have not sufficient belief in their own reiterated assertion that railways ought to be able to charge lower rates to induce them to put their money into a competing line; the Report goes on to formulate as one of the demands of the traders that the companies shall "give no private advantage or favour to any one, even though it might seem for their own immediate benefit to do so." By all means let the traders hammer on an open door if it pleases them. But when their neighbours ask what the noise is about, let us not be put off with a disingenuous insinuation that they fancied the door had been kept shut in their faces all the time.

[3] It will no doubt be said that the existing companies have obtained access to towns which could only be secured nowadays at a cost that is virtually prohibitory. Be it so. Have the North Western proprietors then no right to profit by the fact that they or their fathers had the courage and the foresight to put their savings into building the Liverpool and Manchester line, though the practical men told them that they were going to bury them in Chat Moss?

But even granting the honesty, it is asserted that railway managers lack the requisite knowledge. Doubtless they do. If there be one man who ought to take all knowledge to be his province, that man is a railway goods manager. No doubt it is also true that the goods manager knows less of the iron trade than an iron-master, less of the cotton trade than a Liverpool cotton-broker, less of the corn trade than a Mark Lane corn merchant, and so on. At the same time, it is probable, not only that he knows as much about the transportation of iron or cotton or corn as the specialists, but also that he knows very much more about cotton and corn than the iron man, and very much more about iron than the man who deals either in corn or cotton. No man can know everything, and just as the iron-master, and the cotton-broker, and the corn-factor may all go to the same solicitor and the same counsel for a legal opinion, on matters affecting their respective trades, so it may well be that the best opinion any one of the three can obtain on a question of transportation is that which will be given them by the transportation expert.

Here, as it seems to me, is where the case, put with

When a Lancashire or Cheshire trader devotes years of his life and thousands of pounds to perfecting some new process of spinning or weaving, and his invention at length turns out a success, does he look upon himself as a "virtual monopolist," bound to give the whole benefit to the public at large? Does he not rather congratulate himself that, while his rivals may have to be content with a narrow margin of profit, the superior economy of his process enables him to produce at a cheaper rate goods which command the full price in the market? And as, with a complacent chuckle, he puts the whole of the difference into his own pocket, does he not tell himself that it is to the enterprise of private capitalists, stimulated by a legitimate hope of personal advantage in return, that England owes her commercial supremacy?

great force of language in the Lancashire and Cheshire Conference Report, breaks down. The Report complains that the railway managers claim the right to settle the classification for themselves; that, while they are ready to hear what the traders have to say, they refuse to allow them a voice in the final decision. The writers, however, hardly make out their case. The proceedings of the traders themselves on this very classification question show where their knowledge of the subject falls short. They claimed, for example, that vinegar and British wines ought fairly to be placed in the same class as beer. From the trader's point of view, they were no doubt correct. The articles were not dissimilar in value, difficulty in handling, liability to damage, and so forth. But, from the carrier's point of view, the gap between them was a wide one. The one traffic goes in train loads, the other a barrel at a time. The railway contention, that from the point of view of the carrier British wine is one thing and beer quite another, is surely justified by this single fact. Or take another instance. The tin-plate trade, with their eye on the immense traffic in their staple to Liverpool for export, protested naturally enough against the rate the railways proposed to fix in the schedules. "Quite right," replied the railways, " if all the traffic went to Liverpool in truck-loads, but you forget that a company like the Great Eastern only meets with tin plates in the form of a single box sent down from London to the local tinsmith. You cannot expect the Great Eastern to deal with this traffic at the wholesale rate."

Let it, however, be frankly admitted that, when

all is said and done, the ignorance and the short-sightedness of the goods manager must remain a source of difficulty. He gives a special rate in one place and the traffic grows and prospers under it. But when he invites us to accept this prosperity as a proof of his wisdom, we may reply, " What about the traffic that doesn't go ? What about the traffic which might have been developed at all the other places in the neighbourhood, if it had not been handicapped out of the race by the special rate which you gave to a single point." The question is of course unanswerable. It depends upon a calculus of probabilities whose value every man must estimate for himself. What the goods manager would reply if he is wise, is, that, as the fixing of rates is not an exact science, there must be left a discretion somewhere, and there is no evidence that anyone else would have exercised it better than he has done.

People often speak as though the fixing of rates were something done by a single irresponsible individual, and they say—fairly enough, doubtless, if their premisses were correct—that the task is one which should be entrusted to an individual who represents, not the private interests of the railway, but those of the nation at large. But if there is any force in the considerations which have been urged in the foregoing pages, it should now be evident that fixing rates is not a matter that can be done in the abstract, it can only be attempted by those who are in actual contact with the facts, and in a position to judge what the effect of changing one rate will be not only on the particular trade which is directly affected, but on all the other rates which are left unchanged.[4] Nor is the task one which can possibly be undertaken by a single man, or even by a small body of men. It is safe to say that, if the power to fix rates were given, as is sometimes proposed, to the Board of Trade, that

---

[4] A remarkable illustration of this is furnished by recent American history. When the system of bringing "dressed beef" from the West to the Atlantic cities in refrigerator cars first came into use, the railway companies had to settle what rate they should charge. As far as the individual rate was concerned there seemed to be no special difficulty in fixing it on the ordinary considerations. The traffic was of a high class, and could stand a high rate. On the other hand, it was in full truck loads, large in volume and constant, and the consignors, who employed their own men to keep the cars iced, practically were their own insurers. But there was a further and much more serious question. The "dressed beef" trade, partly from natural and partly from historical causes, was the monopoly of a few immensely powerful Chicago firms. If the rate was fixed at a point which made it materially cheaper to supply New York with "dressed beef," rather than as heretofore to send in cattle "on the hoof," the following result was inevitable. The Chicago firms would be able to outbid the New York buyers in the Western markets. Live cattle would cease to be sent East, and the slaughterers, the tanners, the gut-scrapers, the horn-workers, and fifty trades more, would be ruined. The next stage would be that, having obtained control of the situation, the Chicago houses would be able, on the one hand to dictate to the Western producer what price he should receive for his cattle, and on the other to dictate to the New York consumer what price he should pay for his beef. From this prospect the railway companies, taught by their experience in the case of the Standard Oil Company, recoiled. Their commissioner, Mr. Fink, went to Chicago and took a mass of evidence as to the comparative cost of the two methods of carrying meat to New York, and then the railways deliberately fixed the "dressed beef" rate at a point which, as compared with the existing rate for live cattle, made it precisely as profitable to adopt the one method of transportation as the other. This was certainly claiming to interfere as a special providence with a vengeance, and it was easy to declaim against a deliberate attempt to prevent the consumer from getting the benefit of improved business methods. But on the whole American opinion appears to have approved of the action of the railways. An English observer will, however, naturally think that a policy as far reaching as this ought to be, as it has been for forty years in England, and would be now in the United States (though it probably was not when the event occurred), subject to review by the courts of justice of the country.

board would be compelled either merely to register the decisions of the railway companies, to make itself responsible, that is, for actions whose justice it had no power to check, or else to appoint a staff of inspectors all over the country who would be numbered by hundreds if not by thousands. The task would be an expensive one, for the Board of Trade inspectors could hardly be expected to undertake any other employment. Under present circumstances the railways have their inspectors ready to hand in the station agents, district goods managers, canvassers, and others who cannot help unconsciously assimilating information as to the working of each particular rate in the course of their ordinary avocations.[5]

[5] On this point the evidence of Mr. Fink before a committee of the United States House of Representatives in 1882 is worth quoting. He was dealing with a bill which had been referred to the committee, providing for the appointment of nine commissioners, with power to fix maximum rates throughout the country, and this is what he said: "It would be utterly impossible for nine men to regulate the transportation tariffs over one hundred thousand miles of railroad with the view of making them just to the public as well as to the railroad companies. To perform this work intelligently and properly it would require the duplication of just such an immense organisation as the railroad companies now possess for the very same purpose. Each one of these twelve hundred railroad companies has at least one officer who has special charge of the tariffs of the road, and who often has many assistants, all trained experts in the transportation business, and who from many years' experience on particular roads, understands the wants of the people who are served by these roads. The officers are in constant contact with the shipping [*i.e.* forwarding] communities either personally or through agents especially appointed for that purpose, or through the many station agents located along the lines of the roads. The latter are in constant communication with the shippers [traders], and are in a position to know exactly their wants, receive their requests, hear their complaints, and report the same to the superior officer. In this way all the facts that are necessary to be considered in the establishment of tariffs are brought before the proper authorities, who are enabled to take intelligent action

It may be added that, since Mr. Fink gave the evidence just cited, the United States Commission on Inter-State Commerce has come into operation. It has no control over traffic which arises and terminates within the frontier of a single State, nor does it attempt to fix rates. Apart from its judicial duty of deciding in individual cases brought before it by a specific complainant, it merely collects and files information as to tariffs and rates. Yet for this purpose it requires a staff of scores of clerks. The sum originally set apart by Congress for the expenses of the Commission was 20,000*l.* per annum, and here is what the Commission says on the subject in its first Report:—

thereupon. Assuming that these station agents are located along the line of these roads at a distance of five miles apart, there would be ten thousand agents, who report to the general freight agents, and who bring the shippers in direct contact with the head of the railroad administration, enabling it to judge of the wants of the people and to intelligently establish the tariffs.

It is not reasonable to suppose that nine commissioners, who stand entirely outside of these organisations, who have no such means of acquiring correct information, and who perhaps, in the first place, may have no knowledge of, much less experience in, the transportation business, could evolve out of their own minds just and proper transportation tariffs, or could control, even if they were possessed of the highest accomplishments in that direction, a work that requires the services and agencies of twenty thousand people, who although not exclusively engaged in this business, whose services are necessary for the intelligent and proper conduct of the business. A work of this kind, if it is to be done effectually and properly, cannot be concentrated upon nine men.

In France, with but 12,000 miles of railroad instead of 100,000 miles as in this country, where there is governmental control of the railway tariffs, there is a board composed of thirty-three men, with the Minister of Public Works at their head, all the members being educated experts and men of thorough experience in railroad management. The establishment of such a commission, composed of men who are at least as competent to deal with these questions as the railroad managers themselves, might be justified"—from the point of view, that is, as Mr. Fink went on to explain, of practical possibility, as distinguished from the question of justice or expediency.

"The force of assistants which the appropriation made by the Act enabled the Commission to engage is so small that any steps in this direction of preparing model forms of tariffs and classifications have up to this time been quite out of the question. Some idea of the labour devolved upon this clerical force may be formed when it is known that as near as can now be estimated 110,000 books, papers, and documents showing rates, fares, and charges for transportation, and contracts, agreements, or arrangements between carriers in relation to inter-state traffic have been filed in the office of the Commission, all of which require appropriate classification and systematic arrangement. It has been quite impossible to do more with these than acknowledge the receipt, classify and index them, and put them in order for reference. The organisation of a general system upon which they might most usefully be made has not been attempted, nor even any systematic investigation of their contents for the purpose of observing to what extent the provisions of the Act to Regulate Commerce is complied with in their preparation."

Of course the traders are discontented with the rates as now fixed; it would be no paradox to say that, if they were all equally discontented, that would be the best possible testimony to the skill and impartiality of the existing officials. The business of the goods manager is, as we have seen, to extract a certain revenue, sufficient to pay expenses and $4\frac{1}{4}$ per cent interest on capital, out of A, B, C, D, and the rest of the alphabet. If A is satisfied with the share of the burden that is laid upon him, it is tolerably good evidence that B, C, and D are paying a little more than their just proportion; but if all the lot cry out, an impartial observer will be apt to think that the arbitrator must have adjusted the burden with remarkable equity.

The objection will no doubt here be taken that it is absurd to describe a railway goods manager as an arbitrator. An arbitrator has no interest in the question at issue, the railway manager's business is to extract the utmost possible profit for his company. The answer to this is, that that does not prevent him arbitrating fairly as between the different classes of traders. The master of a house, for instance, might be trusted to bring to the decision of the question, whether a certain domestic operation belonged to the department of the housekeeper or the butler, a mind unbiassed by the consideration that the household collectively was responsible for performing the whole work of the establishment.

Then there are not a few checks upon the arbitrary volition of railway companies. In the first place, there is a most wholesome dread of alienating public sympathy. People talk of the irresponsible tyranny of bloated monopolists, but if any single member of the public will go boldly into the ogre's den, say at Paddington Cross or King's Euston, it is quite possible that he will find the monster cowering beneath the latest onslaught of the "Evening Sputterer." And, indeed, apart from the natural desire to be well spoken of, as a mere matter of self-interest it is well worth the while of any railway company to make considerable sacrifices in order to stand well with the public.

Any one who has paid attention to the subject could give instances where railway companies have obtained very considerable traffic from their rivals, simply on the ground of a reputation for fairness and liberality. Further, it may be said that no railway company has an interest in extorting from the public more than a reasonable remuneration for its services. We have seen already how fractional a part of the whole capital of the companies is that which is paying any exceptional rate of interest; and it must be remembered that if the past is any guide to the future, the 8 per cent. dividends of 1889 will be 6 per cent. when the next wave of depression arrives. No one knows better than the railway managers themselves that any permanent increase of revenue must, in some form or other, be shared with the public.

Let us assume, for the sake of argument, that it is correct that the goods rates have not been reduced for forty years past, that the traders are paying not only the same price, but the same price for the same services, as they did in the year of the Great Exhibition. Even then, there would remain the fact, which every man over fifty can verify from his own personal knowledge, that passenger fares have practically been reduced in the proportion of two or three to one. It is impossible to deny that a third-class passenger of to-day gets, over the greater part of the country, for one penny a mile, accommodation which is better in every respect than the first-class passenger of forty years ago got for threepence. Even supposing class were to be compared with class, the same thing holds to a great extent. A newspaper, a short time back, asserted that "nothing had been done to make the first-class or second-class carriage better or cheaper than it was thirty years ago." The present writer took the trouble to check the statement, and he found that between 1858 and 1888 the amount of space alloted to a first-class passenger on the North Western had risen from 26 to 90 cubic feet, that the fare to Liverpool had fallen from 45*s*. to 29*s*., and to Carlisle from 66*s*. to 40*s*. 6*d.*

The desire to retain the good opinion of the public is not the only influence which operates to keep the railway managers on their good behaviour. Competition is always visible as a warning figure in the background. But competition, say the traders, is of no use. After a time the new company comes to terms with the old, and an agreement is made between them to maintain rates. This, no doubt, is true, but it is also true that at the early period of the competition the rates are usually reduced, and that they seldom go back again to their original point. Witness the rates just quoted to Carlisle and Liverpool, both of which were the result of Midland competition. Again, the construction of a competing line, except in cases where the existing line is absolutely full, is always a very severe blow at the prosperity of the old one. It is common to speak as though, if one line can pay 5 per cent. on a certain capital, two lines between the same points, both equally expensive, should each earn $2\frac{1}{2}$ per cent.; but that this is very far from being the case can be easily shown. As we have seen, under English conditions of service, each train from A. to B. earns five shillings a mile. Now imagine these trains duplicated, and suppose, which fortunately is not entirely true in practice, that they do not develop any new traffic. Their earnings will now fall to 2s. 6d. a mile. For the new company must give as good a service as the old one, if it wants to induce the public to come to it, while the old one dare not reduce its accommodation for fear it should lose even more than half the traffic. Both companies, therefore, instead of earning 5s. a mile, come down to 2s. 6d., and 2s. 6d., as we have seen, while it will pay the whole of the working expenses, will leave nothing whatever for interest on capital.

English people have never seen a case of this kind, because no English company has ever had its lines paralleled from end to end. But this is practically what happened in America a few years back in the case of the West Shore and the "Nickel Plate" railways. The capitalists who found the money for these undertakings reasoned apparently on the theory that if the existing New York Central Company was earning 8 per cent. and they could get half the traffic, they would be able to earn a dividend of 4 per cent. But, for the reasons we have stated, they reckoned without their host. The dividend on the New York Central side of the Hudson River disappeared altogether, but without emerging across the water. Railway managers, however, are fully able to appreciate the significance of these facts, and a railway manager will do a good deal to avoid furnishing the idea of a competing line with a congenial soil to grow in. When, therefore, traders assert that competition between companies affords them no protection, we reply that, even if it were true that competition between existing companies does not—and it is not true because, if a draper who has been accustomed to measure his stuff carefully, begins to sell a yard and a quarter as a yard, it is nonsense to say he has not reduced his prices—competition of non-existing but possible companies affords them a great deal.

There is another protection to which the traders can trust—that, namely, of the law. The law on the subject of discrimination and undue preference has been laid down in the course of forty years in very considerable detail, and the upshot of it all is this:—That a railway company at its peril—and the peril is, as was shown in the Scotch instance quoted some pages back, a pretty serious one—gives to any one trader or any one trade or any single locality a rate which it cannot justify when compared before an impartial tribunal with the rates which it has given to all the other traders and trades and localities over the whole of its system. Now, it is easy to argue, and the point is one that must be dealt with presently, that the Acts of '54 and '73 and '88 have fettered the railways too tight, have kept railway rates up by making a local and tentative reduction too dangerous, but to say that they have left the traders at the mercy of some despotic railway manager is really ridiculous. If the traders of Bradford really feel that they are unfairly treated in comparison with Manchester, if the merchant princes of Liverpool really think that their geographical position is unfairly attacked, they surely can afford to subscribe 1,000*l.* amongst them and test the question. If they will not, or cannot, one may be forgiven for believing that their grievance cannot be a very serious one.

Now of course no reasonable person will argue that the present system of fixing rates is absolutely satisfactory. There are believed to be a hundred millions of them in existence, and in that number it would be very strange if there were not a good many which were too high, a good many which were too low as compared with others imposed under parallel circumstances; a great many, in fact, which for one cause or another could not be justified, in some instances legally before the Railway Commission, in other instances as matter of policy before a tribunal of perfectly enlightened and perfectly dispassionate railway experts. The practical question is, not whether the present system is perfect or imperfect, but whether any system which can be substituted for it would be likely to produce better results.

There seem to be two possible alternatives to our English system of freedom to private managers to vary their rates within the limit of their statutory maxima and subject to appeal to a court of law. The one, the German system of downright State-purchase; the other, the French system of a State Board of Control. Of State purchase, we may have something to say later on. Let us here notice what might be expected to be the effect of the French system. We are not concerned now with the question, whether the English Government, which has done nothing for the companies, would have any moral right to claim such a control. The French people have paid nearly

200,000,000*l.* sterling in capital outlay, and continue to pay some millions per annum in the form of guaranteed interest, to the railway companies, and though some observers may think that they have got uncommonly poor value for their money, no one will deny that at least they have purchased a right to the authority which they exercise.

The question for us to consider is merely whether on the whole the State control of tariffs does or does not benefit the trade of the country. It does not, as we have seen by the instance of the differential rates for Spanish and French wine, prevent the French railways from " favouring the foreigner," who, indeed, is favoured in all directions by special transit rates from Marseilles, from Italy, and Switzerland, to the Channel ports and *vice versâ*. One thing it does do and that a very serious one; it involves the Government of the country in the unpopularity with which these rates there as here are received. Still less does it succeed in producing any of that beautiful mathematical simplicity of rates based on cost *plus* a percentage of profit, which Professor Hunter and his friends so fondly desiderate. According to the writer from whom we have already quoted, 80 per cent. of the total goods traffic of France was in the year 1886 done at special rates. In other words, the Minister with the advice and assistance of his thirty-three experts—and no one who knows the splendid training which French railway men receive will doubt their technical skill—having fixed a tariff to the best of his ability, subsequently finds that Nature is too strong to be held by Government red tape even of the most superior quality, and in four cases out of five is forced either to withdraw or to modify his decisions.

Now it would almost be a sufficient answer to any proposal to adopt the French system here, to point out that, outside the service of the railway companies themselves, this country is incapable of producing, not merely thirty-three, but three railway experts. If it could, there is no reason whatever to imagine that their decisions would be generally acceptable. Here at least we are not without recent experience to guide us. After working at the subject day and night for nine months, Lord Balfour of Burleigh and Mr. Courtenay Boyle did, as representing the Board of Trade, arrive last August—with the assistance of the ablest men at the Bar, and the best expert evidence available in the country—at drafting a schedule, not of rates to be actually charged, but of statutory *maxima* —needless to say, a comparatively simple affair. To any one who is qualified to appreciate the difficulty of their task, the success which they achieved will seem quite remarkable. Even so, there were instances, few no doubt in proportion to the total number of rates, but actually very numerous, in which—as in the example of the rate for grand pianos quoted a few pages back—it can hardly be argued that their decision was in the interest either of the railway companies or of the public at large. But what has since happened? The railway companies and the traders associations have each expressed their profound dissatisfaction. Portions of the case—no one quite knows which—have been reheard *in camerâ*—no one quite knows by whom—and in the Provisional Orders just submitted to Parliament the draft schedules of Lord Balfour and Mr. Boyle have been subjected to wholesale modifications. If railway companies and traders are not still more dissatisfied than before, they certainly ought to be, for the new schedules are unquestionably much less capable of a logical defence than the old. Moreover, their changes are based on *ex parte* statements, which the other side has not only had no opportunity of cross-examining, but even has in some instances had no chance of hearing.

And at this point the case must go before the final tribunal of Parliament. With the considerations which should guide the two Houses in the decision we must deal at a later point. Meanwhile, the present writer will venture on this prophecy—and any one who has studied the history of railway legislation in the Western States of America will be ready to admit its *a priori* probability—that if Parliament passes the Board of Trade Provisional Orders at all in their present form, the agitation on the subject of railway rates will increase tenfold in force and volume. The one man whose rate is raised—and the companies are sure to raise some rates in the attempt to prevent as far as they can a reduction of dividend—will make his disapproval audible above the whispers of satisfaction from the ten who have secured an almost imperceptible reduction; and members of Parliament, who had fondly fancied a disagreeable question settled, will find themselves confronted with the problem in more formidable shape than ever. They will have to face the alternative, either to acknowledge their mistake and to retrace their steps, leaving to the railway companies the responsibility of selling an article of commerce to their customers on commercial terms—subject always to the stringent control of public opinion and the law courts—or else to assume to the State the direct responsibility of managing the railways and paying the interest on 876,000,000*l.* of railway capital.

But of this more anon. Let us go on to notice here one necessary effect which would be produced, if it were proved permanently possible for a Government department to fix rates *ab extra*. Imagine, no impossible supposition, that one member for Liverpool was President of the Board of Trade, and that the same great city had another representative in the Cabinet: would there be much chance of Liverpool being, as its citizens would call it, "deprived of the advantages of its geographical situation," by reasonable concessions to Barrow or to Fleetwood, even though such concessions might not only be for the benefit of these two equally deserving towns, but also for the advantage of the English consumers generally? The question paper of the House of Commons is not too short at present, but imagination shrinks from conceiving the dimensions to which it would grow if the President of the Board of Trade were to be liable to be called to account every afternoon, not only for the rates he had given, but also for those he had refused to give. People may appeal to the analogy of the Post Office, and assure us that this department has been kept absolutely free from the suspicion of political influence. Possibly; and when they can go on to tell us that postage stamps are one of the largest tems in a merchant or manufacturer's expenditure, and that the department is in the habit of selling penny stamps to one man for a halfpenny, and to another man for a penny farthing, for reasons which, however good in themselves, are absolutely invisible to the casual observer, then, but not till then, there will be some point in the analogy.

In brief, the position is this:—A Government department, regulating tariffs *ab extra*, will either permit the present system of discrimination and competition to go on, in which case it will assuredly be accused of acting from political motives, however unfounded the charge may be, or, on the other hand, and this is much more probable, it will, like the German Government, go as near as it can to the cost of service principle. Now this, if the considerations urged in the foregoing pages have any force, is diametrically opposed to the public interest. To alter a tariff, to give a special rate here, some special facility there, in order to develop a new, or maintain an old industry, implies much trouble and much responsibility. To refuse the concession implies neither. It is always easy to say that to grant it would be unfair to someone else.

A railway manager, however, is ready to take the risk, because his will be the credit if, as he expects, the alteration results in benefit to his company; and his directors and shareholders are ready to support him, because they hope for increased dividends. A State official has no such inducement. The blame may be his for not preventing a mistake, the credit of making a success can hardly be so. "Can't you leave it alone?" is his natural motto. This is no mere theory. Professor Hadley, who recognises to the full, as every

American must do, the evils of competitive private management, and is by no means blind to the merits of the Continental system, thus sums up the subject.[6]

"These principles" (of the Continental Governments) "tend to keep rates up. The roads do not lower the local rates to any extent, but rather raise the through ones. They level up instead of levelling down. They are not occupied with the question how to lower rates, but how to keep the right proportion between existing rates. In trying to decide that matter fairly, they are tempted to put everything high enough to leave themselves elbow-room. In their anxiety to decide what is a fair rate in proportion to other rates under existing circumstances, they neglect the question, 'How can we change circumstances so as to make lower rates?'"

"One thing is quite clear"—the words are those of no railway advocate; they are taken from the report made by Lord Balfour of Burleigh and Mr. Courtenay Boyle on the recent proceedings at Westminster—"the special rates are all fixed at the express instigation of the traders. They are granted with the object of fostering the development of trade, and they have the effect of opening up markets which would otherwise be inaccessible to distant traders." If any one, be he trader or only a mere consumer, wishes to put an end to this state of things, and to return as near as may be to the age of gold, when the Middlesex farmers had in the London cattle market the full advantage of their geographical position, he cannot do better than devote his energies to securing a Government control of railway rates.

[6] *Railroad Transportation*, p. 250.

PART II

RAILWAY PRACTICE

CHAPTER VI

SOME EXTORTIONATE RATES

WE have dealt with the question whether English rates as a whole can be fairly called extortionate. Let us now see whether, though inapplicable to the rates as a whole, this condemnation of certain individual rates or classes of rates may not after all be deserved. First of all let us consider what the word itself means. "Extortionate" is sometimes used merely to imply a rate which the trader would prefer not to pay. The leading counsel opposed to the railway company at the recent Board of Trade inquiry expressed very much this idea in the following remarkable words: "Surely a rate that would stop the traffic cannot be a reasonable rate." According to the Board of Trade report, a large section of the traders were of the same opinion. One gentleman, indeed, on their side put his case forward in these words, which deserve to become classic:—

"Berwick.

"What we want is to have our fish carried at half present rates. We don't care a —— whether it pays the railway or not. Railways ought to be made to carry for the good of the country, or they should be taken over by the Government. This is what all traders want, and mean to try and get."

It is interesting to observe *en passant* that the Berwick gentleman has the shrewdness to perceive that railways being taken over by the Government is by no means necessarily the same thing as their carrying for the good of the country. But it is not a little remarkable that so able a man as Mr. Balfour Browne should commit himself, even for a moment, to such a statement as that a rate which would stop the traffic cannot be a reasonable rate, when it is perfectly obvious that with nine-tenths of the potential traffic it always must be a question whether it can bear the cost of transport. No one surely doubts that passengers would travel more if tickets were given away gratis, or that coal is necessarily dearer, and therefore scarcer, in London than at the pit's mouth, because of the cost of carriage. Peat may be had for nothing on the Surrey commons, but delivered in a London park, a cubic yard of it is worth a guinea, and the trees and shrubs have consequently to grow as best they can in the London clay.

To a great extent the rates have in each of these cases stopped the traffic. Is this fact alone sufficient to prove them unreasonable and extortionate? Is it not incumbent on any one who makes such a charge to go on and prove that on these individual rates the company is making an excessive profit? Theoretically, this may be proved in two ways; by working out the actual cost to the company—this, however, as we have shown, is practically impossible—or it may be proved by a comparison with other rates under circumstances as similar as may be. Even this latter course is quite an impossibility to an ordinary person with no special knowledge of the subject. So many considerations come in, that, even for a court of justice assisted by the evidence of experts, it is one of the most difficult things in the world to decide whether the circumstances really are similar, whether or no, that is, the rate is a fair one. Certainly the fact that it stops the traffic is no evidence of unfairness. It was not denied, for example, before the Committee of 1881 that a rate of 40*s*. a ton would have stopped the traffic between Liverpool and London in American beef. Yet, the conduct of the North Western was declared to be unreasonable, precisely because their rate did not stop the traffic.

There are, however, circumstances in which anybody can say that a rate is extortionate. If, for example, as happens repeatedly in America, A. is charged 20 cents, and his neighbour B., alongside, and engaged in the same trade, is charged 16 cents, for precisely similar services, no one will deny that A.'s rate is extortionate. On this point English railway men are as strong as any trader or any court of justice can be. Only they deny that such things happen in this country at all. Before the Committee of 1881, it was put to Mr. Grierson, the late general manager of the Great Western Railway, whether it was not possible for the officials who were responsible for fixing the rates to have friends,

Here is his answer: "If you mean by that, that they would favour any person, I am happy to say that over a period of thirty years, during which I have been manager of railways, I have never known such a case arise either upon the Great Western or any of the lines I have been connected with, and I do not remember such a case becoming public with regard to any other company."

Or again, it may be claimed on behalf of a particular town or district, that its rates taken all round are extortionate; take a higher range, that is, than those given to other districts for similar distances. South Staffordshire, for example, claims that its rates are markedly higher than those of South Wales or Cleveland. Nor is it possible to deny the fact. The only answer is that Nature, not the railways, discriminates against South Staffordshire. If Providence would remove the sea from the neighbourhood of South Wales and Cleveland, the railways might be able to make those districts pay more, and might then be able to afford to let South Staffordshire pay less. Meanwhile the railways have at least done what they can to mitigate the disadvantages of the South Staffordshire position. Thanks to the railways it can compete, not very advantageously certainly, but still it can compete, with Cleveland and South Wales in foreign markets. Without the railways, it is impossible to imagine that it could compete at all.

As a rule, however, it is not a particular person or a particular place which claims a reduction, so much as a particular class of traffic. Railways are told that they ought to carry iron or coal for nothing, or next to nothing, because they are cheap. Or again, fish and milk, because they are dear, and the public cannot afford to buy enough of them. Let us look at these two different classes of traffic a little more particularly. It is of course true, that a main part of the cost of iron-ore or coal is due to railway charges. Still, if it be true, as we have seen in previous chapters, that these articles are already carried at prices which leave less than the average profit for capital, it is evident that the word "extortion" is out of place. For all that the charge is made from time to time. There was one instance before the Committee of 1881; which is worth notice, both for its own sake, and also for the prominent position of the gentleman who brought it forward—Mr. (now Sir Alfred) Hickman. In brief, his complaint was that the railways, which proved by doing it the possibility of carrying traffic at less than a halfpenny per ton per mile, should in another place charge him something like threepence for apparently similar services. When, however, the Great Western general manager got into the box, and was asked what he had to say to the suggested halfpenny per ton for a distance of six miles, he unhesitatingly replied that he would much prefer to be without such traffic altogether. "The traffic would not be worth carrying, it would have and must have the effect of blocking our main line, for the traffic would have to pass up a very heavy incline, and the rate would be too low to block our main line for it."

Here is a typical case. The traffic was for a short distance, over heavy gradients, and passing along a portion of a great through route. Sir Alfred calculated that the engine could take 240 tons of coal, or say a load of some twenty-eight trucks, and on an ordinary road no doubt he was right; but the engineer's calculation is that to haul a load up a gradient of 1 in 50 implies from five to six times the power which is necessary on the level. So Sir Alfred's four-and-twenty trucks shrink to five to start with. Next, he expresses the opinion that "it will cost the same practically per mile in engine power to draw a train a hundred miles as to draw it twenty miles." In fact, he is prepared to maintain that "if an engine has only to draw a truck load six miles distance, you will get as much work out of it as if it went on for a hundred miles right off."

Let us bring this belief to the test of figures, as produced from actual practice before the Board of Trade inquiry last summer. An engine with a stopping goods train takes 11 hours and 20 minutes over the 47 miles between Llanelly Dock and Swansea Valley Junction; a second engine with a through goods train goes from Paddington to Weymouth, which is almost four times the distance, in forty minutes less time. Another engine takes 10 hours 55 minutes in covering the 59 miles from Bristol to Wells and back, while the 194 miles from Paddington to Exeter is done in $7\frac{1}{2}$ hours. Through trains, in fact, give an average of 18 miles an hour; short-distance trains an average of five. Or put the comparison another way. Between Paddington and Didcot the work done per hour by the engine of a stopping train is equivalent to the haulage of 160 trucks one mile. The engine of a through train hauls 493 the same distance in the same time. In plain English, the man who expects as many revenue miles out of the engine of a "pick up" train as out of the engine of a "through goods" is as unreasonable as the man who should expect a letter-carrier to deliver at every house from the Bank to Putney Bridge because that is the average length of a "walk" in the country.

Mr. Grierson's third point is, however, much the most important of the three. "We are not prepared," he says, "to block our main line at this price." If it be true, as we have attempted to prove above, that the low-class traffic at cheap rates seldom or never pays its full share of expenses and profit, but only at best a portion of the latter, we can easily see that no one is ever likely to build a new railway, simply for the accommodation of traffic at a halfpenny a mile. A company having a main line not full to its utmost capacity, may be ready to spend money on improving accommodation at one or two points, in order to get the haulage of coal for 150 miles even at a halfpenny per mile. But it will never increase its accommodation at those points for the sake of coal which is only going over the line for two or three miles. When, therefore, the line is already full, short-distance traffic must expect either to pay high rates, or to be pushed on one side to make room for the through traffic.

A moment's consideration will show that this must be so. Short distance traffic *ex hypothesi* cannot repay fifty or a hundred miles further on the cost incurred for it at its point of origin. There on the spot or nowhere it must yield a rate sufficient to pay working expenses *plus* interest on capital. Now it is safe to say that at the point Sir Alfred Hickman's works are situated between Dudley and Wolverhampton, a new line could not be built for less than the average cost of English railways, or say 50,000*l*. a mile. Take working expenses at 50 per cent. for the sake of argument, this would imply that to pay 5 per cent. interest the line must carry 5,000*l*. worth of traffic per mile *per annum*, or say in round figures 100*l*. worth per week. At a halfpenny a ton this would mean 48,000 tons of coal a week, which on heavy gradients would imply at least 480 trains, or 80 trains *per diem*. Needless to say it is in the highest degree improbable that any such amount of traffic could in fact be furnished. But the matter does not end here. The calculation that a coal train at a halfpenny per ton per mile can be worked for 50 per cent. of the gross receipts is no doubt a fairly accurate one on the understanding that it is for long distances over ordinary gradients.[1] But the engine load in this instance must, as we have seen, be calculated at certainly not more than one-fourth of the average. Further, from the fact of the run being so short, the day's work of an engine must

---

[1] This was Mr. Findlay's estimate before the Committee of 1881, and corresponds with considerable accuracy with the American figures. The Erie Company, for instance, estimates working expenses of freight trains at ·44 of one cent per ton-mile, the New York Central at ·54, and the Pennsylvania at ·47. We shall see later on that, owing to the low class of the traffic and the great length of lead on American lines, a comparison of their freight train expenses with our coal train expenses is not an unreasonable one.

be brought down from 120 to not more than 50 miles. Probably therefore it would be a conservative estimate to put down working expenses at only 75 per cent. And on this basis 96,000 tons of coal per week, or 160 loaded trains *per diem*, would need to be sent over the line to pay the capitalists who built it a reasonable return for their money. In fact our analysis comes to this, that no one can afford to build a line for short distance traffic at any rate at all like a halfpenny per ton per mile, unless there is a certainty that the line will get as much traffic as it can carry, and be able to work that traffic in the most economical manner in full train-loads.

On the whole, however, there is but little discontent with local rates for low class articles. A somewhat remarkable instance of this fact is afforded by evidence given in reference to Sheffield. Few towns have been harder pressed of late years. More than one famous undertaking has found itself compelled by the cost of carriage to move its works, for articles such as rails at least, from Sheffield to the sea-coast. Why this step was taken it is easy to understand. Other countries have begun to catch up England in the manufacture of the coarser and heavier kinds of ironwork, on which a few shillings more or less in carriage will make all the difference between getting and losing a contract. Then Nature, and not the railways, is responsible for the fact that the iron mines of Cleveland and West Cumberland, which are near the sea, have been found of late years to be very suitable for the manufacture of steel. Further, the adoption of the principle of compounding in marine engines has, for the present at least, decisively given back to sea-transport the accustomed advantage over land-carriage in point of cheapness of which the invention of railways seemed for a time almost to have deprived it.

But, whatever be the reason, the effect on the trade at Sheffield was equally serious. And yet the goods manager of the Manchester, Sheffield, and Lincolnshire Railway was able to tell the Committee of 1881 that, in spite of advertisements issued by the Railways' Rates and Charges Committee of the Chamber of Commerce, and by the Railway Freighters' Protection Society, inviting complaints with the object of bringing them before the Parliamentary Committee, "Throughout the whole of the Sheffield district there has not been a single complaint of a single overcharge upon anything in connection with the Sheffield Railway either over the railways or over the canals."

The most serious complaints—those which have been most frequently and persistently pressed upon the public notice, have come from persons engaged in industries to which the cost of carriage can never be a matter of more than secondary importance. This can, I think, be readily shown. The rate—10*l.* per ton—for bullion from London to Liverpool was quoted some time back. It may safely be taken as representing a standard of charge unknown in the case of any other less precious commodities. Yet as a tax upon the article transported it represents but one hundredth part of 1 per cent. of its value. For articles of ordinary trade, we may say that 50*s.* per ton from door to door, from the docks in London to

K

the warehouse in Yorkshire; or *vice versâ*, is certainly a good deal above the average charge. Now 50*s.* equals 600 pence, and, therefore, a 50*s.* rate per ton is in other words a rate of $\frac{600}{2240}$, or, say, $\frac{2}{7}$ of a penny on every pound weight conveyed.

Consider at what rate this charge works out to the consumer. Is it not a percentage of the total sum which he pays so small as to be scarcely noticeable? Take tea, for instance, sold in the North of England at 2*s.* per lb. The railway charge on this amounts to little over 1 per cent. of the retail price. Is the Yorkshireman soft-headed enough to believe that, if the railway carried his tea gratis, he would get the very slightest concession in price from his friend the grocer? Or turn it the other way round: the Bradford goods which go up to London to pay for the tea are worth on the average certainly not less than 2*s.* 6*d.* per lb., and out of this the railway claims once more $\frac{2}{7}$ of one penny, or less than 1 per cent. Is this a rate which is likely to stifle trade? If it were cut down by one half would the manufacturer be likely to raise his wages?

But we are often told—though the reasons for a statement which on the face of it is questionable are never produced—that it is not fair to calculate percentages on retail cost: we must consider the weight of the burden laid upon the wholesale dealer. Let us do so, therefore, and imagine a London commission merchant engaged in the Bradford trade and turning over, say, 150,000*l.* per annum. This, at 2*s.* 6*d.* per lb. once more (and though some of his goods may be worth a little less, the finer qualities will be worth ten times as much), would imply that he sold 536 tons per annum. Suppose that half of it comes to London at the local rate of 43*s*. 4*d*. and half at the export rate of 35*s*., his total expenditure, therefore, on railway carriage and cartage is a little over 1,000*l*. a year. Now imagine an all-round reduction of 10*s*. per ton in these rates—and the chairman of the Railway Committee of the Bradford Chamber of Commerce declared in 1881 that such a reduction would bring salvation to a rapidly perishing industry—the London merchant would save 268*l. per annum*, that is, assuming that he kept the whole of the gain to himself.

But—in the witness-box at least—no trader ever desires to act as anything more than a conduit pipe through which the whole benefit of cheap rates may flow uninterruptedly to the consuming public. We must not, therefore, imagine a reduction so trifling as a mere 10*s*.—even though it be sufficient to sweep away almost the whole of the railway profit—for 10*s*. per ton, when reduced to the price per yard, is an amount too fractional to be represented in English currency. Let us adopt the doctrine and the language of the gentleman from Berwick, and without " caring a —— whether it pays the railway company or not," let us imagine the goods brought to London gratis. In that case there will be 1,000*l*., or 960,000 farthings, to divide among the purchasers of 1,200,000 yards of woollens—taking a yard as roughly weighing a pound. Not a farthing a yard, unfortunately, so, pending the adoption of a decimal system, it really seems as though, if the consumer is to be benefited, it would be necessary to call upon the altruistic merchant to contribute 240,000 farthings more from his own exiguous profits. What matter though railway shareholders and merchants be ruined, so long as the consumer can effect a total economy of three farthings on the cost of a pair of trousers?

Take another instance, that of the Lancashire cotton trade. Manchester has fully persuaded itself that the cotton rates are extortionate, and, largely in consequence of that belief, has invested some eight millions sterling in the construction of its new Canal.[2] Let us see what these rates are, as testified by Mr. Harrison, Mayor of Blackburn, and himself a cotton spinner, before the Committee of 1881. Cotton, he tells us, is first carried from Liverpool to Oldham; there it is spun into yarn, and thence it goes to Manchester for sale; then from Manchester to Blackburn to be woven; back to Manchester to be sold and packed for export. Sometimes the cloth, after being sold in Manchester, is sent out again to Bolton or the neighbourhood to be bleached, or even to Lanarkshire to be calendered, before finally returning to Manchester for the third time to be packed.

Now, the fact that the trade is conducted in this manner is fair evidence that the railway rates are not

---

[2] As a mere spectator, one is bound to wish all success to the bold endeavour of the Lancashire men to place themselves on the sea, and so in a position to dictate rates to the railways. If they succeed, they will only have done for the railway shareholders of to-day what the original railways did to the canal proprietors of 1830 and 1840. But one remark is not out of place, that the natural disadvantages of an inland situation will be brought more forcibly home than ever to the minds of the inhabitants of, say, Birmingham, when they see, as they must see —railways being commercial concerns, and exposed to commercial competition—the companies raising their Birmingham rates still higher, in order to recover some portion of their loss in Lancashire.

much to complain of. If they were, is it conceivable that Lancashire could afford to play battledore and shuttlecock with its cotton in this fashion? Would not Oldham weave as well as spin, or would not Bolton and Blackburn arrest the bales on their passage from Liverpool and refuse to let them go till the whole of the processes of manufacture had been completely carried out? Is it not evident that, if the cost of carriage were a point as vital as we are told it is, the Manchester capitalists would forego the trifling advantage which they gain by this local distribution of the trade, and the trifling further advantage which they gain by buying their yarn or their cloth in bulk instead of from sample, in return for the immense saving which they would effect in the cost of carriage? So, at least, one would have imagined if Mr. Harrison had not also told us how fractional the cost of all these numerous journeys—averaging nine times on and off a cart, and five times on and off a railway truck—is when compared with the total value of the product. His figures broadly give 60*l.* for a ton of raw cotton, 21*l.* for labour, 64*s.* 4*d.* for railway rates, as the expenses of placing on board ship in London a ton of cotton cloth valued at 100*l.*[3]

There is no need to labour this point further. Let

[3] There has been a reduction in the cotton-rates since these figures were given, but too small to affect a rough calculation like the one in the text. Indeed, though sixpences and ninepences per ton no doubt make a serious difference to railway companies, whose sole business is the sale of transportation facilities, it is difficult to believe that to the cotton-spinner, in whose expenses, as we have seen, transportation occupies but a very small place, any practicable reduction of rate can have any effect which will be visible in his balance sheet, however great be the subjective effect produced on his imagination.

any one remember that a charge of one penny *per lb.* would mean a rate of over 9*l.* per ton, let him realise that it is only an infinitesimal fraction of the total traffic which pays a rate as high as one-third of this amount, or 60*s.* per ton, that the average amount paid to the railway is much more like 6*s.* per ton, and he will be able to see for himself that, with the exception of fuel, and in a much less degree of flour, there is no single necessary of life whose cost is at all largely due to railway charges, while when we come to articles, whether they be produce or merchandise, grapes or salmon, Nottingham lace-curtains or Bradford woollens, whose value is reckoned by shillings per lb., the charge for conveyance shrinks into absolute insignificance.

There is, however, one article in reference to which we have heard so much of extortionate railway charges, that it is perhaps as well to examine the case in somewhat more detail. That article is fish. There are four main sources of supply for Billingsgate market—as far, that is, as it is served by railway. Herrings come chiefly by the Great Eastern from Yarmouth and Lowestoft; mackerel by the Great Western either from Cornwall or from Milford; trawl and line fish, such as cod, haddock, and whiting, from Grimsby *viâ* the Great Northern or the Midland, and lastly salmon, either from Ireland or from Scotland. Now let us see what the railway rates are. Roughly they may be put down as follows:—

Herrings from Yarmouth, 10 lbs. for 1 penny.
Mackerel from Cornwall, 3 lbs. for 1 penny.
Live cod from Grimsby, 4 lbs. for 1 penny.
Salmon from Wick, Stornoway, or Ireland, 2 lbs. for 1 penny.

It is not worth while, in face of these figures, whose accuracy can easily be tested, to enter into arithmetical calculations to prove that, whatever Fish Traders' Associations may assert to the contrary, the railway charge for carriage is not the reason for the preposterous price of fish in the London shops.

Any one who chooses to go into the matter for himself, who will go to the fishing ports and see the barbarous arrangements in force there, and then on his way back look in at Billingsgate about six or seven in the morning, will have no difficulty in understanding why fish is dear. He will see on the one hand everything done that can be done to load the producers with unnecessary expense. Fish out of condition, undersized, broken perhaps by the tread of heavy fishing boots, covered with dirt from a filthy quay—fish which, to start with, was only fit to be sent to a manure factory—is packed in one box with good sound fish, and the whole is hurried off to London and sold in a lump together. Then at Billingsgate the fish supply for five millions of people is all brought to a market whose area would be insufficient for the supply of Leicester or Nottingham, where the idea of a new-comer being able to get a footing either as buyer or salesman is physically out of the question.

There may not be—gentlemen who ought to be in a position to know assert that there is not—any such thing as a Billingsgate Fish Ring. But one thing is certain, that, if there is not, the Billingsgate salesmen have unaccountably neglected—or perhaps one should say, with singular public spirit have refused—to avail themselves of their unequalled opportunities of setting on foot such an organisation. Here, however, I would venture to repeat a suggestion that I made some years ago, to the effect that the Fish Traders' Association should be invited to analyse the cost of a ton of fish sold by retail. Take mackerel for instance, sold at 6*d.* each fish, weighing say 1 lb. : the retail buyer pays 56*l.* per ton, out of which the extortionate railway company takes, allowing for weight of packages, &c., certainly not more than 5*l.* How is the remaining 51*l.* divided? If it be true, as the fish-traders assure us, probably with perfect accuracy, that the fisherman does not get as large a share of the price as the railway company's charges amount to, there must be left a sum of 46*l.* per ton to be shared amongst the various middlemen. Is this an ideally just division? And is it not conceivable that the fisherman's dinner ought to be added to by the sacrifice, not of the ewe-lamb—the 5*l.* of the railway company—but of a portion of the well-fed flock from the rich pastures of Billingsgate?

Perhaps the same Association would at the same time answer a further question. Last mackerel season the railway rate from Cornwall was reduced 10*s.* per ton, which meant to the company a loss of 14 per cent. of their gross receipts, and of fully 28 per cent. of their net profit from the traffic. Has the price of mackerel to the public been reduced one iota? Have the fishermen sold their fish to better profit in consequence? Or has a single new boat been put on, or a single new hand been attracted into the business, either in Mount's Bay or at St. Ives? And, if not, into whose pocket has the 10*s.* per ton reduction gone?

Buried in the Appendix to the Report of the Select Committee of 1882 there is a letter from a gentleman named Barclay, which undertakes to answer the question as to the distribution of the price paid for fish, as far as the Montrose cod fishery is concerned. This is the substance of it: The wholesale Billingsgate price is $1\frac{1}{2}d.$ per lb. *Before leaving Billingsgate the three-halfpenny pound of fish stands at sevenpence.* Out of the $1\frac{1}{2}d.$ the railway takes $\frac{13}{32}d.$, the fish curer takes $\frac{17}{32}d.$, and $\frac{18}{32}d.$ are left for the fishermen who "own and man their own boats." To the prime cost of the fish, delivered at the quay, the curer thus adds 95 per cent. as his own gross profit. Out of this he has to provide boxes, to pack the fish, to pay the fishermen a bounty of 14*l.* per boat for the season of seven months, and to pay carriage across London of $\frac{1}{37}d.$ per lb. The total amount of these expenses is, says Mr. Barclay, "very small." He continues: "Parliament is urged to compel the railways to carry at one-third (1*s.* 3*d.* per cwt.) less, and thereby to increase the curer's profit of 95 per cent. to about 115 per cent., that they (the curers) may be enabled to bend a bigger stream of cod-fish at $1\frac{1}{2}d.$ per lb. upon London. The plain inference of this being that London, in offering only 95 per cent., is outbid by other markets. An ordinarily accepted wholesale profit is 10 per cent.; if the article dealt in is risky, it may reach 20 per cent. Comment on this is superfluous." Mr. Barclay probably overstated his case, but at least he gave definite figures, which, if inaccurate, should be capable of statistical disproof. It would be well if Fish Traders' Associations, before next they come forward to abuse the extortionate railways, would produce positive evidence where the money paid by the public for fish does actually go to.

Perhaps, however, enough has been said to show that, from the point of view of the consumer, rates are not extortionate, that in other words the influence which they exercise in enhancing the price which he pays for commodities is almost invisible. There is, however, another point often taken, which may be fairly put in the following form: "If a ton of coals can be profitably carried a mile for a halfpenny, is not a rate for fish of 3*d.*, or six times as much, on the face of it unjustifiable?" It may, on the contrary, be answered without much hesitation that the coal is the more profitable traffic of the two. A train load of coal probably averages not less than 250 tons, a fish "special" probably does not average 25. Further, coal is a steady and unvarying business. Nothing is so uncertain as fish. Sometimes, as for instance in the North of Scotland, an engine and train may be sent 100 miles to meet an expected catch of fish that never comes to port at all.

When it does come, one day's catch may be ten times as big as the next. At Milford, for example, the weight of fish landed on seven successive days, a short time before the writer last visited the place, was 634, 596, 351, 27, 45, 14, 436 tons. Take another instance, which was given in evidence before the Board of Trade tribunal. On December 9, 1889, the amount of fish sent up to Paddington from Cornwall was 14 tons. Three days later there were 43 tons, then next day 216 tons, and the day following the amount dropped again to 39 tons. Does it need any argument to prove that a traffic so variable as this must be exceptionally expensive to work? The pier or station accommodation, the supply of engines and trucks, the staff of men engaged to load them, all must be sufficient to cope with the *maximum* traffic; and yet in the course of a season, which itself only lasts a third of the year, that *maximum* amount occurs perhaps half a dozen times. Then, when the fish gets to Paddington, 100 vans are required to hurry it down to Billingsgate, and these vans must be hired at a fancy price wherever they can be obtained.

Further, the coal jogs up to London at a steady 15 miles an hour, at times when the line is not wanted for other traffic. The fish "special," as it flies past at thrice the speed, leaves behind it in every siding along its path coal trains, goods trains, sometimes even passenger trains, with their engines—worth 5*s.* an hour apiece at the lowest computation—idly blowing off steam, till such time as they are allowed to resume their interrupted journey. It is safe to say that, if the railway manager did as the theorist bids him; if he ascertained—that is, estimated—the exact cost of working the fish traffic, and then added the proper percentage of profit in order to fix the rate, a much larger proportion of the fish landed would be sent to the manure factory than goes at present, even in the imagination of the Fish Traders' Association.

Here are some further calculations, which, if the subject has not been worn threadbare in the preceding pages, should not be without interest. Four years back, in July 1886, Mrs. Barnett, of St. Jude's, Whitechapel, published in the "National Review" some specimen diets of a labourer's family, consisting of man, wife, and eight children, in the East End. They are given below in the tables marked I, II, III. I have imagined the family to live one-third of the year on each of three diets, and have taken out the total weight of food so consumed. Then, after transferring the family from Whitechapel to Birmingham, as the point furthest inland, and where the cost of railway carriage is likely therefore to be on the whole the heaviest, I have calculated, on the basis of the rates actually in force from the point from which the food of each kind would most naturally come, the total railway charge on the food of these ten persons for the entire twelvemonth.[4] The result, which will be found in table B, shows that the family uses something over two tons of food, that its cost is just under 43*l.*, and that the proportion of this due to railway carriage is 37*s.* 11·95*d.*, or 4·44 per cent. In other words, if the railway shareholders would forego the whole of their income, each member of the family might conceivably save 1*s.* 11*d. per annum* ; if some beneficent fairy would in addition work the lines for nothing, the saving would amount to no less than 3*s.* 10*d.* It should of course be remembered that this is an extreme case. If arrowroot were substituted for oatmeal, asparagus for onions, and salmon for herrings, while the gross charge for carriage would be increased, the percentage of cost of carriage to the total retail price of the article would be very much less than 4½ per cent.

[4] The railway rates will be found given with greater fulness in the Appendix at the end of this book.

SOME TYPICAL MENUS

I

Food	Weight per day	No. of days	Weight for twelve months	Cost per day	Cost per year
	lbs.		tons cwt. qrs. lbs	d.	£ s. d.
Breakfast—Oatmeal Porridge					
Oatmeal	1¼	122	1 1 12½	2½	1 5 5
Tinned milk	1½ pts.	122	One hundred and eighty three pints	1½	15 3
Treacle	½	122	2 5	1½	15 3
Dinner—Irish Stew					
Meat	1¼	122	1 1 12½	8	4 1 4
Potatoes	4	122	4 1 12	2½	1 5 5
Onions	1¼	122	1 1 12½	1	10 2
Carrots	A few, say 1¼ lbs.	122	1 1 12½	1	10 2
Rice	½	122	2 5	1	10 2
Bread	1½	122	1 2 15	2¼	1 2 10½
Tea—Bread and Coffee					
Bread	2½	122	2 2 25	3¾	1 18 1½
Coffee	2½ oz.	122	19	2½	1 5 5
Tinned Milk	1½ pts.	122	One hundred and eighty three pints	1½	15 3

II

Food	Weight per day	No. of days	Weight for twelve months	Cost per day	Cost per year
Breakfast—Bread and Cocoa					
Bread	2½	122	2 2 25	3¾	1 18 1½
Cocoa	1½ oz.	122	11½	1½	15 3
Tinned Milk	1 pt.	122	One hundred and twenty two pints	1	10 2
Sugar	2 oz.	122	15	½	5 1
Dinner—Lentil Soup, Toasted Cheese					
Lentils	1½	122	1 2 15	3	1 10 6
Cheese	1	122	1 0 10	8	4 1 4
Bread	1½	122	1 2 15	2¼	1 2 10½
Tea—Rice Pudding and Bread					
Rice	¾	122	3 7½	1½	15 3
Tinned milk	1½ pts.	122	One hundred and eighty three pints	1½	15 3
Sugar	2 oz.	122	15	¼	2 6½
Bread	1½	122	1 2 15	2¼	1 2 10½

III

Food	Weight per day	No. of days	Weight for twelve months	Cost per day	Cost per year
Breakfast—Hominy, Milk, Sugar	lbs.		tons cwt. qrs. lbs.	*d.*	£ *s.* *d.*
Hominy . . .	1½	121	1 2 13½	¾	7 6¾
Tinned milk . .	3¼ pts.	121	Three hundred and ninety-three and a quarter pints	3¼	1 12 9¼
Sugar	6 oz.	121	1 17	1	10 1
Dinner—Potato Soup, and Apple and Sago Pudding					
Potatoes . . .	5	121	5 1 17	3½	1 15 3½
Tinned milk . .	1½ pts.	121	One hundred and eighty-one and a half pints	1½	15 1½
Rice	3 oz.	121	23	¾	7 6¾
Dripping . . .	3 oz.	121	23	1½	15 1½
Apples	2½	121	2 2 22½	3¾	1 17 9¾
Sago	6 oz.	121	1 17	¾	7 6¾
Sugar	6 oz.	121	1 17	1	10 1
Tea—Fish and Bread					
Fish	2½	121	2 2 22½	7½	3 15 7½
Bread	2	121	2 0 18	3	1 10 3
Tinned milk . .	1½ pts.	121	One hundred and eighty-one and a half pints	1½	15 1½
Sugar . . .	3 oz.	121	22½	½	5 0½
Total . . .	—	—	2 1 2 25	—	42 19 1¼

In face of these facts, which can hardly be disputed, remembering too that the market salesman, whose capital outlay consists of the purchase of a desk, a hammer, and a note-book, charges a commission, usually of 5 and sometimes rising as high as 10 per cent., merely for selling the goods, while the gross profits of the retail dealer certainly do not average less than thrice this latter figure, the English railway

NOTE.—C. and D. means collected and delivered; S. to S. means station to station; O. R. means owner's risk.

	Total weight for the year				Total cost for the year			Railway rate to Birmingham	From	Cost of railway carriage on the particular weight	
	tons	cwt.	qrs.	lbs.	£	s.	d.			s.	d.
Apples		2	2	22⅓	1	17	9¾	17s. 6d. deld. in B'ham	Liverpool	2	4·36
Bread		12	2	1	8	15	1½	Flour, 11s. 3d. C. and D. 4 ton lots	Liverpool	7	0·44
Carrots		1	1	12⅓		10	2	11s. 8d. S. to S.	Sandy		9·53
Cheese		1	0	10	4	1	4	20s. 10d. deld. in B'ham	Liverpool	1	1·62
Cocoa				11½		15	3	22s. 6d. C. and D.	London		1·39
Coffee				19	1	5	5	22s. 6d. C. and D.	London		2·30
Dripping				23		15	1½	Not received by railway	—		
Fish		2	2	22½	3	15	7⅓	Herrings, 41s. 8d. O. R., S. to S., min. 1 cwt.	Yarmouth	5	7·52
Hominy		1	2	13½		7	6¾	Grain, 11s. 3d. C. and D., 4 ton lots	Liverpool		10·94
Lentils		1	2	15	1	10	6	19s. 2d. C. and D.	London	1	6·79
Meat		1	1	12½	4	1	4	30s. deld. in B'ham, 10 cwt. lots and upwards	Birkenhead	2	0·51
Onions		1	1	12⅓		10	2	12s. 6d. S. to S., 1 ton and under 2 tons	Leighton		10·21
Oatmeal		1	1	12½	1	5	5	30s. 10d. S. to S., 4 ton lots	Alford	2	1·19
Potatoes		9	3	1	3	0	8½	11s. 8d. S. to S., 2 tons pkd. 3 tons loose	Sandy	5	8·31
Rice		1	2	7½	1	12	11¾	18s. 9d. C. and D.	Liverpool	1	5·63
Sago			1	17		7	6¾	22s. 6d. C. and D.	London		5·42
Tinned milk	Fourteen hundred and twenty-seven and a quarter pints				5	18	11¼	28s. 4d. C. and D.	London	3	1·17
Sugar		1	1	2½	1	12	10	20s. C. and D. in cases, cks., or bags	London	1	3·27
Treacle			2	5		17	3	17s. 6d. delvd. in B'ham	Liverpool		5·72
Total	2	1	2	25	42	19	1¼	—	—	37	11·95

Percentage of yearly cost . . 4·44 per cent.

In calculating the railway rate it has been assumed that the trader in Birmingham will receive the goods in quantities over 500 lbs.

manager may be forgiven if he sometimes feels inclined to sympathise with Mr. Fink, who on one occasion frankly stated the issue before a committee of the United States Senate in the following words: "The shipper is never satisfied as long as he has to pay anything. You will find this the case here and all over the world. The shipper's business is to get the rates down as low as possible, and to get as much service as possible for the least money. The middlemen, the merchants and shippers, stand between the railroads and consumers, and whatever deduction in charges the railroads make the middleman generally puts in his own pocket. . . . That is the reason why he is so interested in getting the rates down. He generally represents himself, however, as doing it for the benefit of the people, when it is really for the benefit of himself. The people at large are generally satisfied with the transportation rates, and have reason to be so. . . . But some of these middlemen go before the working people and talk of the exactions of the railroads. . . . The middlemen that produce nothing are the men who arouse dissatisfaction among the working men by telling them that the railroad companies are their enemies, and are ruining them, and are taxing them to death, while the fact is that the railroads have been instrumental in supplying the labouring men with cheap food."

The truth is that the Traders' Associations are in a dilemma. Either they can charge the public with the cost of railway carriage, or they cannot. If they can, they are not hurt, and have no reason to cry out. If they cannot, the public have no special interest in the contest, and can stand by and see fair play between the two contending parties. But when asked to give sympathy to one side or the other, they can pause to remember that the middlemen, too numerous as they doubtless are, are yet a much smaller proportion of the inhabitants of the country than the railway shareholders, and that if one side or other must go to the wall, the public can do without the middleman very much better than they can without the thrifty investor.

CHAPTER VII

COMPETITION AND COMBINATION

"WHERE combination is possible competition is impossible." Such was the famous aphorism of Robert Stephenson in the early days of railroads. Since that time it has gone the round of two continents. Here in England more particularly its absolute truth has been not infrequently accepted without question by hasty observers who have taken it for granted that, as combination has in fact been possible, competition must therefore have ceased to exist. We have been assured accordingly on all hands that it has actually so ceased, in spite of the fact that we can see with our own eyes that it is as active and as likely to live at the present moment as it was a quarter of a century back. Even men as clear-sighted as those who formed the Joint Committee of the two Houses on the Amalgamation projects of 1872—probably one of the very strongest committees that ever sat in this country, for ten out of the twelve members either were or have since become Cabinet Ministers, while the eleventh was Lord Redesdale—did not rise entirely superior to the popular impression. In their report occur the following passages: "The direct action of competition by which in ordinary cases the price of articles to the consumer is reduced to such a point as will afford a fair profit to the producer and no more, does not exist and cannot be relied on in the case of railways. . . . . There is little real competition in point of charges between railway companies, and its continuance cannot be relied upon; there is at the present time considerable competition in point of facilities, but security for its permanence is uncertain. . . . Competition cannot be relied on to secure proper service and a fair price."

Now what are the facts? Companies have combined and do combine every day; but for all that they have competed, do compete, and, as far as we can see at present, are likely to continue to compete to the end of the chapter. Will any Lancashire trader go into the witness-box and declare that the Lancashire and Yorkshire and the North Western never make any attempt to get hold of each other's traffic? And yet all the world knows that, from a time whereof the memory of man runneth not to the contrary, these two companies have agreed to divide the traffic at competitive points. Was there ever a time when the East Coast and West Coast routes to the North renounced competition? Yet one of the most famous agreements in railway history is that under which the two systems accepted the award of Mr. Gladstone as to the proportion of receipts which should be allotted to each. Was the "Race to Edinburgh" of two years back merely a bouquet of fireworks let off by enthusiastic locomotive superintendents, or had the desire of the North Western and the Caledonian to get hold of a larger share of the Edinburgh traffic anything to do with the occurrence?

Take one more instance, perhaps still more familiar to the public. The much discussed Continental Agreement between the South Eastern and the Chatham and Dover, which settles the proportion in which the two companies are to share the receipts for all traffic to the Continent passing over their lines through any out-port between Margate and Hastings, is solemnly scheduled to an Act of Parliament, and has been judicially considered by every court in the country up to and including the House of Lords. Yet is it not matter of common knowledge that the South Eastern and the Chatham each fight their hardest to divert the stream of traffic from the rival line? We have taken instances from passenger traffic, as likely to be most familiar to the ordinary reader; but every trader knows that the exact same thing takes place with goods. In fact, a common count in the indictment against the railway companies is found in the fact that they fight too much, and that, whichever wins, the public is always called upon to pay the stakes. In face of this, is it not absurd to continue to quote Robert Stephenson's saying as proof of the fact that the companies, instead of competing, combine against the public?

Of course there is a sense, and a most important sense, in which the saying is practically true. The English companies do combine to maintain rates, as is done by competing railroads—those which are State property just as much as those which are in private hands—all over the continent of Europe, and as not only American railway managers but the American public fondly hope to see happen in America in some more fortunate, if still far distant future. It is true the English companies are not always successful; a new company may sometimes appear upon the scene, and upset the harmony of the old agreement. The opening of the Midland route to Scotland, for instance, implied a large reduction on the fares for the whole of the through traffic. Only last year the opening of the new Barry Railway and Dock brought down the rates charged upon the South Wales coal trade—a matter of 15,000,000 tons per annum—by something like 25 per cent.

Still on the whole there can be no question that English railways maintain rates with a steadiness which is regarded by the only other nation living as we do under a competitive railway system—a system, that is, in which the bulk of the traffic is competitive, and not as on the Continent only small portions here and there—with the highest admiration. This may seem on the face of it to be almost a paradox. At first sight one is naturally inclined to imagine that a system under which the rates on two competitive lines are driven down as though by a Dutch auction, must be eminently desirable in the interests of the consumer. Sir Bernhard Samuelson, for instance, was evidently of this opinion, when, as a member of the Committee of 1881, he asked Mr. Findlay: "What would be the effect if, instead of competing as to speed and agreeing as to rates, the railway companies were to adopt the opposite course of agreeing as to speed and competing as to rates?"

It might be possible to answer the question by asking the interrogator what would happen if the consulting physicians of London, instead of charging the guinea fixed by the Royal College, were each to advertise in the morning papers a reduction upon their neighbour's tariff of yesterday. Or, again, what would happen, say, in the engineering trade, if the Amalgamated Society withdrew its scale of wages altogether, and left each workman, according as he happened to be more esurient and impecunious than his mates, to underbid the rest. Or we might ask him what did happen in the London docks not so long ago, when there was practically no fixed scale of wages, and hungry men fought like wild beasts to wrest work from one another. In this case his reply would probably be that public dissatisfaction was justified in putting an end to a system which was bad for the employers, bad for the employed, and bad for the public whom they both served; as any system which refuses to give an honest day's wage for an honest day's work must always be bad.

But instead of dealing with analogies, which must always be more or less liable to mislead, it would perhaps be more profitable to invite Sir Bernhard to consider the actual teachings of railway history on this subject. We have not, as has been said, much experience of rate-wars in England of late years. But from earlier history we can see something of their obvious results. It might be very convenient, for example, to the inhabitants of Glasgow to be carried to Edinburgh for sixpence; but the passenger who was charged as many shillings by the same train from an intermediate station, and refused redress by the Court of Session, was probably far from satisfied of the equity of the system; and similar anomalies, it is evident, must always recur in similar circumstances. For if a railway reduces its rates to competitive points, it may be implicitly trusted to maintain its local fares at their former height, even if it does not attempt to raise them still higher in order to recoup itself for the profit lost on the competitive business. Take another instance:

Twenty years back there was a fight between the Midland and the Great Northern over the South Yorkshire coal traffic, and rates fell in the course of a few days to something like half their normal figure. That the two companies lost goes without saying; but whether anybody gained is problematical. The South Yorkshire coal-owner could hardly do so. His output was fixed; his contracts probably made some time in advance; he dare not expand his undertaking to meet a state of affairs which might be altered any day, and which he knew for certain would not be permanent. Supposing that he had ventured to do so, when peace was re-established and rates restored to their former level, he would have been left face to face with an increase of expenditure to obtain an increased output for which there was no market whatever available. Meanwhile, the collieries of Derbyshire, of Staffordshire, of Durham, and of Wigan, all of which are competitors in the London market, would have been utterly disorganised.

To imagine that the London consumers gained

anything like the amount which the railways lost is almost absurd; a sudden and temporary reduction of price never reaches the consumer. Even the coal-merchant, who unquestionably would put additional profit into his pocket to start with, would do it at the price of having the whole of his business arrangements upset. A, who was selling coal that he had brought into London while the rate was 7s., would evidently be in a very different position from B, who had replenished his stock at a 5s. rate, while C, who had waited till the rate had fallen to 3s. 6d., would be in a position to laugh at both of them. But none of the three would dare to live more than a hand-to-mouth existence, or to renew his stock till he saw what course events were going to take.

But there is no need to go to ancient history for our examples. Competition in rates is going on under our eyes at the present moment in America, and it may safely be said that, though the railways like it little, the general public likes it even less. No one, the present writer least of all, can wish to deny the merits of American railway management. But the demerits are at least equally patent; and if there is one cause more than another that is responsible for them, it is that the American railways, for reasons on which it would now be too long to enter, fail to keep their frequently renewed agreements to maintain rates. Hence has ensued wholesale bankruptcy of companies, with enormous loss to innocent shareholders; reckless discrimination between local rates and competing rates; flagrant dishonesty in preferences given to big traders over smaller rivals; secret rebates and discounts which have sapped the very foundations of commercial morality; and uncertainty which has made what should have been legitimate trading often little better than mere Stock Exchange gambling. This is strong language, so it is perhaps as well to produce some evidence to justify it. As for the bankruptcy of companies, let this one fact suffice. Between Chicago and Cairo, a distance of 367 miles, there are twenty-two railway companies whose lines cross that of the Illinois Central. Eighteen out of the twenty-two have passed into the hands of a receiver since the year 1874.

As for rates, take these instances. From Chicago to New York, 15 cents; to Pittsburg, which is half the distance, 25 cents. From the same point to Kankakee, 56 miles, 16 cents; to Mattoon, 172 miles, 10 cents. Cotton from Memphis to New Orleans, 450 miles, 1 dollar per bale; from Winona to the same city, 275 miles, travelling possibly in the same train with the Memphis bales, 3·25 dollars. At times in America it has been no unusual thing for freight to be invoiced to a competitive point, and thence sent back again for a considerable distance over the route by which it has come, for the sake of economy.

Of personal preferences, take the following, proved before the Hepburn Committee of the New York State Legislature by the production of the books of the companies concerned. Five firms at Binghamton and the same number at Elmira had special rates varying from five-ninths to one-third of the published tariff. At Utica three drapery firms had rates of 9 cents and a fourth a rate of 10 cents for traffic which was taken for the outside public at 33, 26, and 22 cents, according to its class. Five firms in the grocery business in Syracuse also paid a 10 cent rate, while the published charges varied from 18 to 37 cents. At this latter town in one instance it was proved that a special rate existed which was literally one-fifth of the amount in the published tariff.

No one needs to be told that the meaning of rates such as these is that the man who fails to get them is driven out of the business, as no economies or energy on his part can possibly enable him to sell at the same price as his favoured rival. It would be bad enough if these rates were given and entered in the ordinary manner on the customer's invoice. But in fact all kinds of deliberate deception have been resorted to in order to keep them secret. At one time a consignment note acknowledges the receipt of seventy barrels of flour; sixty-five only are shipped, and the railway company pays damages for the loss of the five non-existent barrels. At another time the cashier of an important firm is made a nominal agent for the railway company, and under the name of commission to him an enormous rebate is allowed for all the business his employers send over the line. Or, again, the goods are paid for at the published rate, and after the transaction is complete an agreed rebate is paid over in cash to the freighter and no receipt taken. Or, once more, the railway company purchases from a favoured trader its supplies of the goods in which he deals at a fancy price.

Within the last few months a chief official of one of the great railways and a prominent Chicago merchant have been sent to prison by the United States Court for refusing to give evidence as to transactions of this nature, on the ground that they were not prepared to incriminate themselves. Writing only a week or two back, the American "Railroad Gazette" referred to this matter of corrupt bargains between railroad officials and traders, and after pointing out that the officials were not alone to blame, added: "Should the roads use the evidence in their possession, in many cases it would carry consternation into the ranks of the shippers."

In England, on the other hand, a committee largely hostile to the companies sits for two sessions, examines scores of hostile witnesses, and ends by reporting: "No witnesses have appeared to complain of preferences given to individuals as acts of private favour or partiality." It is undeniable that agreements have been made between English companies to keep rates up; that the fights between American companies have brought rates down; and that on the whole it is better to have low rates than high ones. But, for all that, if the merits of English and American railway management could be balanced against one another before an impartial tribunal, it is not the English railways which would need to be afraid of the decision.

Last and worst of the results of the system of competition in rates which Sir Bernhard desires to see introduced into England, American experience entitles us to place uncertainty. An English trader would as soon think of asking what was the premium on sovereigns as compared with Bank of England notes, as of inquiring how much the railway rate has risen or fallen since his last shipment. In America rates vary from day to day as wildly as the price of fish fluctuates at Billingsgate. Not so many years back, in the course of a single week there were four different published rates from Chicago to New York, at 6, 8, 10, and 12 cents respectively; and it may be added that the highest of them represented about half the out-of-pocket cost of doing the business. The present writer was talking a short time back to a linen merchant in a large way of business in New York. The merchant mentioned that, a day or two before the McKinley Bill came into force he had been compelled to set to and pack his goods himself. The writer innocently asked why speed was of such extreme importance, once the goods had passed the New York Custom House. "Oh, you see," was the reply, "a rate in America is only good for the day it is made, and if my customers wire me to forward a consignment, and I don't send it till next day, and the railway rate has been raised in the interval, they would expect me to be responsible for the difference."

Witness after witness before the Hepburn Committee told the same tale: "Every shipment," said one merchant, "is a special rate; we don't know what we have to pay to-day or to-morrow." Asked by a member of the Committee, "Do you pay no attention to the schedule?" he replied, "I don't think I ever saw a schedule. I don't know anything about them;

they are like the weather, I presume." Here is another trader's evidence :—

Q. In every instance when you ship from the West do you make a special contract ?
A. Always.
Q. You never confine yourself to schedule rates ?
A. We know nothing about them ; I never saw a schedule rate ; I know nothing about that.
Q. How long have you been in business ?
A. Twenty years, more or less.
Q. And during those twenty years you have never known anything of schedule rates ?
A. I have been in this country since 1866, and have never known anything of schedule rates, and never saw a schedule rate.

It is perhaps superfluous to ask the English trader whether he thinks a system such as this would be an improvement on our own. English observers have seen the marvellous cheapness of American railways, they have failed to notice the price at which this benefit has been obtained. The Americans themselves know better. One could fill pages with extracts from American utterances to the effect that what they want is not cheapness but reasonable rates, combined with equality, publicity, and permanence. A few quotations, however, it is worth while to give. Mr. Cole, a former President of the New York Produce Exchange, used these words before the Hepburn Committee : " I am not speaking in any way antagonistic to a railroad or to a railroad interest, I think their interests are identical, I only hope to see a fixed rate brought about. I think they are bringing their goods low enough. The average merchant would be willing to pay a larger rate than he is paying to-day." " Steadiness and reasonable permanence in the prices of transportation services," writes Mr. Dabney,[1] formerly Chairman of the Committee on Railways and Internal Navigation in the Legislature of Virginia, " are the chief essentials of success in any legitimate business in which transportation by rail constitutes a considerable element; *steady rates are far more desirable than much cheaper but more uncertain rates.*"

Here is another quotation, which I take at second-hand from Mr. Jeans: " Producers and consumers are more interested in having rates for transportation *uniform, steady, and reliable,* than in having them *low*.[2] " The Inter-State Commerce Commission, in its first report, after describing in scathing terms the existing system, and pointing out the difficulty of putting an end to it, summarises as follows the public opinion which compelled the passage of the Act to which the Commission owes its existence: " Nevertheless it was a common observation, even among those who might hope for special favours, that a system of rates open to all and fair as between localities would be far preferable to a system of special contracts into which so large a personal element entered or was commonly supposed to enter. Permanence of rates was also seen to be of very high importance to every man engaging in business enterprises, since without it business contracts were lottery ventures. It was also perceived that *the absolute sum of the money*

---

[1] *The Public Regulation of Railways.* By W. D. Dabney. Putnam's Sons, New York, 1889. P. 177. An excellent little book, written from the point of view not of the railways, but of the public interest.

[2] *The Relation of Railways to the State.* By W. P. Shinn. P. 11.

charges exacted for transportation, if not clearly beyond the bounds of reason, was of inferior importance in comparison with the obtaining of rates that should be open, equal, relatively just as between places, and as steady as in the nature of things was practicable."[3]

Nor are the railway men themselves behind the outside public in the eagerness of their yearning after the exact condition of things which exists in England, with which, however, we here are dissatisfied. " The element of stability of rates," says the " Railway Review " of December last, " is promised as a feature of the new agreement; a feature as important as the absence of discrimination, and which when lacking is equally destructive to the interests of the commercial world as is the other when present. It is of little value to A to know that B pays the same rate as himself unless he is also assured that C will pay the same to-morrow." Here is an extract from the report of the Illinois Central Railroad for the year 1890: " Your directors feel satisfied that competition among Western Railways, which has heretofore been almost entirely on the line of reduction of rates, is coming to be, as in Great Britain and Eastern States, one of adequacy and frequency of service, and that in such a struggle success lies in furnishing the best service."

Mr. Fink's writings are filled from end to end with the same idea. Here are one or two extracts : " By guaranteeing the separate existence of a great

---

[3] If this be true in America with an average haul of 127 miles, and where the vast proportion of the traffic is in commodities of as little value as wheat and iron, must not the consideration apply with tenfold force here to our traffic, which is largely in valuable merchandise over a distance which can hardly average more than 25 miles?

number of competing roads, and preventing their consolidation under a single management, the spirit of competition is necessarily kept alive. But it is not to be exercised hereafter by paying rebates to shippers, and by trying to take underhand advantage of each other, but by endeavouring to improve and increase the facilities of transportation, and thereby retain or increase the claims of each road upon public patronage." Here again: "It is much more important that the rates should be steady and permanent, that merchants should be able to calculate with some degree of certainty as to what would be the rates of transportation at all seasons of the year, than that they should be excessively low at one time and correspondingly high at another, and that no one at any time can know what they will be the next hour."

"These railroad wars," he says again, "are most injurious to all interests, and the shippers understand this well enough. They are most satisfied when they have uniform rates and when these rates are permanently maintained. Although, strange to say, while they want uniform rates permanently maintained, they also want competition between the railroads—that is to say, they want the railroads to underbid each other. It is clear that they cannot have both peace and war between the railroads at the same time." "Steady and fixed rates," the quotation is this time from a document put forth by the Directors representing the United Sates Government on the Board of the Union Pacific, "even though they are high, are much more conducive to a healthy and prosperous condition than the unsettled and fluctuating rates, however low, which are brought about by the competition of railroads."

But enough of America, though it has been worth while dealing at some length with American experience in order to show that there are two sides to most questions; that, when a German official writer declares the "primary requisites of a goods-tariff" to be not cheapness, but "fixity, intelligibility, and unrestrained publicity of every rate," he is not speaking without ample justification;[4] and that, if Sir Bernhard Samuelson got his way and the English railway companies took to competitive rate-cutting, the gain to the English trader would be very far from unmixed.

There are not a few critics, however, who take a different line. They see that rate-cutting is impossible as a permanent policy, but they maintain that the existing competition in facilities costs the trader more than the facilities are worth to him, and that it is in the public interest that competition should be put an end to altogether. The railways, say they—the point, for instance, is strongly urged in the Report to the Lancashire and Cheshire Conference—agree not to cut rates, but as they are, in Irish phrase, spoiling for a fight, they cannot resist the temptation to spend a shilling in order to rob their neighbours of three pennyworth of traffic; and in the long run the public, which has no control over the rates, is called on to pay the entire fifteen pence. The statement is not only plausible, but undoubtedly has in it a considerable element of truth. It has been mournfully acknowledged, for example, over and over again,

[4] *Archiv für Eisenbahnwesen*, March and April 1890, p. 275.

by railway men themselves, that the competition in express trains between, say, London and Manchester or Manchester and Liverpool, is extravagant. A third of the number of trains could carry the whole of the traffic, and even then give a service sufficiently frequent to deprive the public of any right to grumble.[5]

Or, again, it is said, goods trains are run at high speeds, in other words with light loads, and therefore at increased expense; and the trader who would be equally well satisfied if his goods arrived a week later, has to pay the extra cost of the speed which is caused largely, not by the real necessities of the trade, but by the desire of each company to surpass its rival. Or, once more, a railway company establishes a new goods station in the heart of the business portion of some great city where land is at a fancy price, and the traffic of the company as a whole has to pay for the expenditure. Small blame to the trader, for whom the old station on the outskirts was equally convenient, if he feels aggrieved that expense is incurred from which he can receive no benefit, while indirectly he must be called upon to pay his fraction of it. The answer, however, to be made on behalf of the railways is, as I conceive, the following:

As for competition, there can be no question that it is wasteful. *On a toujours les défauts de ses qualités*, and if human beings were angels the waste of compe-

---

[5] The present writer must confess to scant sympathy with these lamentations. To demand simultaneously the advantages both of monopoly and competition is to expect to make omelettes without breaking the eggs. As well complain of Nature herself, whose tornadoes, while they sweep away the stagnant and fever-laden miasma, are apt to be reckless of snapping trees and unroofing houses.

tition might be at once eliminated, and each man left to do his best because it was his duty and pleasure to do so. Mankind, however, have not reached this point yet—at least in the railway world—and universal experience shows that, failing competition, railway facilities improve but slowly, and even in some cases actually deteriorate. Readers of Mr. Farrer's book on European expresses [6] will remember how remarkably his statistics bear out this conclusion. Mr. Farrer shows how in Germany the express services had actually in some cases retrograded between 1875 and 1888; how the best of the trains then existing were relics of the free competition of an earlier date; how in France, at Bordeaux, in the Auvergne, at the Swiss frontier, wherever in short two competitive routes came in contact, the service had improved enormously; how, on the other hand, the wealthy and powerful Paris and Lyons Railway had treated Marseilles and Toulon, Cannes, Nice, and Monte Carlo, with absolute neglect, while by the opening of the St. Gothard route even the Paris and Lyons itself had been forced into giving a creditable service through the Mont Cenis to Italy.

Mr. Foxwell's portion of the work, which deals with English expresses, when compared with his book of five years earlier on the same subject, shows what may be called the reverse side of the German picture. The best trains of 1883 made but a poor showing beside the best trains of 1888. Hardly a single town of importance throughout the British

---

[6] *Express Trains, English and Foreign.* By E. Foxwell and T. C. Farrer. London: Smith, Elder, & Co., 1889.

Isles is as far from London nowadays—for distance is to be reckoned not in miles but in hours—as was the case at the earlier period. Not only are the trains faster, but there are more of them, the accommodation for passengers of all classes is remarkably improved, and the proportion of expresses which still exclude third-class passengers has now become more infinitesimal than ever. As far as passenger services at least are concerned, it is impossible to question that competition in England gives better results than State regulation gives in France or State ownership in Germany. The comparison cannot be so easily made in the case of goods, but there seems no *a priori* reason why here too the same rule should not apply, nor would it be easy to show *a posteriori* that in fact it does not; but of Continental goods services we must speak later on.

Meanwhile, this point deserves notice here. Italy has had more experience of different methods of railway management than any other country on the face of the globe. It has tried State ownership and private ownership; it has tried allotting a district to a company as in France; and it has held an investigation into the whole subject unparalleled both in its extent and minuteness. It has laid under contribution the railway experience gathered in the course of fifty years by every nation in the world, and the conclusion to which Italy came in 1885 may be expressed as follows: "State management is more costly than private management, the State is more likely to tax industry than to foster it. Private management, therefore, must be accepted, and the only force powerful enough to at once restrain and stimulate private management is competition." Acting on these principles, the Italian Government, having first got all the railways of the peninsula into its own hand, has divided them out between two great companies, operating, the one along the East Coast, the other along the West, but meeting and competing at all the main points, at Milan and Florence, at Rome and at Naples. And though this system has only been in force for about five years, its effect in improving the Italian services has already been all that its originators could have reasonably hoped for.

One might be content, therefore, to rest the case for the English system of railway management on this point alone; that efficiency and progress cannot be secured under any system of monopoly, whether that monopoly be in the hands of the State or of private companies; that competition, therefore, is necessary to prevent stagnation. Now competition may take the form of rate-cutting or of improvement in facilities. The former, if American experience goes for anything, is a two-edged weapon, with the sharper edge turned against the interests of the public. We are shut up, therefore, to the latter form, and if we are told that it is wasteful that two trains should run each earning 5*s*. a mile, when one might just as well carry all the passengers and earn the whole 10*s*., leaving a substantial balance of profit to be applied in reduction of charges elsewhere, we reply that Continental experience shows that what would in fact happen would be that the one train would be so bad and so inconvenient that only 4*s*. worth of passengers would travel at all.

But there is a further answer than this. In one sense it is no doubt true that the public pays for both trains, that is to say, that, if the public ceased to pay for them, the accommodation would be withdrawn; but it is also true—and the truth is proved by the experience, not only of the Continent, but of districts in these islands where no competition exists —that if the second train were withdrawn, the public would pay precisely as much for the remaining one as at present it pays for both. Look at examples in the case of other competing enterprises. The proprietor of a restaurant, let us say, spends 50,000*l*. in marble and gilding, and unquestionably he does so in the hope of recouping the expenditure out of the mutton chops of the public: but for all that, do we in fact find that in the marble halls a mutton chop is any dearer or any worse than in the dingy old coffee-house across the way?

Or, again, take two fairly comparable articles of trade, such as coffee and cocoa. One hardly ever sees an advertisement of coffee. The cocoa manufacturers must spend tens of thousands a year in advertising. Theoretically, the public ought to get its coffee either better or cheaper because this wasteful expenditure is not incurred. Does it do so as a fact? Do any of us believe that, if coffee were advertised with the ingenuity and persistency which is displayed in the case of soap, either the quality would be reduced or the price to the consumer would be advanced? Are we not morally certain that the cost of advertising would in fact come, either out of the profit of the vendors, or else out of the economies effected by the better methods of manufacture or of distribution which are the natural results of increase of competition? And if this be, as it is commonly accepted as being, the universal law in ordinary business, why should we doubt that it applies even when the business is on a scale as large as that of the North Western or the Midland Railway?

One may carry the case, however, one stage further, and deny that any of the competitive expenditure of railway companies is in fact a pure economic loss like money spent in advertising. Take this very question of rival express trains for instance. Before the Midland built its new line to London, Scotland and Yorkshire and Lancashire were already in possession of an adequate express service. The new Midland expresses were, we are told, simply so much waste. Is this so? What, then, about the intermediate stations? Compare, for example, the Bedford of to-day, which is within an hour of London, with what it was when passengers crawled round by Hitchin or Bletchley. Whatever gentlemen who manipulate figures in their studies may think, the inhabitants of Chatham and Canterbury cannot be expected to admit that there is no need for a route competing with the South Eastern to Dover, nor those of Salisbury and North Devon to confess that a second series of expresses to Plymouth is a superfluity.

The same point may be made *à propos* of the multiplication of stations. It is preposterous, we are told, that the South Eastern, with a route 67 miles long, should compete for traffic from Reading to London, when there is a direct route to Paddington whose length is only 36 miles. Whether, however, the Deptford Tramway Company, for instance, would be as well pleased to have its hay delivered at Paddington as close to its door at Bricklayers' Arms, is another question. It is true, no doubt, that it would have to put up with the Paddington delivery if our railways were organised on the French or German system, but could it fairly be expected to accept the change as an improvement?

Take another instance, of which a good deal was made before the Board of Trade tribunal last year, that namely of receiving houses. Of late years, urged on, doubtless, by the force of competition, our railways have established in the great towns, in London more especially, a series of receiving houses where goods and parcels are taken in, and which practically act as subsidiary stations. Some of them are established in situations where the rent is enormous. Surely, it is said, the public should not be called on to pay for this extravagance, which is little better than a form of advertising. Or, again, a company builds warehouses adjoining its stations, and, provided it can thereby induce traders to send traffic over its line, it is not over punctual in demanding a proper warehouse rent. Or, again, it establishes a depôt for flour, say, or Bradford woollens, where without charge, or for a merely nominal one, it keeps on hand two or three weeks' stock for its customers. Surely, it is urged once more, the general public who have no wish to avail themselves of these facilities ought not to be made to pay for those who do.

The answer once more is that business is business. The railway company is only a great shopkeeper, and though, considering the scale on which its shopkeeping is done, no one can dispute the right of the public and the law courts to supervise the operations in a way that is neither possible nor desirable with a private enterprise, the principles which must be applied to both are the same. A shopkeeper must adapt the course of his business to the demands of his customers as a whole. He cannot make a reduction to one because the brightness of the plate-glass front had no attraction to him, to another because he carries off his parcel under his arm instead of leaving it to be delivered by the shop-cart. The result of any such attempt would, it is easy to see, be that the complexity in organisation and account-keeping would be so great as to absorb any reduction which the less exacting customer might otherwise be entitled to.

But a more serious charge than those last mentioned is to the following effect: The whole system of English goods management is wasteful and extravagant. In their mad race to outstrip each other in accommodation the companies postpone the collection of goods till the latest possible hour of the evening, load them up by the use of expensive machinery in the minimum of time, and then hurry away the waggons two-thirds empty, in trains only half the length of what the engine could take, in order that they may deliver the goods next morning in Leeds, say, or Liverpool, ten minutes or a quarter of an hour earlier than the rival line can promise. That such is the English system there is no denying. That compared with the leisurely Continental methods, of which more anon, it is an expensive system, there is no doubt whatever. Whether, however, it is wasteful depends entirely on whether the accommodation afforded is worth the price paid for it. On this point it is almost impossible for an outsider to judge.

That speed is of very great importance in many branches of business may be taken as proved by the fact that our rapid English services have not been volunteered by the railways, but forced upon them by the demands of the traders; by the fact that a considerable proportion of Continental traffic pays the *grande vitesse* rates, which are never less than double the ordinary ones, for a service which even then is much slower than ours; by the fact that the proportion of business correspondence transacted by telegram is rapidly increasing, and that notoriously it is becoming less and less common for merchants and shopkeepers to keep large stocks on hand. But in the nature of things precise information on the subject is unattainable. Next, however, to precise information, the best evidence that one can have is the opinion of those who from their position and training are best qualified to judge, and the writer accordingly has taken steps to ascertain the opinion of five firms of the first rank as warehousemen in the city of London. Here is in brief substance what they one and all report:

"It is of the very utmost importance that goods should be delivered the day after they are handed to the railway company, or in the case of Scotland the next day but one. We have become so accustomed to this prompt delivery that promises are made to customers who call and to those in the country, that goods sold from sample shall be delivered the following or the second day, as the case may be, and the customers rely on this being done. To go back to slower methods would entirely upset the trade, and cannot for a moment be thought of. In innumerable instances our country customers order goods by wire, and if we have not got them in stock, we wire forward to the manufacturer. Ordering by telegram has very much increased of late years, especially since the introduction of sixpenny messages.[7] In consequence of telegrams and quick trains consignments are very much smaller than in years gone by. We could not contemplate for a moment the introduction of the slower Continental method of transit, even though it might enable the railways to reduce the rates. It is altogether out of the question."

It should be noted, however, that one firm is of opinion that perhaps 25 or 30 per cent. of its consignments are not of special importance, and might without inconvenience be sent at a slower rate. On which

---

[7] As illustrating the practical influence of railway rates on the cost of manufactured goods, it is worth noting that the man who orders a roll of cloth, weighing say 1 cwt., from Bradford by telegram instead of by letter pays 6*d*. per cwt., or 10*s*. per ton, extra to save one day's delay. And apparently the time is worth the money. But for all that, English traders, from Sir Bernhard Samuelson downward, think it right to compare English charges for goods carried from London to Leeds between Monday night and Tuesday morning with French or German charges for goods carried from Paris to Calais, or from Crefeld to Bremen, in the sufficient interval which elapses between Monday and Friday.

the obvious comment is once more that a business must be managed as a whole. If four men want all their goods carried full speed, and the fifth wants three-quarters of them so carried, there is no gain either in economy or convenience in organising a slow service for the benefit of only a fraction of the traffic. Two of the firms above mentioned expressed their opinion on another point, that namely of the railway depôts. It was necessary, they said, that such depôts should exist somewhere. Either the railway company must provide them, and charge for it in the rate, or else they must enlarge their own premises and pay for the accommodation in the form of rent.[8]

Here is another instance of what traders are ready to pay for speed when it is entirely optional with them to do so. From a printed tariff of the rates in force between Berlin and London I take the following:—

Time on journey	Charges per 100 kilogrammes (say 2 cwt.)	s.	d.
6 to 7 days,	*Stückgut* (ordinary goods train)	8	6
4 to 5 ,,	mixed express	14	0
3 ,,	*Eilgut* (fast goods)	37	2
2 ,,	*Courirgut* (express)	74	4

I am informed by one of the largest firms of Continental carriers that a considerable percentage of

---

[8] Here is an actual instance of how business is done, which happened at the time the writer was inquiring into the matter. On Thursday, November 13, a customer wished to purchase twelve pieces of stuff from Messrs. —— & Co., warehousemen. The latter had the class of material in stock, but it was slightly finer, and consequently ½d. a yard too dear. Messrs. —— & Co. accordingly wired to the manufacturer in Fife, who had the exact article in stock, and promised their customer delivery on Saturday, the 15th. The goods were duly sent off, but went astray and were not delivered in London till the Monday. Meanwhile, the customer had claimed delivery on the Saturday, and had been supplied with the better class article at the price of the coarser quality, and then the railway company was called upon by the warehousemen to pay the difference.

the total traffic pays the " mixed express " rate, and that not a little comes even at the 74*s*. 4*d*. rate. Further, that Berlin would be able to command a much larger share of our millinery trade than it does at present if it were not handicapped by the great difference in the time in which goods can be obtained from Paris.

Here are two other instances of the way in which English trade is actually conducted, which have happened at different times to come under the writer's own notice, and which seem to be germane to the present question. I understand that even in a city like Dublin tailors have ceased to keep a stock of cloth, and only show patterns. A customer comes into the shop in Grafton Street and chooses the stuff for a coat or a pair of trousers. The tailor wires to London for the two or three yards required. The parcel is immediately sent to the nearest North Western receiving house, leaves Euston at 6.30 the same evening, and next morning the Dublin tailor sets to work to cut out the garment. Again, I was told in Aberdeen that it was no uncommon thing for a number of errand boys to await at the station the arrival of the night mail from London in order to get their parcels to the shop half an hour earlier than would be the case if they waited for the company to deliver.[9]

In face of facts like these, it is surely nonsense to claim that the railways would be acting in the public interest if they adopted slower but more

---

[9] This was when the mail did not get in till 9.55 A.M. No doubt the accelerations of last summer may have made a difference.

economical methods of working. The whole question of facilities *versus* low rates might fairly be put like this. The North Western or the Midland can raise money at a fraction over 3 per cent. The trader expects 10 or 15 per cent. on his capital. Accordingly he keeps down his warehouse accommodation and his stock to the lowest possible figure, and by the help of the elaborate and costly organisation of the companies, turns over his capital many more times in the course of the year than is possible to his rival in France or Germany, who is shut down to the possibly cheap but certainly nasty accommodation afforded by Continental railways.

The truth is, the more we can bring ourselves to realise that a railway company is only a shopkeeper on a large scale, anxious to make the best profit it can on the solitary article in which it deals, transportation, and desirous like every other shopkeeper to give better value to the public for its money than the rival shopkeeper in the next street—the more we can bring ourselves to realise this, the less shall we be inclined to lay down for the railway company *a priori* rules how it ought to conduct its business. If our grocer moves into larger and more expensive premises, if he adds new departments of trade, or opens branch establishments in another part of the town, we take it for granted that he knows his own business best. He has opportunities which no outsider can have of feeling the public pulse.

So, too, if a railway accelerates its trains and increases their number, if it opens new stations and sets up receiving houses and inquiry offices at every street corner, if it warehouses goods for nothing, and sends a van, with a horse, a man and a boy, half across London to deliver a single trunk, we may safely assume that it does so because it believes that by so doing it is ministering to the public convenience and so indirectly increasing its own custom. We may assume, too, that, though one man may object to one facility being given and another to another, in each case because he does not expect to be in a position to take advantage of it himself, the railway manager, who, through his innumerable agents scattered all over the country, is in constant contact with every class of his customers, is—not of course an infallible judge, but the best judge that can be found in this fallible world, as to whether any particular facilities are wanted or not. And by " wanted " we must understand " such as the public is prepared to pay for directly or indirectly at the price they cost." But this brings us back once more to the point whether the price which the British public pays for the unquestionable facilities it enjoys is not excessive, a matter on which we shall be better qualified to pronounce when we have drawn a few comparisons with the Continental and American railway systems.

CHAPTER VIII

CONTINENTAL RATES

THE warmest admirer of English railways would find it difficult to express his admiration of the statistical information which they furnish. Professor Hadley, for instance, a critic certainly by no means unfavourable, complains of the "secrecy of English railroad accounts," which makes it impossible to tell whether the companies have or have not for years past been paying dividends out of capital. That, however, is not our point here. We are here concerned with the fact that the refusal of English companies to furnish statistics on the same basis as those given in almost every country in the world makes it impossible to institute a comparison between the average cost of carriage—either the gross cost to the public or the net cost to the railway—in England and in foreign countries. In England, as elsewhere, it is possible to obtain figures giving the gross number of passengers and of tons of goods carried, and also the number of miles the trains have run, and the expenses which have been incurred in working the traffic. From these three sets of figures we can ascertain, by simple processes of division, how much the English company has received, how much it has spent, and what therefore is its percentage of profit per train-mile.

But there our knowledge stops. Now, this information, indispensable though it is to the railway manager himself, as the barometer to show whether the prosperity of the undertaking is increasing or diminishing, is perfectly valueless to the outside public. The trader knows nothing, and cares nothing, about train-miles. His interest is to know what it costs the company, and what the company charges, on the average, per ton. Out of England, accordingly, calculations to this effect are almost always made. A record is kept of the distance each consignment is moved, and the number of tons carried is multiplied by the number of miles which they travel. The result is to give the number of ton-miles. For instance, 100 ton-miles may mean 1 ton conveyed 100 miles, or 100 tons conveyed 1 mile, or any other possible combination of these two factors. Now, it is evident that, once we obtain the number of ton-miles, knowing as we do already the gross receipts of the goods traffic, we have only to do a simple division sum to ascertain the average charge per ton per mile. Again, knowing as we do the gross number of tons conveyed, by dividing this sum into the gross number of ton-miles, we can ascertain the average distance which goods are carried. When we get these figures, but not till then, we shall be in a position to compare English railways with those of any other country on a basis of fact, instead as at present of mere surmises.

Mr. Grierson, before the Committee of 1881, was examined at considerable length as to why this information was not given, and replied with perfect frankness: "We used to keep it, and we gave it up. It cost us a great deal of money. We kept probably as elaborate statistics as were ever kept by a railway company, but we could not make any use of this. . . . The average sum for carrying traffic for one mile, that again is perfectly useless. The figures are very interesting, I have no doubt, but they are perfectly useless. I assure you, there is no indisposition on the part of any railway company to keep any statistics. They would be only too glad, being the parties themselves most interested." Now, from one point of view, Mr. Grierson was no doubt right. It is true that the American railways—and no one will question the technical ability with which American railways are managed—do base all their calculations, not on train-mile, but on ton-mile figures. But it is more than likely that train-mile statistics are on the whole the most useful for the railway manager's purpose.

There is, however, another point of view of equal importance, whose existence Mr. Grierson absolutely ignored. Railways are shops for the sale of transportation, no doubt, but they are shops with, practically speaking, a licensed monopoly of the sale of an article of public necessity, and as such the public has a natural right to overhaul their accounts. This in a rough way ton-mile figures would enable it to do, just as the train-mile figures enable the railway manager to check in a rough way the expenses and the profits of his business. Professor Hadley has put the whole question with his accustomed clearness: [1]

[1] *Railroad Transportation*, p. 156.

"The English companies do not furnish, or even compile, ton-mileage statistics. This is no mere accident of practice; it is characteristic of the principle on which English railways are managed. There is a fundamental difference of purpose between train-mile and ton-mile statistics. The train-mile is, in a rough way, the unit of *railroad* service—so much work done by the railroad. The ton-mile (or passenger mile) is, in the same rough way, the unit of *public* service—work done for the public. Now, the whole theory of the English railroad system starts from the principle that railroads are to be managed as business enterprises, not as matters of public service; hence their impatient rejection of the idea that they should compile a set of statistics arranged from an outside point of view, but with little inside interest."

It is five years since Professor Hadley's book was written, and in the interval English railway managers have moved a long distance away from their former untenable position, that railways are ordinary private commercial undertakings. But to the height of giving us ton-mile statistics they have not yet risen. Till they do, any comparison between English and Continental railways can only be matter of guess-work. As the guesses, however, are usually made by writers not over friendly to the English companies, perhaps these latter would be wise in their own interest to produce the information required. Failing their action, the Board of Trade might do worse than take into consideration the question of exercising its authority under section 32 of the Railway and Canal Traffic Act of 1888, and amending the returns now required by law of the railway companies, in such a fashion as to include the missing statistics.

Even in their absence there are, as has been said, some writers who believe themselves in a position to pronounce positively on the subject. Sir Bernhard Samuelson, for instance, writes as follows: "Except as to iron-ore, coal, and coke, in certain cases, and a few other articles under special circumstances, the rates are so much lower in the countries of the North of Europe which compete with us for the trade of the world, as to place our traders at a serious disadvantage." Mr. Jeans too is able, after a series of possibly more rather than less accurate guesses as to the length of haul and average rate per ton per mile, to dismiss the whole question with the following airy conclusion: "So far as the nations of Continental Europe are concerned, we have no need to go into details. Suffice it to say that the average ton-mile rates in Belgium, Germany, and Holland, are much under our own."[2]

On the other hand, Gustav Cohn writes as follows: "Whether the existing freight tariffs of the English railways, compared with the earlier ones or compared with Continental tariffs, are high or low, is a question the answer to which is exceptionally difficult, and is wont to be given without hesitation only by those who fail to understand the difficulties.[3] Now, with all respect to Sir Bernhard Samuelson and Mr. Jeans, we may venture to say that Gustav Cohn knows a great deal more about the subject than they do. He has given the best years of his life to the

[2] *Railway Problems*, p. 449.
[3] *Die englische Eisenbahnpolitik der letzten zehn Jahre*, p. 87.

study of our English system. His book is, in Professor Hadley's opinion, "an admirable book, probably the most careful investigation of railroad problems from the standpoint of political science which has anywhere been made." Moreover, he is no partisan, being indeed convinced that State ownership of railways will be found in the long run the only possible policy.

Now, the present writer is firmly persuaded of his own inability to offer even a plausible guess on this subject. It is true that he did happen the other day to notice that the charge for carrying a horse from Berlin to Flushing is 230 shillings, while from London to Perth, which is a very similar distance, it is 111*s.*, and this little fact hardly seems to him to square with Mr. Jeans's large theories, but beyond that fact he has no wish to go. It occurred to him, however, that, a comparison of average rates over the whole country being impossible, a comparison of certain selected instances might not be without value. He has therefore, through the kindness of a friend, himself a foreigner and concerned all his life with the transportation business both here and on the Continent, obtained the following series of comparisons. Whether they are fairly chosen, the reader must judge; but from the tone in which the comparisons are drawn—for the present writer has done nothing to them but make mere verbal alterations—it is evident that the author of them is not so much impressed with the superiority of Continental railways as might naturally be expected in one possessing such a close familiarity with them.

"London—Aberdeen. The third-class rate between London and Aberdeen, a distance of 528 miles, or

850 kilomètres, according to the official tables, is 70s. per ton, including collection and delivery. For this distance the *Stückgut* (small consignment) rate in Germany is 95s. 6d., not including collection and delivery, which may be considered as worth between 5s. and 10s. per ton extra. Even if the goods are of a class for which in Prussia reduced rates are in force for quantities under 5 tons, the rate for this distance comes to 70s., not including collection and delivery. If the goods are sent in quantities of 5 tons the net rate for 850 kilomètres is 59s., but in such cases senders and consignees have to load and unload the goods themselves, or, if they prefer, they may have it done at their own risk by the railway company at a cost of 5d. per ton at each end, or in all 10d., so that the actual cost of transportation comes to 59s. 10d.—*plus* collection and delivery. Add collection and delivery charges and we bring the rate up to 65s. to 70s. This however is at owner's risk. If these rates were transferred into "company's risk" rates, according to the English Clearing House scale, they would amount to between 72s. and 87s. 6d. For quantities of 10 tons in one truck the Prussian rate would be 53s. 2d. Add once more cost of loading and unloading, collection and delivery, and transfer to "company risk" scale, and we should have a rate for 10-ton lots of between 65s. 10d. and 80s. In other words, the Prussian rate on 10-ton lots is higher than the English for consignments of over 500 lbs. Further, it must be remembered that it is almost impossible to get 10 tons of ordinary goods into one of the German

covered waggons. It is necessary therefore, in sending consignments of 10 tons, to use open waggons; hence tarpaulins are required, and the use of these is by the German railways charged for separately, at a rate of 4s. each for every 200 kilomètres or fraction thereof. Now, if the goods are to be properly protected, at least two tarpaulins are required, so that the cost of covering between London and Aberdeen will amount to 40s., or 4s. per ton additional. Now, to compare with Austrian rates; between Vienna and Brody, 848 kilomètres, they are as follows:— For common cotton goods, iron-ware, and other articles belonging to the third class of the English classification, 41·15 florins. This is equivalent to a rate of about 72s. 2d., station to station, or, allowing once more for collection and delivery, 7s. to 12s. higher than the English rate. For toys, leather in cases, and other articles for which the English rate would be the same, the Austrian rate comes to 51·61 florins, or about 80s. 6d., a difference once more of 15s. to 20s. in favour of England. In the through tariff between Germany and Austria, we find rates between Vienna and Ems, 855 kilomètres, of 89s. and 85s. per ton—or, say, making allowances once more, 20s. to 29s. more than the English. In France we find that, for the distance of 850 kilomètres between Paris and Marseilles, the rate applicable to goods not specially reduced is 117·50 *fcs.*, or 94s. In the through tariff between Paris and Germany similar figures are found: for instance, between Paris and Augsburg, 855 kilomètres, the rate for goods not specially reduced is 113·70 *fcs.*, or 90s.

"London—Penzance; distance 326 miles, equal to 525 kilomètres. The English charge for third-class goods is 60s. per ton, including collection and delivery. The German rate is 59s. 10d., station to station, for quantities under 5 tons; or, say, 64s. to 69s. collected and delivered. For articles for which reduced rates apply—iron, coal, grain, timber, &c.—the station to station rate is 44s. for lots under 5 tons. For goods in quantities of 5 tons the German rate is 37s. 2d., and for 10-ton lots 32s. 8d.; add collection and delivery, loading and unloading, and for 10-ton lots the cost of two tarpaulins at 12s. each, we get a rate of 38s. per ton for 5-ton lots, and 35s. 11d. for 10-ton lots, equal to about 41s. to 48s. collected and delivered at owner's risk, or 45s. to 60s. at company's risk. In Austrian traffic the rate for the similar distance between Vienna and Arad, 520 kilomètres, amounts to 37·90 florins, or about 66s. per ton station to station. In France, between Paris and Lorient, 523 kilomètres, the rate for articles not specially reduced is 79·30 fcs., or 63s. 5d. per ton. For a similar distance between Germany and Austria, e.g. between Frankfort and Teplitz, the station to station rates are 60s. 3d. and 58s. 6d.—once more, therefore, higher than the English. Between Belgian and German places, they are on much the same scale. Between Bremen and Brussels, for instance, 519 kilomètres, the rate is 66·25 fcs., or 53s. station to station, or, if collection and delivery be added, practically the same as the English rate.

"Birmingham—Edinburgh; distance 293 miles, or 471 kilomètres; third-class rate 55s. per ton. The ordinary German rate for this distance is 53*s*. 10*d*. station to station, the reduced rate for virtually the same distance is 39*s*. 8*d*. station to station, while the special English rate for hardware is 45*s*. collected and delivered. Between France and Germany the rate between Paris and Cologne, a distance of 487 kilomètres, is 61 *fcs*. station to station—say 70 *fcs*. or 56*s*. per ton collected and delivered. In Austria the rate for exactly the same distance of 471 kilomètres, from Vienna to Schoenau, is 28·80 florins, or 50*s*. 5*d*. per ton for ordinary goods, 22·70 florins or 39*s*. 9*d*. for hardware; both these rates, making allowance for collection and delivery, being about equal to the English ones. The through rates between Germany and Austria are higher. Between Cassel and Aussig, for instance, 476 kilomètres, the rate is 53*s*. 8*d*. for ordinary traffic and 52*s*. 11*d*. for hardware, both station to station only. The French rates for the distance of 473 kilomètres between Paris and Marennes is 89 *fcs*., equal to 71*s*. per ton.

"Leeds—Northampton. The principal traffic moving is dressed leather, which is carried at a rate of 30*s*. collected and delivered, or 25*s*. station to station. The distance is about 130 miles, equal to 209 kilomètres. The German rate for this distance is exactly 25*s*. per ton, station to station. The French charge between Paris and Le Mans, 210 kilomètres, is 34 *fcs*. or 27*s*. 2*d*., station to station. Between Dusseldorf and Antwerp the rate is 29·50 *fcs*. or 23*s*. 7*d*.

"Birmingham—Coventry. Where short distance traffic exists to a certain extent—for example, between Birmingham and Coventry—hardware packed is 10*s*.

per ton collected and delivered. The distance is about 18 miles, or 30 kilomètres. The North German rate amounts to 4s. 6d. per ton, station to station. The French rates for the same distance amount on the average to 6·50 fcs., say 5s. 2d., but in each case collection and delivery must be added."

So much for what Continental railways charge in comparison with English. This, however, is only one-half of the question. It is at least equally important to know how the accommodation which they give in return compares with ours. On this point my informant continues as follows:

"In comparing Continental rates with English rates, the following points have to be considered: (1) the time of delivery; (2) the responsibility the railways undertake for the delivery of the goods in good condition; (3) the accommodation and facilities afforded to the public.

"1. *Time of Delivery.*—It is a well-known fact that in England between the more important places, even at a very great distance, goods are delivered within twenty-four to forty-eight hours. On the Continent, and especially on the German, Austrian, Dutch, and Belgian systems, goods sent by *petite vitesse*, or goods service, are not delivered within these times. Their times of delivery are made up as follows:

For handling at despatching station.	1 day.
For carriage for the first 100 kilomètres.	1 ,,
For every additional 200 kilomètres, or part thereof.	1 ,,
For handling at receiving station.	1 ,,

"The day on which the goods are delivered to the company is not counted, and the time of delivery is not considered to have expired if an advice can be sent to the consignee within the appointed time that the goods have arrived. Taking our former examples, the time allowed in each case would be:

	German	French
London to Aberdeen	7 days	9 days
London to Penzance	5 ,,	7 ,,
Birmingham to Edinburgh	5 ,,	9 ,,
Leeds to Northampton	4 ,,	4 ,,
Birmingham to Coventry	3 ,,	3 ,,

The day on which the goods were delivered to the company in each case not being counted.

"If goods are delivered after the legal time, but not more than three days late, the railway may be made responsible to the extent of one-quarter of the charge for carriage. If the goods are delayed for more than three, but less than eight days, the consignee may recover half the charge. If the delay exceeds eight days, he may recover the whole. But he cannot recover more than the amount paid for carriage, unless he insures an 'interest,' so-called, in prompt delivery. The charge for such insurance is, for every 10 marks insured, 1 pfennig for the first 50 kilomètres, $\frac{1}{2}$ pfennig for the next 225 kilomètres, $\frac{1}{2}$ pfennig for each 375 beyond. For instance, in the case of a consignment to Aberdeen, with an insured value of 25*l.* the additional charge would be 1*s.* 6*d.*; between London and Penzance it would be 1*s.*

"Of course, compensation is only paid when there is proof of loss, and only to the extent that the loss is proved. In England, when goods are not delivered within a week, they are very commonly thrown on the company's hands altogether, and the company may be thankful if by the sale of them it can get back half the money which it has to pay to the consignor.

"All the Continental railways, especially the German ones, have a quick service called *Eilgut*, or *grande vitesse*, the charge for which in Germany is usually only twice the ordinary rate, but in many parts of Austria, Belgium, and France, rises to as much as three times the *petite vitesse* rate.

"The time allowed for *grande vitesse* or *Eilgut* traffic is fixed as follows: Booking one day, and for every 300 kilomètres or part thereof one day. The day of despatch is never counted, so that practically, even for short distances, goods sent off on Monday cannot be claimed before Wednesday night or Thursday morning. It is only fair to mention that the railway companies do not in practice avail themselves of the full time allowed them by law; but in many instances they do take the larger part of the time allowed them, and the fact that the *Eilgut* service is not really the quickest possible mode of conveyance is proved by the fact of the existence of a *Courirgut* service, that is, *Eilgut* carried by passenger or express trains. For this the charge is twice the rate for *Eilgut*, at least four times, that is, the ordinary tariff. Of course, goods are only consigned by *Courirgut* for longer distances, and this method of forwarding is very expensive; for instance, between London and Aberdeen the English charge by passenger train is 11*s.* 8*d.* for 1 cwt., the *Courirgut* rate would be 19*s.* 6*d.*, the French *grande vitesse* rate 16*s.* 3*d.* To Penzance the English rate is the same as to Aberdeen; in this case the German *Courirgut* rate would be 12s., the French *grande vitesse* rate 9s. 5d., but to these charges in both countries must be added the cost of collection and delivery. Of course, in England, where the goods service is so expeditious, a very small proportion of goods is sent by passenger train. The proportion on the Continent is much larger, more especially in the case of valuable goods. Besides, in consequence of the non-responsibility of Continental railways for loss or damage of goods, everybody is anxious to shorten the journey, and therefore the risk of transit, as much as possible. But this brings us to the second point of the liability which attaches to a railway company as a carrier.

"The Continental railways, especially those of Germany, Austria, and Holland, are not responsible for any greater sum than 3*l.* per cwt., and if goods are damaged, the railways pay any claim, if they pay at all, only on this scale. For instance, if goods weighing 1 cwt., and worth about 30*l.*, get damaged, and the expert who is called in to arbitrate considers that the damage amounts to half the value of the goods, the Continental railway will pay, not the full 3*l.*, but only 50 per cent. of that sum, viz. 30s. If the trader pleases, he can insure his goods for a higher amount; but a premium is charged for this of 2s. per 1,000*l.* for every 150 kilomètres or fraction thereof. For instance, for a ton of Bradford goods, worth 300*l.*, between London and Aberdeen, the premium would be 3s. 7d., between London and Penzance 2s. 5d. Further, it must be remembered that, even where insurance is effected, it only covers the risk while the goods are in transit on the railway. The Continental railways, which only carry from station to station, run no risk of damage through loading and unloading on the sender's and consignee's premises.

"Nor is this all. When a trader obtains a lower rate for a 5-ton or a 10-ton lot, he must undertake the loading into and out of the railway truck himself. It is true that the railway company will do it on payment, where it suits them to do so, but even then they do it at the customer's risk. And if the railway company has not got convenient accommodation, or does not see its way to make a profit out of the transaction, it stands aside and leaves sender and consignee to do their own work. For these truck-load and half-truck-load goods the railway declines all liability, so that the rates applied to them are practically like the Owners' Risk rates in England. There is yet another charge which the railway is allowed to make. They have the right, according to their regulations, to forward certain classes of goods in uncovered trucks. If the sender wishes them to go in a covered waggon, he is charged an additional 10 per cent. But if, either because the railway has not sufficient covered trucks on hand, or because those which they have are not large enough to contain the 10 tons which they nominally carry, the trader is obliged to use an open truck, he is not entitled to any reduction on that account; on the contrary, as has been mentioned before, he is charged a considerable additional sum for tarpaulins to protect his goods from the weather.

"In comparing the accommodation offered by English and Continental railways respectively, the following point should be considered: Continental railways, even in large places, have seldom more than one station—have at the utmost only two—at which goods are received for despatch, or whence they must be fetched by the consignee after arrival. The English companies, on the other hand, in any place of importance have a number of stations, and thus offer to everybody facilities for delivering and fetching away their goods. Further, the English lines afford proper siding accommodation for station to station traffic. On the Continental lines, such accommodation is often very bad indeed, and the loading and unloading of goods is interfered with every minute, and often entirely stopped, by shunting and other work done by the company for its own convenience. There is another way in which the English companies meet the convenience of their customers: goods collected quite late in the evening are nearly always despatched the same night. The Continental companies require all goods to be delivered by an early hour. English railways again lay themselves out to benefit their customers in the matter of warehousing goods, and by executing special instructions respecting delivery to other warehouses, to docks, wharves, &c., without extra charge—facilities which are quite unknown in any other country. The Continental railway companies make extra charges for everything they do outside their regulations."

"Ten years ago," says Mr. Jeans "a distinguished

French economist estimated the mean goods tariff on British railways at 21 per cent. higher than that of the French lines; and since then the difference appears to have become still more adverse to England." As we have seen already, an economist, however distinguished, can only estimate; the exact facts are unattainable. But let us assume that he is correct. Let us assume further—in face of Mr. Scotter's evidence before the Committee of 1881, that from the office of the Manchester, Sheffield, and Lincolnshire Company, in the five years between '76 and '81, there were sent out notices of 56,942 reductions as against fourteen advances, a still more questionable assumption—let us assume that Mr. Jeans's estimate is also correct, and that the French rates are nowadays 30 per cent. lower than ours. To this concatenation of assumptions it might fairly be answered: "Is that all the reduction that is offered to induce traders to accept a Continental instead of an English standard of service? If Continental traders could send their goods by *grande vitesse* or *Courirgut*, which is certainly not faster than the ordinary English goods service—if they could get English accommodation in stations, in insurance, in general readiness to oblige exchanged for bundles of official red-tape, and all for an addition of only 30 per cent. to their present rates—how much traffic, one would like to know, would be left to go under the conditions of the existing *petite vitesse* services?

Two more points in connection with German railways should perhaps be noticed. Mention has already been made of the fact that an English town has many more different stations than a German one. It is also worth while to recollect where those stations are. Some fifteen or twenty years back the Great Eastern Railway spent about 2,000,000*l*. sterling in order to bring its passengers from Bishopsgate Street to Liverpool Street, half a mile or so nearer to the centre of the City. Liverpool Street Station, having already become too small for its traffic, is at this moment being enlarged at a cost of about another 1,000,000*l*. sterling, three-quarters of which sum goes in the purchase of land. In Germany also the traffic is growing; at Frankfort, for instance, it has been necessary to build a new station very much larger than the old one. When it was opened a year or two back, its size and magnificence was trumpeted in every journal in Europe. But the reporters forgot to mention that the new station was half a mile further from the centre of the town than the old one. Lest it should be supposed that this case is exceptional, I will give another instance. At Hildesheim, a town which, after sleeping for centuries as soundly as Barbarossa in the enchanted cavern of the Kyffhäuser hard by, has in the last few years awaked to new commercial life, there also has been erected a splendid new station. As at Frankfort, it is half a mile further from the centre of the town than the old one; the former site, having been cleared and levelled, is now available for sale as building allotments.

Now, if railways worked on these principles are no cheaper than English lines, they most certainly ought to be—cheaper at least as far as the direct railway charges are concerned. For, if the law which holds elsewhere holds inside a town, that wholesale carriage by railway is cheaper than retail carriage in cabs and carts, it is difficult to believe that the German policy, which, though possible to a State monopoly, is fortunately impossible for our competitive English companies, can be cheaper in the long run. If, for example, in the case of Frankfort, we were to add together the extra cost to the travelling public, both in time and cab hire, the extra cost of carting goods, the extra expenditure on the maintenance of the additional length of street, and capitalise the whole at, say, 4 per cent., it is probable we should arrive at a sum representing the value of a good many acres of land adjoining the old station.[4]

Another and a more important point is this. The

---

[4] This point the English traders' advocates very wisely ignore. The Lancashire and Cheshire Conference Report, for instance, condemns in no measured terms the system by which the English railways not only deliver goods at stations in the heart of the great towns, but actually expect their customers to pay for this service, instead of leaving the traders to cart their own goods to the stations in the outskirts. I have made a rough estimate of what the adoption of the new system would mean in London. I find that the northern companies bring into and take out of the City something like 3,000 van-loads of goods per diem. If the traders did their own carting it would mean at the very lowest, for traders' waggons would rarely get full loads, even one way, 10,000 additional vehicles daily between the City and the northern termini. It has been calculated on good authority that the total number of vehicles passing through the Strand in the 24 hours is only 12,000. This one fact, then, is surely sufficient to prove that the streets from the City to King's Cross and beyond would be entirely inadequate for the enormous additional traffic which would have been thrown upon them had the railway companies stopped short to the north of the Euston Road. And if the millions which have been spent by the railways in bringing their lines into the City had been spent in street improvements, and charged on the parish rates, instead of, as now, being included in the railway charge, would the London public have secured any great gain in economy? That they would have lost in expedition and convenience is of course undeniable.

published statistics of the German railways are very far from representing the total sum which is paid for railway accommodation by the public. "The traffic in commodities in Germany," says Sir Bernhard Samuelson, "is carried on under rates founded upon intelligible principles." Let us endeavour therefore to understand them. Neglecting altogether traffic in coal, lime, ironstone, farm manure, and similar raw materials of production, and dealing only with what may more properly be called merchandise—ignoring also the very numerous exceptional tariffs of which we have already spoken—we find that the German system works as follows :—For goods carried in small quantities (*Stückgut*) there is—in addition to the charges for terminals, covering, weighing, insurance, &c.—a fixed rate of 2·123d. per ton per mile ; for loads of 5 tons the rate comes down to 1·283d., and for loads of 10 tons to 1·162d. Or, let us say, in round figures, that the charge for small consignments is not far short of double the charge for 5-ton and 10-ton lots.

Now, it is obvious that in the case of an ordinary merchant or manufacturer's business, a consignment of 5 tons, and still more of 10 tons, to a single customer must be very exceptional. It was stated, for example, before the Committee of 1881, that the average weight of a single consignment, apparently including minerals as well as goods, was only 7 cwt. on the South Eastern Railway. More recently the South Western has taken out the weight of all the goods passing through Nine Elms Station on Friday, October 4, 1889. The number of consignments of merchandise, properly so-called, was 5,798, and the weight 854 tons, or, say, roughly an average of 3 cwt. per consignment. Probably the circumstances of Germany are not so very dissimilar.

To the man then who wants to send 3 cwt., the offer of a cheap rate for a consignment of 5 or 10 tons is absolutely illusory. Still, the difference between the *Stückgut* and the truck-load rate is so enormous that some attempt was bound to be made to make these latter practicably available to the public. What has in fact happened is this. There have sprung into existence, since the introduction of the "Reform" tariff, a number of forwarding agents, or *Spediteure*. Their business is to collect or receive goods from the public, to make them up into lots of 5 or if possible 10 tons, and then hand them over to the railways for carriage. Their profit consists of so much of the difference between the very high *Stückgut* rate and the comparatively low truck-load rate, as they can persuade the public to leave in their hands. Roughly speaking, it is estimated that the *Spediteure* do in fact succeed in retaining, not of course as net profit, from a half to two-thirds.

There is no need for us here to investigate in detail this highly artificial system. Still less is it necessary to say one word against the *Spediteure*, who have done what is in their power to bring the most unnatural, however "intelligible," system of the German Government into conformity with the hard facts of this workaday world. But the following objections are obvious at the first glance. In the first place, instead of dealing direct with a railway company, a large and conspicuous public body, easily accessible to control by public opinion and by positive statute law, the trader is at the mercy of the *Spediteur*, who makes his own rules, and occupies no public position whatever. Secondly, the system leads to enormous delay. A consignment, for example, going, say, from Potsdam to Düren, near Cologne, would probably first be taken at the *Stückgut* rate back to Berlin, then be sent as portion of a 10-ton load from Berlin to Cologne, there once more unpacked and sent on to Düren at the *Stückgut* rate, or possibly it might be detained in Cologne till a 5-ton load for Düren had time to accumulate. Instances are mentioned in which freight consigned from New York to Berlin took longer over the last 234 miles from Bremen than over the whole of the ocean voyage thither.

Another objection, and no slight one, is the uncertainty of the system. The *Spediteure* have got to live, and the possibilities of making up 10-ton loads —of transacting their business, that is, in the most economical manner—vary very considerably from time to time. Accordingly, their tariffs are revised from year to year. Further, they are not the same necessarily in both directions. From Mannheim to Berlin, for instance, the *Spediteur's* rate per ton is 42*s.*; from Berlin to Mannheim it is 55*s.* 6*d.*

Here let us leave this matter. The main point is to notice that the ton-mile statistics of the German railways by no means represent the whole sum that the German public has in fact to pay for railway carriage; and that the low rates for 5 and 10-ton lots, which look so well on paper, are not directly available to the German public at all; and that the fraction of benefit derived from them, which in fact the public does obtain, can only be obtained on condition of paying for the maintenance of an immense organization of parasites to perform functions which in England are performed as a matter of course and without extra charge by the railway companies as part of their everyday business.

One word may, however, be added: that if anybody is anxious to see the German system introduced into England, it is more than possible that his wishes will be gratified within the next few years. For one at least of our most experienced general managers is of opinion that if the maximum rates are reduced any further, the railway companies will be forced to abandon their present position as public carriers, and to return to the status which they occupied fifty years ago as carriers' carriers. Messrs. Pickford, and Chaplin & Horne, and their rivals, would then load and unload, fetch and deliver, insure, and perform all the other functions which they once performed in England, and which the *Spediteure* now perform in Germany. To obtain the necessary accommodation, they would rent the goods stations of the existing companies; nor would they have any hesitation in paying a handsome rent for them, for, whatever Traders' Conferences may say, there is a good deal of traffic in England which might be made to bear rates much higher than those at present in force, if the inconvenient restrictions imposed on the railway companies by the legislation of the last half century could be quietly left on one side; if the railway companies simply charged their statutory tolls for the use of the line and the provision of locomotive power, and the irresponsible carriers exacted what terminals they pleased and adopted such classification as they found convenient.

It is, however, pretty safe to say that no one wishes to see the *Spediteur* acclimatised in England. Writing *à propos* of the precisely similar system which up to the year 1847 maintained a struggle for existence on the English lines, Professor Hunter says :[5] " The carriers tried to keep the railway companies as nothing more than sub-carriers, responsible only to them, and having directly no contact with the customer. Such a view was not likely to commend itself either to the directors or shareholders of the railway companies; they entertained the not unnatural fear that under this arrangement, after they had borne the brunt and heat of the day, in introducing at their own risk a vastly improved machinery for the conveyance of goods, the carriers would interpose between them and the public and secure a large share of the profits which might legitimately find their way into the railway exchequer. . . The subject engaged the closest consideration of Select Committees of the House of Commons in 1839 and '40. . . . The Select Committee of 1839 heard much evidence on the comparative merits of these systems, and declined to express any opinion until further experience was obtained. The Committee of 1840, however, arrived at a decided opinion. They declared against the views of the carriers, and held that the railway com-

[5] *Railway and Canal Traffic Act*, 1888, pt. i., pp. 11, 12.

panies should not be prohibited from collecting and delivering goods at the termini."

Consequent on this decision there was a struggle for a few years, followed in the course of nature by the survival of the fittest, and the extinction in this country—except for mere parcels traffic—of the *Spediteur*, only to reappear forty years later in Germany, galvanized into life by a system which—" natural " though it may be, and "intelligible" though it may be—has yet embodied the mistake, common to all powerful and highly organised bureaucracies, of assuming that the customers were made for the railways, not the railways for their customers; which lays down a cast-iron scale of rates, proper at all times and seasons and places, for consignments of small amounts, of five tons, and ten tons, respectively—a scale whose abstract justice it evolves from the depths of its own inner consciousness—and expects the public to govern itself accordingly.

But probably enough has been said to show that an attempt to compare the railway systems of two countries merely on the basis of their printed tariffs is as preposterous as though a foreigner should write an essay to prove that London cab-fares are extortionate, on the ground that, while an omnibus will carry a passenger from Charing Cross to Liverpool Street for a penny, the driver of a hansom expects for the same distance eighteen times as much. Or, as though one should argue—as indeed has actually been done more than once—that the North Western must be extravagantly over-capitalized at 53,000*l*. per mile, seeing that the Americans can lay ten miles of "track," as they appropriately call it, across a Texan prairie for the same figure. It is worth while, however, noticing very briefly where this paper comparison of tariffs would really land us.

The Cape Government Railways, for instance charge 6*d.* per ton per mile for articles such as cast-iron grates and kettles. On imported coal the tariff is 3*d.* per ton-mile, while the native article is let off at the reduced rate of 28*s.* 6*d.* for 180 miles, as against 7*s.* 2*d.* for a similar English distance. In Ceylon again the average rate for the whole traffic, the vast bulk of which consists of rice and similar low-class commodities, is 4*d.* per ton-mile. In the Argentine Republic there are rates in force rising as high as 8½*d.*, while in New South Wales the last report of the Government Commissioners boasted that the highest rates had been brought down from 9*d.* to 7*d.* The Australian coal rates were referred to at some length before the Committee of 1881. For distances of 150 miles they vary from 9*s.* 5*d.* in the case of Queensland to 31*s.* 3*d.* in the case of South Australia, which, on the other hand, responds by charging ploughshares at 39*s.* 6*d.*, as against a rate of 103*s.* 4*d.* in Queensland. Is it really possible to found any serious argument on such figures as these? Would the coal merchant in Queensland be justified in declaring the South Australian Government three times as extortionate as his own, and the South Australian manufacturer of agricultural instruments in maintaining that the proportionate extortion was accurately stated, only that it applied the other way round?

Or, take another instance: the Indian rates are in

many instances enormously less than those obtaining in Europe. Shall we therefore say, with Aristotle, that the deficiency which is Indian is bad, that the excess which is Argentine or Australian is bad also, and that the mean which is displayed in England is right and proper? Shall we not rather examine the conditions under which the rates apply, and taking for example the lowest rate for passengers of, say, $\frac{1}{4}d.$ per mile in India, as against four times that amount in England, go on and compare the circumstances of the two countries? And when we do that, what shall we find? That in the one country a workman's time is worth about $2d.$ a day, while in the other it is worth about $9d.$ per hour. That the Indian, therefore, who sacrifices half a day to save three-halfpence is a gainer, while the Englishman who wastes an hour to gain sixpence is a loser. Then, with this idea in our minds, we shall compare the train services of the two countries, and we shall find that in India the trains run so seldom and stop at so many intermediate stations, that they can accumulate loads of 400 or 500 passengers, so returning to the railway an income of something like 10s. per train mile; that in England, on the other hand, where passengers cannot afford to waste a day in waiting for a train, and where they demand to be carried to their destination with the utmost possible speed, trains must run so often and so fast—that is stop so seldom—that an average express carries barely fifty passengers, has to be content in other words with earning only 4s. a mile.

And if, in so simple and straightforward a matter as passenger traffic, we see that how far mere paper comparisons of fares charged might lead us astray, shall we not be wise if, in the immeasurably more complicated and more recondite matter of goods traffic, we distrust those who on mere paper comparisons of printed tariffs—and much more on comparisons of printed tariffs with surmises as to the average rates charged in this country—invite us to pronounce dogmatically as to the justification or non-justification of the charges made by our English railways?

CHAPTER IX

AMERICAN RATES

" IF," says Mr. Jeans, in the " Nineteenth Century " for September 1890, " the traffic carried on the railroads of the United States in 1888 had paid the same average ton-mile rates as they (*sic*) did twenty years before, the people of that country would have been charged for the transportation of the products of their fields, factories, and mines, about 192,000,000*l.* sterling more than they actually did pay in that year." An equally valuable and veracious comparison would show that, if the 800,000,000 passengers whom the railways of the United Kingdom carried in the same year had been called on to pay the fourpence a mile which they would have paid to the old stage-coaches, instead of the one penny per mile with which the railway companies were content, the English people would have been charged for their transportation about 80,000,000*l.* sterling more than they actually did pay in that year. Needless to say, however, that —imposing as the long row of figures may look, and accurate from an arithmetical point of view though the multiplication sum may be—the one calculation and the other are equally devoid of practical value. The English railways have not remitted this vast tribute of 80,000,000*l. per annum*, for the simple reason that at stage-coach rates the passengers would have stopped at home. So, too, in the case of the United States. The Western farmer has had a hard enough struggle to make both ends meet even with the present rates of carriage. Had the railway rates remained what they were in the days when the West was first opened up after the Civil War, the buffalo would still be roaming over the wheat-fields of Iowa and Wisconsin.

But, to drop imaginative statistics and to come to plain and literal fact, it is undeniable that at the present moment the average rate per ton per mile for the carriage of goods in the United States—including under the term "goods" not only coal and wheat but furniture and millinery—is in round figures something like one halfpenny. Mr. Jeans gives it at ·91 cent for 1888. The Statistical Bureau of the Inter-State Commerce Commission puts it at 1·001 for 1888 and ·922 for 1889. If we add to this, as we ought to do to make the comparison a fair one, the receipts of the express companies and the carting agencies, we shall probably not do more than bring up the ·922 to an even cent.

Now, as has already been said, no accurate comparison with these figures is possible in the case of the English railways, because the necessary statistics are not in existence. We know that in round figures 300,000,000 tons were carried at a cost of 40,000,000*l.* sterling—at an average cost, that is, of 2*s.*8*d.* per ton. Supposing the average distance travelled to have been twenty miles, this would be roughly equivalent to $1\frac{1}{2}d.$ per ton-mile ; or, supposing the distance to have been thirty-two miles, it would be equivalent to one penny. Probably the truth is that the distance was nearer the shorter than the longer figure. If we say that English traffic paid on an average $1\frac{1}{4}d.$ per ton per mile—that is, a good deal more than double the American average—our guess will probably be as near the truth as it is possible to go. The fifty or sixty per cent. reduction which the American railways have achieved is therefore without doubt a feat of which they have every right to be proud. Let us realise what it means.

One commonly sees in the City intelligence of the newspapers the information that the Chicago rate has been cut to 16 or 18 cents, or again has been restored to 25 cents. This is to say, in other words, that 100 lb. of wheat is carried from Chicago to New York, a distance of between 900 and 1,000 miles, for 25 cents or in English figures 22s. 6d. per ton.[1] Now, the Chicago rate to New York is the basis on which the whole of the through tariffs over the larger part of the United States depend : for example, when the rate from Chicago to New York for wheat is 25 cents, it is 23 cents to Philadelphia, 22 cents to Baltimore, and 20 cents to Albany, and as the New York rate moves down, all these other rates move down proportionately with it. Then again other towns and distributing centres in the West are charged fixed proportions of the Chicago rate. Taking the Chicago standard as 100, St. Louis pays 12 per cent. more,

---

[1] Per "gross" ton, that is, of 2,240 lbs. The ordinary American reckoning is 2,000 lbs. only to the ton.

Cincinnati 13 per cent. less. We may say therefore that, while the trade of the country as a whole is carried at $\frac{1}{2}d$. per ton per mile, or roughly the English price for coal in full train-loads, the grain traffic on the through routes between the great producing and distributing centres is carried at a price of something between a farthing and a third of a penny.

Further, it must be acknowledged that, unlike Continental rates, which need when compared with English ones to have additions made to them for terminals, for loading and unloading, for sheeting, for weighing, for checking, &c., &c., these American rates are inclusive. It is true they do not include—and the exception is of course a very important one—collection and delivery.[2] In the case also of rough freight, such as firewood or paving-stone, and also sometimes in the case of perishable produce, the railway does not undertake to load and unload. Moreover, a considerable proportion of the traffic is carried only at owner's risk; not as with us in the alternative, but the "release," as it is called, of the company is made a *sine quâ non*. But the whole of the services rendered by the company, whatever they be, are covered by the inclusive rate quoted in the tariff. The 22s. 6d., for instance, from Chicago to New York includes sending the railway truck alongside the elevator in Chicago and delivering the wheat in lighters alongside the steamer in New York harbour.

[2] There are, I am informed, three places in the States, two of them important, and one most unimportant, where collection or delivery, as the case may be, is included in the rate—Baltimore, Washington, and Watkins Glen; the reason in each case being different, but of a purely local nature.

Such being the rates which the American railways have perforce to be satisfied with, the question which naturally occurs to an Englishman is, How do they live? Badly enough, it must be confessed, seeing that the profit on railway investments is steadily but not slowly diminishing year by year, and that in the last year for which statistics are available the average rate of interest paid by the United States railways was on ordinary stock 1·91 per cent., on preference stock 2·11, while on the whole capital invested, both in stock and bonds, it was only 3·10. Of the stock, nearly two-thirds paid no dividend whatever, while more than 18 per cent. even of the bonds were in default. And this, be it remembered, in a country where the average rate of interest on investments of other kinds is at least half as high again as is the case with us.[3]

Still, though the shareholders may not be to be congratulated on the results of their enterprise, the American railways do continue to live—to pay, that is, their working expenses and their fixed charges—even at this extraordinarily low tariff. Further, it

---

[3] It has often been asserted, and is commonly, I think, believed in this country, that American railway stock is mainly "water." Unquestionably there is a very large amount of stock in existence not representing hard cash put into the line; on the other hand, hundreds of millions of dollars, which were honestly invested, have been wiped out under foreclosures and reconstruction schemes. Which of these two items is the larger no man can say. Professor Adams, the statistician to the Inter-State Commerce Commission, probably the most competent authority in the country on the point, professes himself unable to make even a plausible guess. Meanwhile, this at least is certain, that if we apply the only practical test, the price for which they could be replaced, the railways of the United States are worth to-day far more than their capital value.

may be said that a few exceptionally favourably situated lines—the Pennsylvania, and the New York Central, with its allied companies, are the most conspicuous instances—succeed in living very comfortably. What is more, even in the West, where the normal condition of the railways is chronic bankruptcy, certain old-established lines, such as the Illinois Central and the Chicago and Alton, still continue to pay good dividends. How much longer they will continue to do so, depends on two considerations: the first, whether the inexhaustible credulity, the inextinguishable ardour for investment of the British capitalist, will continue to multiply indefinitely competitors for whom there is no traffic actual or potential available for some time to come;[4] the second, how far the profound dissatisfaction of the Western farmer is likely to push a policy of confiscation. For it is one of the most striking features of current American history that in the New England States, where the rates are practically almost as high as in England, and where dividends are satisfactory, the railway companies are very fairly popular. In the West, on the other hand, where the rates are so low that the public practically gets its service merely at the price of working expenses, a politician out of place, bidding for popular support, can find—not before a town rabble, but before an audience of sober, God-

---

[4] There is, of course, this to be said for the capitalist: the States are developing so fast that a line which is bankrupt to-day may be a "bonanza" to its proprietors in ten years' time. A man may be wise to deliberately forego a dividend for the next few years, provided he can gain and hold possession of the strategic points—if there are any still left unoccupied—on the natural lines of communication of the great West.

P

fearing farmers, whose fathers were in all probability New England Puritans—no more attractive topic than proposals for the further spoliation of those "vampire foreigners," those "robber barons," the railway companies.[5]

But the point of interest to us here is not so much the profit which the American railway shareholders secure for themselves, as how they manage to carry on their services at all at the price they receive. To answer the question within any reasonable limits of space is a task of the utmost difficulty. "On account of the great extent of territory," says Professor Adams,[6] through which the railways run, and the great variety of conditions, both social and industrial, to which their business must be adjusted . . . . an average taken for any class of facts reported for all the railways of the United States has but little meaning. It is typical of nothing in the sense that it is a measure with which corresponding facts for individual cases may be compared." This very average of one halfpenny per mile, for instance, is made up out of an average charge of one farthing on the New York, Chicago, and St. Louis, and twenty-one pence on the Pittsburg and Castle Shannon. But then the former line is 523 miles long and carries 800,000,000 tons one mile ; the latter is 9 miles long and carries 95,000.

[5] The last report, for instance, of the Railroad Commissioners for the State of Connecticut gives the average ton-mile earnings as 1·69 cents, while on seven out of the ten lines it is over 2 cents, and the average dividend as within a fraction of 5 per cent. According to a recent statement of Mr. Jay Gould, there is, on the other hand, not a single Texan line which pays a dividend, and only half of them are able to meet their bonded indebtedness.

[6] *Statistical Report of the Inter-State Commerce Commission for* 1889, p. 38.

Between these two extreme points there are all possible variations. There are roads earning 5d., 10d., and 15d. per ton per mile. Quite considerable systems even have a high average rate. On the Connecticut River line, for instance, it is 2·73 cents, on the Denver and Rio Grande 2·2 cents, and on the Long Island Railway, where the great bulk of the traffic is in coal and building materials, 3·91 cents. But the enormous volume of the long-distance trunk-line traffic swamps these totals and brings down the average for the entire country to, as has been said, one halfpenny.

It might therefore fairly be urged that, though an English railway expert may learn very much from American experience, the task of comparing American railways with English is one which implies such an amount of detailed description, such a mass of exceptions and qualifications and explanations, that it cannot profitably be attempted by a layman writing for laymen at all. If any one could accomplish it satisfactorily, it would be Professor Hadley. And yet Professor Hadley writes:[7] "Any attempt at comparison of freight charges would be long, technical, and unsatisfactory. On high-class freight it is altogether impossible, because the English rates for such goods include collection and delivery. No one can tell how much we should allow for cartage, or whether we should take American freight rates or express rates as our standard of comparison. An extremely rough estimate, not making allowance for any of the disadvantages to which English railroads are subject, would indicate that their charges per ton-mile on all

[7] *Railroad Transportation*, p. 158.

traffic average from 50 to 75 per cent. higher than ours." Still, perhaps a few pages devoted to the subject should enable us to achieve, if not positive, at least negative results; and, considering the number of English critics who ignore such trifles as cost of cartage altogether, even that will be something. We can hardly do better than begin with an analogy.

Most people know the American hotel system, if not by personal experience, at least by description. For a sum of 18s. or 1l. a day, a visitor to Washington or Chicago is made free of the house. Within wide limits, he has his meals when he pleases, and takes his choice of any or all dishes on the *menu*, which comprises all the delicacies of the season. From the oysters at the beginning of his dinner to the grapes and peaches at the end, everything is served absolutely without stint. Extra charges for baths or lights, for coffee after lunch or after dinner, are practically unknown. In fact, in a country where wages and rent are very much higher than is the case in England, life at an hotel is a great deal cheaper. On the other hand, if one goes to an hotel organised on the European principle, one pays for one's room much the same as in the other case one pays for everything, while the prices for each individual article of food are such as would make the experienced *boulevardier*, accustomed to the charges of Bignon or the Café Riche, stare and gasp.

The truth is that the plastic American intellect has introduced the wholesale principle into regions where the slower-witted nations of Europe have never thought of applying it. The factory life of

England is new; and our manufacturers fully appreciate the economies to be effected by turning out pins by the million gross, cotton yarn by the million pounds, and steel rails by the tens of thousands of tons. But the Americans have applied the principle to businesses which have existed since the dawn of civilization. Their hotel-keeping is wholesale; their farming is wholesale; and, most of all, their transportation system is wholesale. The English farmer still looks upon the railway train as only a slightly magnified carrier's cart, and persists in sending his basket of eggs or his hamper of vegetables to market, as his grandfather did when George III. was king. The American farmer does his business in car-loads.

How far the new departure is due to the voluntary action of freighters themselves, how much to pressure put upon them by the railroad, no one can tell. But the result is to-day that the Pennsylvania Railroad, a company with probably a larger local and short-distance traffic than any other railroad in the States, reports that 80 per cent. of its business is done in car-loads, that is, in minimum quantities of ten tons. No doubt the introduction of this system has been rendered easier in America by the fact that the English companies inherited an old-established business in a settled and thickly populated country, while in America the railroads went first, and the population and the business only followed after them. Still, in the older parts of the country there was a certain amount of *vis inertiæ* to be overcome. A gentleman, for instance, now high up in the service of the Pennsylvania Railroad, told the present writer a month or two back that he occupied a position as local freight agent when the rapid diminution of rates forced his company to realise that they could no longer afford to go on hauling the small old-fashioned cars. It was his business to break the news to the farmers in his district. They were in despair. It was impossible, they said, for one man to furnish the loading for a ten or twelve-ton truck. He put it to them that the way out of the difficulty was to be found in combination. Let three or four of them agree together to order in a truck of coals or to load out on a certain day a car-load of produce, and then they could share amongst them the fruits of this economy. In a very short time the farmers fell into the new system, and all trouble on the subject was at an end.

And to-day, while the English farmer and market gardener goes on in the retail methods of his ancestors, selling his fruit by the sieve and half-sieve, his celery by the basket, and his peas by the bag, his American rival deals in the same commodities by the car-load. There lies before me, for instance, as I write, a list of the strawberries sent up last summer in the course of a fortnight from Swanwick in Hampshire to London. So extravagant was the method of packing and loading adopted, that it required 11 trucks to convey 5 tons of strawberries, or an average of a little over 9 cwt. per truck. One day there were 24 packages, weighing 10 cwt. amongst them; a day or two after there were 52 packages to carry less than one-quarter of the weight. The growers, no doubt, grumbled at the rate, which works out at exactly 3*d.* per ton-mile; but the railway company, which received a gross return of under 10*s.* per truck for a total journey of nearly 180 miles (for of course the trucks would have had to go down empty), had at least an equally good right to grumble.

When an American railway deals with a traffic of this kind, it either charges a car-load rate and leaves the shipper to get in as many tons as he can, or else it charges a rate per 100 lbs., which is very much higher than anything to which we are accustomed on this side of the Atlantic. But, in truth, the American public has learnt its lesson. Our railways waste their time with fractions of hundredweights. If the Lancashire and Cheshire Conference got its way, they would be required, if I mistake not, to work out fractions of a penny. The American railways fix a minimum charge of 1*s.*, and a minimum weight of 100 lbs.

In fact, as has been said, the real American unit is the car-load, or say 10 tons. Butter, eggs, vegetables, are all forwarded in this manner. Either the grower produces sufficient of the single article to furnish a car-load himself, or, if he cannot do this, he sells to the dealer at the local centre, who makes up a car-load from the contributions of the neighbourhood. If this too is impossible, as in the case of a commodity like eggs it well may be, the local dealer in his turn sells to a travelling agent, who comes along the line and stops his car at four or five different points, and so makes up the full load amongst them. Much the same in its effect is the Chicago system of grading wheat. Once a farmer's wheat reaches Chicago, its identity is lost. He gets from the broker, not a receipt for his wheat, but a certificate for so many bushels of "number 2 spring," or "number 1 Turkish red winter," and the whole of the grain of the same quality being then mixed together in the elevators, all expense of identification and possible small consignments is avoided.

The same principle might be carried through innumerable instances. Mr. Grierson, for instance, told the Committee of 1881 that the chairs his company brought up, presumably from Wycombe, occupied 827 cubic feet to the ton weight.[8] Chairs also come into New York by the tens of thousands from the great Michigan factories, but no chair is ever to be seen in the railway freight-sheds. There are bundles upon bundles of backs and seats, of legs and staves, which as soon as they get to New York will become chairs; but the finished article is nowhere to be found. So too with wooden pails for stable or domestic use. A glance at the American classification explains the reason. Chairs "set up," in less than car-loads, pay 2½ times first-class rate. Chairs completely "knocked down"—that is, in pieces—if in car-loads, pay fourth-class rate. The difference, that is, is that in the former case the railway charge would be, from say Lansing, 178 cents, and in the latter case 33 cents per 100 lbs. carried. Or, take another instance—they can be found by dozens by any one who will look through the classification

---

[8] On the ordinary shipowner's principle of 40 cubic feet to the ton, these chairs, it should be remarked, would pay as for a weight of 20 tons.

for himself. There is a demand, let us say, for stovepipes at Croton Falls, 48 miles from New York. If a private individual thinks proper to order his stovepipe ready finished direct from New York, he will pay 38 cents for every 100 lbs. If, on the other hand, the local ironmonger will order a carload, cut into shape but not riveted up, so that it will lie close, and a reasonable weight can be got into a car, the freight per 100 lbs. comes to only 10 cents.

If, however, the public declines to take a hint, and to send its commodities the way the railway wishes, then the company puts its foot down peremptorily. Our own Chambers of Agriculture complained bitterly the other day that, while their cheese went in the third-class, cheese " packed in hampers, boxes, casks or cases," that is to say, practically the American article, was charged at a lower rate. In vain the railway representatives explained that they could fill a truck to the top with cheese in boxes, while for many months of the year the English cheese, which is sent loose, is so soft that it sometimes breaks to pieces by its own weight, and that it is as a rule impossible to put one layer on top of another. Nothing would satisfy the farmers. They were convinced that the railways made the difference from their instinctive desire to " favour the foreigner." It was of course inconceivable that the farmers should follow the suggestion of the railway managers, and, abandoning the traditional methods of their great-grandfathers, pack their cheese in boxes just as if they were mere Yankees. Now let us glance at the classification in use throughout the Western States, and we shall find the whole question decided in four words, "cheese loose not taken." The same note is to be found against statuary marble. Had the position been the same in England, the House of Lords would have been spared the decision of the interesting case of Peek *v.* the North Staffordshire, and the question, whether conditions exempting a company from liabilities must be reasonable, might have remained until this day undecided.

But enough has probably been said to show that, both by the railways and by their customers, every effort is put forward to manage the transportation of the country on wholesale principles. Whether the English railways would be wise in facing the unpopularity which they would inevitably incur, if they endeavoured to persuade or force their customers into adopting similar methods in this country, is a question which it is almost impossible to decide. That economy might be thereby effected is obvious. Whether the game would be worth the candle is another matter. After all, one does like to order one's own dinner sometimes, and even if Bignon's be dearer than a dinner at an hotel run on the American system, it is a great deal nicer. With us, the cost of carriage is in any case but a small matter. With American distances it is a case of life or death; and just as the working man, to whom a new pair of boots is a serious affair, has to be content with a ready-made pair at 15*s.*, while his richer neighbour cheerfully pays three times as much for a pair, hand-sewn and shaped on his own last in Bond Street, so the English merchant may be well advised in having his own small consignment called for at his own door, at the hour he pleases to name, and delivered next morning as punctually as the letters at his customer's warehouse in Manchester. But in reason let him not claim to be given the retail service at the price of the wholesale one.

Nor is the fact that a customer must adapt his arrangements to the convenience of the railroads, instead of the railroads studying the convenience of each individual customer, the only disadvantage of the American system. In the nature of things, the wayside stations can never do anything but a retail business, and the American roads have consequently yielded to a natural instinct and neglected local business in favour of the large towns. And from the point of view of national interest, a system which develops the towns at the expense of the country can scarcely be admired. Roadside stations, in our sense of the word, are in America almost non-existent. On the main line of the Pennsylvania, on the great highway between New York and Philadelphia, one passes through station after station that consists of nothing better than a rough board shed, and where accommodation for goods seems to be absolutely non-existent. Enquire how the goods service of these places is carried on, and one learns that, once in the day, there comes what is known as a "way-freight" train, and the conductor and his brakesmen turn out on the roadside what consignments they may have, to wait till the consignee thinks proper to fetch them.

Supposing it should be raining and the consignee not in attendance, the goods will probably be taken on to the next important station, and brought back thence the next fine day—a system which might lead to considerable delay in, say, Lanarkshire or Lancashire.

Nor is any time for delivery guaranteed, and in actual practice goods for non-competitive points are usually kept back till the company can get something like a profitable load. If local stations want a quick and reliable service, they must send by " express ; ' and the express rates may be anything up to six times the ordinary freight rate.[9] In rates, too, the short distance traffic suffers severely. Cotton, for example, carried into New Orleans from points not more than 200 miles distant, is made to pay a rate of between 1½ and 2 dollars per bale, or say 32s. per ton ;[1] while from Cairo to New York, which is six times the distance, the freight is a good deal less. Or, again, for the 1,000 miles from New York to Chicago, the rate for drapery goods is about 67s. 6d.; but it costs on an average 28s. per ton to distribute them from Chicago to points fifty miles distant. If a Penzance draper were to wish to send a ton of goods to a customer at Wick, he would assuredly be charged a good deal more than 67s. 6d. for the service ; but, on the other hand, if a draper at Bedford was charged 28s. from London, *plus*, say, an additional 9s. for cartage and delivery, he would not be much mollified by being

---

[9] A fuller account of the American "express" system will be found in the Note at the end of this chapter.

[1] From London to Manchester or Oldham, a similar distance, the rate is 25s. per ton, inclusive of collection in London and delivery in Manchester.

told that he ought to live in a great trade centre and do his business in car-loads.²

The truth is that the American companies have been left to develop their traffic on purely competitive business principles, with an unfettered freedom of which we in England have no idea. An Oriental despot, a Baber or an Aurungzebe, did not make and unmake cities with more absolute and irresistible power than an American railway king. Few campaigns in history have been more momentous than the great "Rate War," fought by the New York Central under Vanderbilt, and the Erie under Jewett, to protect the ocean trade of New York against the encroachments of Baltimore and Philadelphia. But those wars could only have been carried on—and even now they are not altogether things of the past—on condition that the local stations furnished the sinews of war. Chicago possibly gained by sending its wheat to the seaboard at 7s. a ton; but the intermediate points, which simultaneously were paying perhaps five or six times as much, unquestionably suffered. We are often told that the American railways have ruined the English farmer; people forget that they have ruined the American farmer also. Between 1870 and 1880, in spite of an increased area of two million acres under cultivation, agricultural land in the State of New York alone depreciated in value to the extent of 45,000,000*l.* sterling. And all this while the American people looked on and did nothing—it cannot be said they made no attempt—to stop it.

---

² The Bedford rate for drapery is actually 21s. 8d., or 25s., according to class, inclusive of collection and delivery.

In England for nearly half a century the railways have been restrained by law from giving free play to competition. Let us take some instances and see what this means. From Buffalo on Lake Erie, just above the point where the Lake narrows into the Niagara River, to Chicago, a distance of 500 miles, there used to be a great trade in coal by water. The bulk of that coal now goes by land. The change, so the writer was informed, came about as follows: Chicago sends eastward to New York on the average three tons of freight for every ton that New York sends back; in other words, a vast number of cars, especially at the season when the grain crop is moving, go west empty. The manager of one of the lines came to the conclusion that almost any price for a back load was better than nothing, and accordingly offered to take coal for the 500 miles at a dollar a ton, or say 4s. 8d.[3] His neighbours declared the action madness. The rate was scarcely half a farthing per ton-mile. But he persisted, being satisfied that it more than covered the difference between the cost of hauling an empty waggon and a full one. For it should be observed that American farmers cannot afford to be particular, and make no difficulties if coal is loaded in wheat-cars and stock-cars.

The idea took. Railways could be depended upon, while a ship might be wind or weather-bound, or blocked getting through the Detroit River. Further, the railways had sidings into every works. The ships could only deliver on the quays, and there was further

[3] It should be remembered that the American ton is only 2,000 lbs., as against the English 2,240 lbs.

expense and breakage in getting the coal to its destination. So gradually the railway traffic grew at the expense of the water carriage; then the railway ventured to advance the rate, and nowadays it succeeds in obtaining 2 dollars a ton, which, as American through rates go, is quite a tolerable price. Now, under the existing law it is practically impossible for an English railway to attempt to develop a similar business. If, for example, the Midland were to give an exceptionally low rate for coke from Sheffield to Barrow, in order to get a return load for the trucks that bring the hæmatite "pig" into Yorkshire, it might find itself called upon to reduce scores and hundreds of other rates, on the ground that it was giving Barrow an undue preference. Parliament and the Courts have always been more careful to protect individuals against undue competition, than to benefit the public by reducing the general average of charge.

Take for instance the well-known case of Budd *v.* the London and North Western Railway. The plaintiff had works 12 miles out of Swansea on the North Western line to Liverpool. He was charged to the latter place a rate admittedly fair in itself, but lower than the rate past his works from Swansea. The company pleaded that they would have been only too glad to charge the Swansea traders more, but that, if they raised the rate, the Swansea traffic would go by sea. It was held, however, that the Swansea traders were unduly preferred to Mr. Budd, and the rate was disallowed. Or, take another and more recent instance. The representatives of the grain trade in Liverpool complained a short time back to the Railway Commission that they failed to get their fair share of the business of Birmingham, owing to the low rates which were given from Cardiff to that town. The company's reply once more was that the Cardiff rates were controlled by the water competition of the Severn and the Birmingham and Gloucester Canal. But the excuse was disallowed, and the result of the action has been that, sooner than lower the rate from Liverpool, on which of course an enormous amount of money depends, the North Western has abandoned the comparatively unimportant Cardiff trade altogether.[4] Now compare this with a recent decision of the American Inter-State Commerce Commission. Messrs. King & Co., traders, situated at Readville, eight miles from Boston on the road to New York, complained that, while the railways were carrying flour from New York to Boston for 9 cents, from New York to Readville the rate was 18 cents. The Commission refused to interfere, holding that the local rate was not unreasonable in itself, and that, as the circumstances and conditions of the two cases were not substantially similar, the provisions of the Inter-State Commerce Act did not apply. The fol-

---

[4] The rate of 8s. 4d. and 8s. 10d., including delivery, has been cancelled, and a rate of 12s. 6d., station to station, substituted. Presumably the Cardiff traffic continues to go at the old rates by the other routes. The net results of the action may therefore be summarized as follows: (1) Liverpool gains nothing; (2) railway companies have been notified to be very careful how they reduce rates; (3) the North Western has been compelled to give up a certain amount of traffic on which it presumably earned some profit, even though a small one; (4) the traders for whom the North Western stations at Cardiff and Birmingham were more convenient than those of the other companies, have been compelled to incur the inconvenience and expense of going elsewhere.

lowing extract from their judgment is worth quotation:

"The Commission has repeatedly held that, where the competition of an independent water line, not subject to the provisions of the Act to Regulate Commerce, is actual with that of a rail-carrier for traffic at a point reached by it, and for traffic important in amount, that then the rail-carrier, if necessary to meet such competition, may lower its rates at that point without doing so at other points on its line at which no such competition exists, and at which other points the rail-carrier could not so reduce its rates without a large loss of revenue." After citing previous decisions, the judgment goes on to say: "A full discussion of the rule and grounds upon which it rests will be found in these decisions, and it is unnecessary to repeat it at length here. The principle found running through them all is that, the statute in express terms having provided that the circumstances and conditions must be substantially similar in the performance of each service in the longer as in the shorter haul, that the existence of such competition as above stated at one point, between a carrier subject to the law and one that is not subject to the law, creates at that point circumstances and conditions which are substantially dissimilar, in the service performed by the rail-carrier, to those existing on other points of its line where no such competition exists. That in such a case the railway carrier is not obliged to go out of the business at a point where such competition with an independent water-line prevails, leaving the water-line a monopoly

Q

of that business; nor is the rail-carrier, on the other hand, compelled to lower its rates at other points along the line, where no such competition is found, to the standard of the rate it is compelled to make to meet the competition of the water-line at the point where such competition does exist; but the rail-carrier may lower its rates at the point at which it has to encounter such competition, and in lowering them may make such just and reasonable rates, in view of all the circumstances and conditions surrounding its business, as will enable it to meet the competition of the independent water-line at that point."

Now, needless to say, the present writer has no intention of arguing that in Budd's case, or the Cardiff case, the law was wrongly interpreted. Nor would he venture to assert that the Inter-State Commerce Act, which practically was founded on our English Acts—the clauses of which relating to undue preference it repeats almost *verbatim*—really gives the American Commission the power to sanction discrepancies of rates as startling as those in the Readville case. He would not even go so far as to express a positive opinion that the American decision was better for the public interest than the English one.

It is evident that a system which gives to Boston not only the advantage of low water-rates, but also the benefit of rail-carriage on almost identical terms —for the railway rate of 9 cents was made in competition with a steamer rate of $8\frac{1}{2}$ cents—tends greatly to enhance the natural advantages of Boston's geographical position. Now, to swell the great towns at the expense of the smaller ones is in itself a disadvantage. Further, as long as the fixing of rates has to be left in the hands of fallible, possibly even not entirely disinterested, mortals, a system which so largely ignores cost of service as an element in fixing a rate—which recognises so fully the right of a railway company to sell its services for precisely what they will fetch—such a system cannot but give rise to the possibility of abuses, and, at least till such time as every citizen becomes a philosopher and a political economist, to the certainty of discontent.

The point is that we should recognise that the question has two sides. The Germans have endeavoured to introduce a cast-iron system, eliminating competitive rates altogether. The Americans, on the other hand, have given free play to competition. In England we have taken a position midway between the two. It will not be denied that in return the Americans obtain their transportation on terms very much lower than the Germans; nor can it, I think, fairly be disputed that—when quality of service is taken into account—in price too the English railways occupy the intermediate position. Every time we yield to German ideas, and move away from the American principle of giving competition full swing, every time we cancel a rate such as that from Cardiff—and there have been scores of such rates cancelled as the result of direct decisions, and hundreds upon hundreds withdrawn or never given as an indirect result—we may do justice between two competitors, whether they be individual traders or rival towns, but we unquestionably raise the general average of English rates.

But to come back to the American railways. There are, of course, many other reasons why their work is done so cheaply. It needs no argument, for instance, to show that the percentage of the total cost, due to the provision of station accommodation and the cost of handling at either end, must be greater, where the traffic goes, as it does in England, for an average distance of perhaps 25 miles, than in America, where the average length of haul is 127 miles. How serious a matter terminal cost is, American railway men know, even if the English trader does not. To give one instance: as between the companies themselves—for the outside public has nothing to do with the arrangement—5 cents per 100 lbs. for terminal services at New York are allowed before the rest of the rate is apportioned on a mileage basis. In other words, the railways which bring the wheat half-way from Chicago are content to acknowledge that the terminal service in New York is worth as much as the haulage for 250 miles.

"We calculate," said one of the best known railway men in the States to the present writer, only a few weeks back, "that it does not make any practical difference to us, once we have incurred the heavy terminal expense at New York, whether we haul a whole train 100 miles, or haul half of it 50 miles, and then go on with half a load." "With the constant cheapening of movement expenses," wrote the "Railroad Gazette" in October last, "charges for terminal handling form every year a larger portion than the whole." "You will note," said President Roberts, at the last meeting of the Pennsylvania Railroad Company—the greatest corporation, not only of the United States but of the world—"that the rates per ton per mile on the Main Line have now been reduced to about 6 mills (·6 of a cent); that the cost of transportation on the Main Line has been reduced to about 4 mills; and that on the United Railroads of New Jersey the cost of moving traffic between Philadelphia and New York is over 1 cent, as against 4 mills on the Main Line. This indicates the great expense attending the management of a line located between two large cities like New York and Philadelphia, and which has entailed upon it the maintenance of expensive terminals in such cities, and the cost of handling the traffic thereat, a matter that is not generally understood by the public. I think I am not wrong in stating that every ton of merchandise secured in Philadelphia to be transported westward has to be hauled 70 miles, before the revenue received therefrom equals the actual cost of handling in Philadelphia." The English reader scarcely needs to have drawn for him the moral that, with an average haul of 25 miles, the English railway cannot afford to forego altogether a charge for terminals of a still more expensive character.

Another important point in making a comparison is to be found in the actual haulage itself. As we have already seen, in dealing with Sir Alfred Hickman's claim that a rate which was fair for 50 miles might be taken as the basis of a rate for 5 miles, short distance traffic is always much more costly to work than long. Engines cover 5 miles an hour instead of 18. A truck that has travelled from

Liverpool to Oldham takes just as long to unload, and has to wait just as long before it can be sent back, as one which has come through from Minneapolis or Kansas City to New York. In other words, the one may be on the average earning revenue for two hours out of every five, and the other for two hours out of every hundred.

Here is another point. Every manager knows that the greater the difference between the speed of his fastest and slowest train, the less is the carrying capacity of his line. The Metropolitan, for example, can work seventeen trains an hour over the same pair of metals, at 12 miles an hour; the North Western can send three expresses from Euston to Crewe within ten minutes; but when it comes to one train at 12 miles an hour and another at 50, the results are very different. With a traffic such as exists in England, with coal trains at 12 miles an hour, goods at 18, fast goods and stopping passenger trains at 25, and express trains at 50 miles an hour, all mixed up together in something like equal proportions, it needs very careful management to get in an average, not of seventeen, but of five trains an hour. Now, in America, as a rule, the line is almost wholly given up to freight. The New York Central thinks itself entitled to boast itself "America's greatest railroad," on the ground that eight expresses depart daily from New York to the north and west. There are something like 30 from Euston to Rugby. In other words, one pair of rails in America can be made to carry a much larger volume of traffic than is possible here.

Another difference may be found in the fact that the percentage of mixed goods to the total is very much larger in England than in America. On the Erie line, for instance, which returns 6,700,000 tons of merchandise carried as against 9,580,000 tons of coal, merchandise proper was less than half a million tons. The balance is made up of grain and flour, lumber, iron-ore, building materials, and 215,000 tons of live-stock. In a word, the English railways carry manufactured articles for half the civilized world; the American surplus over consumption is in corn and "hog-products."

Now, manufactured articles go as a rule in comparatively small, raw produce in comparatively large, quantities. How immense is the difference in point of economy between the two systems, it is difficult for any one without actual practical experience to imagine; there, however, are some figures "found as facts" in a recent judgment of the Inter-State Commerce Commission: "The cost of loading 1,769 cars, of which six per cent. was car-load freight, at Duane Street, New York, was shown to be 62·1 cents per ton. At Dock No. 6, Jersey City, the cost of loading miscellaneous freight was 58·3 cents per ton. At Dock No. 5, Jersey City, the cost of loading car-load freight . . . was 16·3 cents per ton. On this basis the cost of loading miscellaneous freight is from 42 to 46 cents per ton [say 2s. per English ton] greater than loading car-load freight. The relative cost of unloading and delivering car-load and less than car-load freight at Chicago was shown to be 23 cents a ton for less than car-loads, and 9 cents per ton for car-loads. . . . With reference to transportation alone, exclusive of loading and unloading, the following results appeared. The general average of car-load shipments was, from the tables in evidence, nearly 15 tons for car-loads and about 5·8 tons for less than car-loads, or miscellaneous freight. . . . . The cost of hauling the freight would be in the first case 0·276 cents per ton per mile, and in the latter 0·471 cents per ton per mile. . . . . The average difference in earnings per car, from an average load of car-load freight, and an average load of less-than-car-load freight, is *not far from* 100 *per cent.*"

Again, nothing is so expensive as to keep abreast of a demand which at one time of the year is twice what it is at another. An English railway is expected to handle all the traffic offered it, however great, there and then; in America the customers, even of a line like the Pennsylvania, take it as a matter of course that the railway will be unable, in the autumn at least, to give them all the accommodation they ask for. "It is a fact," says the last report of the Erie Company, "that for the larger part of the year the trunk lines have been unable to furnish equipment to move the tonnage offered."[5]

Then again comes in the system of working. With lines immeasurably more crowded and more cut up with junctions and sidings, in a climate in which for months of the year dense fogs are of

---

[5] I have quoted so much from the Erie Company that it is perhaps as well to say that, whatever may have been its financial offences in the past, it is recognised to-day as being one of the most efficiently managed railroads in the States.

almost weekly occurrence, the English railway companies are able to boast that their traffic is carried on at one-third of the risk, whether for passengers or employés, which is incurred in America, according to American figures. But this result has not been achieved without expenditure. The cost of establishing and maintaining the block system alone would go far towards furnishing the entire "maintenance" expenditure of an American railway. If we added the money spent on ballast which shall not subside, and bridges which shall not break down under an advancing train, it would more than do so. Not that the English public is contented even now. "It seems to me," so wrote a month or two back, *à propos* of the Taunton accident, a correspondent of an engineering journal, " that whatever difficulties may occur, and at whatever cost it may entail to the railway companies, the public, and possibly in the end the legislature, will not rest satisfied until all the railways have their lines signalled, interlocked, and worked in such a manner that accidents such as those that have occurred during the last week will be impossible." Be it so. The railways have no need to complain as long as the public will understand that the excess cost, incurred in the further protection of its skin, must come in the long run out of its own pocket.

There is another point, perhaps of even greater importance than any of those hitherto referred to. In the United States, "when railroads began to be built"—I quote once more from the first report of the Inter-State Commerce Commission—" the demand for participation in their benefits went up from every city and hamlet in the land, and the public was impatient at any obstacles to their free construction, and of any doubts that might be suggested as to the substantial benefit to flow from any possible line that might be built. . . . For a long time, the promoter of a railway was looked upon as a public benefactor, and laws were passed under which municipal bodies were allowed to give public money or loan public credit in aid of his schemes, on an assumption that almost any road would prove reasonably remunerative, but that in any event the indirect advantages which the public would reap must more than compensate for the expenditure." Now, in England this state of things has never existed. From the earliest time, railways have had to encounter the fiercest opposition from vested interests. Carriers and stage-coach proprietors banded together against them; one duke saw in "those d——d railways" mischief to his favourite canals; another to his still more beloved fox-covers. Engineers were hunted off the ground with sticks and stones; their lines were bidden with contumely to beware of touching the sacred limits of Lichfield, or Worcester, of Eton, or Oxford.

It is not only the costs which the English railways incurred in their early days, for which their customers are at the present time paying the bill; it is not only that the capital account of the American railroads has been kept down by the amount of those early subsidies, while the present shareholders have many millions of acres of land still left to sell; but the same spirit which prompted, and the same legislation which permitted, Lord Petre to levy blackmail on the old Eastern Counties to the tune of 100,000*l.* has survived in England from that day to this. The present writer was discussing with the general manager of one of our great lines a short time back the prospects of a proposed branch in one of the most out-of-the-way portions of the kingdom. "What price do you allow for land?" he asked. "It would not be safe," was the reply, "to calculate on anything less than 500*l.* per acre." The price is something more than a willing purchaser pays as a rule for moor-land to a willing vendor, and 10 acres of land to the mile of line at 500*l.* per acre would account, to start with, for a capital sufficient to lay and equip a mile of railway in the Western States.

Here are two companion pictures from very recent history, to show the different points of view in the two countries. The London public claim, whether rightly or wrongly is here beside the question, that their railway accommodation at this moment is deficient. A new railway, the Manchester, Sheffield, and Lincolnshire, is anxious to come in and supply the demand. The London County Council has resolved to petition Parliament not to pass the bill, except on terms that the company shall pay to the local authority compensation for closing its streets, and give an equivalent of open space elsewhere for the gardens which may be built over. Now, considering that the only property the local authority has in the streets is the right of user for purposes of traffic, and that carriages and carts will have no reason to circulate within the precincts of the proposed station, that on the other hand the local authority will be relieved of its present expenditure for maintenance; considering further that the only gardens proposed to be taken are those which are attached to private houses—this is surely what the Americans would term "a large order." For all that, it is typical of the attitude of Englishmen, whether in their private or public capacity, to every line which is promoted; and yet we wonder that the competition of new railways does not result in the lowering of the prices.

Now turn to the companion picture. One of the greatest railway centres in the States, the point at which traffic leaves the Great Lakes to go eastward either by rail or the Erie Canal, is the City of Buffalo. There are the lines of ten different companies within its precincts already. Needless to say, they all cross the streets "at grade." Application was made by an eleventh, the Rome, Watertown, and Ogdensburg, last December, to be admitted in the same fashion. The matter was referred to a special committee of the municipality. Evidence was given by prominent citizens that the new railway would be a convenience. Then counsel for the company summed up. It was true, he said, that Buffalo had a good deal of railway accommodation already. There were 642 miles of track within the city boundaries as it was. Level crossings were certainly a nuisance, and it was undeniable that, if this new one were sanctioned, accidents would occur from time to time. But, he continued, it was impossible for the railway to come in on any other terms. The citizens must either take the line with its acknowledged disadvantages, or go without it altogether. Their city had grown and flourished in the past because of its railway facilities. Were they prepared to take the responsibility of checking its growth? They were not, and the application was unanimously granted.

The British public may depend upon it, that it is upon radical distinctions like these, and not upon comparative trifles such as the size of the trucks in which the traffic is carried, that the difference between English and American charges depends.[6] The particular fad of big bogie-trucks has, however, been pushed with such pertinacity in England of late that it is worth while to say a word or two on the subject, and to mention in the first place more particularly that the "tubular-frame car," whose merits have been so loudly trumpeted here, is, prophet-like, not much honoured in its own country. The present writer can claim to have walked, within the last few months, through some miles of freight-yards, and he never was fortunate enough to catch sight of a single tubular-framed car. He questioned several railway officials on the subject. "Yes, they had heard of them," was the effect of the answers; 'believed they had been tried, but people did not seem

---

[6] The statement that the size of the truck is a "comparative trifle" may seem inconsistent with what was said on p. 214 as to the Pennsylvania Railroad being compelled to adopt big cars for the sake of economy. But in America cost of haulage is a very much larger item of the total expenditure than with us. The problem for an English manager is how to make up anything like a full load for the present engines. His colleague in the States is occupied in designing engines and rolling-stock to enable him to increase still further the enormous weight of his existing trains.

to like them, and certainly they had not come into general use."

But on the broader question whether English goods managers would be wise to use American wholesale machinery for doing English retail work, there is more to say. "Had I your traffic," said the chief goods manager of one of the trunk lines to the present writer, "I should use your trucks." "It seems to me," said a well-known railway engineer, "that all this talk about light loading does not come to much. One of your small trucks weighs 5 tons and carries 2 tons of general freight; with us a 10-ton car as a rule takes about 4 tons. Nor is there any economy in first cost. Our cars cost about 140*l.* to start with, and even then the wood is so green that you can almost see the water oozing out of it, and they only last about twelve years." On the other hand, an American gentleman has been good enough to give evidence on the matter before the Board of Trade tribunal, and to read a paper before the Institute of Mechanical Engineers, and his conclusions are very different. "I have claimed," he writes in "The Engineer," on November 28, "and now assert that fully $67\frac{1}{2}$ per cent. can be saved in the working expenses of British railways, by discarding four-wheeled rigid waggons and adopting a proper bogie-truck."

This sounds startling. Let us see what it means. The working expenses of British railways amounted in 1889 to $30\frac{1}{2}d.$ per train-mile. A reduction of $67\frac{1}{2}$ per cent. would bring them down to $10d.$ Now, according to the Board of Trade Returns, general charges—expenses, that is, of administration, directors, secretary's staff, and so forth—Government duty, compensation, legal, Parliamentary, and miscellaneous expenses, amounted to something over $4\frac{1}{4}d$. The shape of the goods trucks could hardly produce any effect on reducing these items. We are left, therefore, with a sum of $5\frac{3}{4}d$., to cover an expenditure which under our present antediluvian methods amounts to $2s.\ 4d$., so that the reduction is really not one of 67 per cent., but of something like 78 per cent. Let us admit that the new trucks run so easily that locomotives would be a superfluity even for passenger trains, that they glide so smoothly over the ground that the road would never wear out, and that the bridges would never need repainting or repointing, and of course that they themselves are imperishable—even so we should only save about $16\frac{1}{2}d$., and we have got to effect an economy of $20d$. It really looks as though, in some mysterious manner, the company which was bold enough to introduce tubular-framed trucks would find its passengers ready to carry their own portmanteaux, and the consignees of its goods ready to make out their own invoices and carry the price direct to the company's bankers.

But, in fact, such statements, though they do well enough for a text on which to hang a sermon preached to a sympathetic Chamber of Commerce, on the exorbitance of the English railway charges, are hardly worthy of serious refutation. The real question, stripped of rhetorical exaggerations, is this: big bogie-trucks being impossible for ordinary everyday traffic, is there a sufficient quantity of wholesale traffic to make it worth while to complicate matters by having two different sets of goods-trucks in use simultaneously and to incur the expense of altering existing terminal accommodation to suit the new system? The present writer confesses to the opinion that it is quite worth while making an experiment on a sufficiently large scale, say with the shipping coal traffic of Cardiff or Newcastle. At the same time the question is so largely one of detailed calculation—" what capital outlay would be required, and what economy in locomotive expenses might possibly be secured in return?"—that it is quite impossible for an outsider to speak with any confidence on the subject. Perhaps it will be of more general interest if we conclude this chapter with a few comparisons between rates charged in England and America for traffic of a similar character and under as far as may be analogous circumstances.

Let it be frankly confessed that in one sense the rates which follow cannot be asserted to be typical of American rates. As has been said already, the average American rate is $\frac{1}{2}d.$ per ton per mile, and if the rates given below appear to be, as they in fact are, a great deal higher than this, there must of necessity be an equal number of other rates so much lower than the $\frac{1}{2}d.$ as to redress the balance. Still, it is, I believe, fair to say that they do show the rates which in America are thought reasonable, where traffic is either in small quantities, or for short distances or expensive to handle, or, it may be, merely able without difficulty to bear a high rate, and where, too, the standard of charge is not kept down by the impossibility of making too sharp a distinction—as is the case on the main trunk lines—between the rates for local traffic and those in force between the great centres of the East and West. Here, any way, are rates actually in force. If they prove nothing else, they at least prove this, that it is as easy to produce figures to show the moderation of English charges, as it is to find others to convict them of being excessive and extortionate.

The coal rate from Wilkesbarre in the anthracite coalfield to Philadelphia, 105 miles, is 7s.;[7] to New York, 150 miles, the charge is the same. From Pantyffynon, also an anthracite district, to Birkenhead, 153 miles, the charge is 6s. 4d.; but, as this does not include waggons, while the American rate does, it may fairly be said that the two are identical. But there are many rates in England lower than the Philadelphia rate: for instance, Bedworth to London, 107 miles, for 6s. including waggons; or Wigan to Coventry, 106 miles, for 6s. 5d. Take another article, milk. The charge into London on the Northern lines ranges from $\frac{3}{4}d.$ per gallon under 20 miles, to $1\frac{1}{4}d.$ for over 50. Into New York the rate is uniform for any distance, and amounts to 32 cents per can of ten gallons on the New York, Ontario and Western, and to 35 cents on the New York, New Haven, and Hartford. In other words, the American farmer is charged a minimum rate of $1\frac{2}{5}d.$ and $1\frac{3}{4}d.$ per gallon in the two cases respectively, with the additional disadvantage that he must pay full rates even if his cans are half empty.

Take another instance. The tariff for drapery

---

[7] If the Board of Trade held sway in the United States, its new Provisional Orders would bring down this rate to 5s. $10\frac{1}{2}d.$ as a maximum.

and other goods of the same class out of Chicago for a distance of 50 miles works out as equal to 28*s*. 6*d*. per ton. From Manchester to Lancaster the distance is 51 miles, and the rate of 20*s*. includes collection and delivery. If we compare similar distances out of London and out of New York, we shall find some remarkable contrasts between Bedford, which is on the Haarlem branch of the New York Central, 40 miles out, and Leighton, which is distant $39\frac{1}{4}$ miles from Euston. For instance, carrots are 11*s*. in the former case as against 5*s*. in the latter; hay and straw in America 18*s*. 5*d*., in England 6*s*. 8*d*., 10*s*. 10*d*., and 12*s*. 6*d*., according to quantity and method of packing. The American farmer pays 18*s*. 5*d*. to send in his beef and mutton, and 16*s*. 7*d*. to send his pork at his own risk. The English company charges 20*s*., which includes not only the risk but collection and delivery. For butter the American pays, according to method of packing, from 16*s*. 7*d*. to 36*s*. 10*d*. The highest English rate is 26*s*. 8*d*., while the lowest is 10*s*. less, and in every instance the English company takes the risk and does the carting at both ends in addition.

We have heard a good deal in England about the extortionate rates which are killing the fruit trade. The American rates appear to be higher in almost every case. Here is one comparison. Kirkwood to Jersey City, 141 miles: peaches in less than car-loads owners' risk 55*s*. 2*d*., company's risk 82*s*. 10*d*.[8] In

---

[8] The present writer laughed when he was given a rate for peaches in less than car-loads, and asked whether anyone had ever seen a car-load. The answer was that a single company had carried

England raspberries and strawberries from Wisbech to Manchester, 142 miles, owners' risk 40s., company's risk 47s. 6d.; Stanbridgeford to Manchester, 147 miles, plums and gooseberries, at company's risk 29s. 2d. The American rates are quoted as by special fast train, the English by goods train; but of course the English service delivers first thing next morning, and the American fast train cannot do more. An ordinary American goods train would be liable to take a couple of days. The American rates exclude both loading and unloading. The English include not only these services but collection and delivery as well.

In the case of fish, the English rates look lower, but it is perhaps not quite fair to compare them, as the special English rates are usually given only for large consignments, while the Americans quote theirs per barrel or per box. Here, for curiosity's sake, is what the Americans would call a rate for medium distance: Oranges, Callahan to Washington, 827 miles, 57s. 6d. per ton; London to Wick, 754 miles, 60s., but at company's risk, and including collection and delivery.[9]

One more comparison of a different kind. The class rates throughout the district governed by the Southern Classification—broadly speaking, the whole of the country east of the Mississippi, and south of the latitude of Washington—were given the other day in a judgment of the Inter-State Commerce Com-

---

9,000 "straight" car-loads (say 8 tons each) from a single district in a single season. One more instance of the fact that the Americans have laid to heart the doctrine that a railway train is not a carrier's cart.

[9] The detailed comparisons from which these few illustrations are extracted will be found given at length in the Appendix.

mission, as averaging something like the following scale:

Louisville to Selma, 490 miles.

Class 1 . . . 88s. | Class 3 . . . 70s. | Class 5 . . . 47s.
,, 2 . . . 83s. | ,, 4 . . . 57s. | ,, 6 . . . 37s.

Below let us put some English rates for comparison, noting that the numbers in the two countries run in opposite directions.

London to Blair Athole, 489 miles.

Class 5 . 126s. 8d. | Class 3 . . 73s. 4d. | Class 1 . . 43s. 4d.
,, 4 . 105s. 0d. | ,, 2 . . 55s. 0d. | Special Class . 35s.

In making the above comparison, we must remember that all the English rates are at the company's risk, and all except the last include collection and delivery. In the American case, on the other hand, not merely are many articles only taken at owner's risk, but also light or valuable goods are sometimes charged up to four times the 1st class rate. Further, as will be seen more fully later on, a very much larger proportion of the American traffic is charged under the higher classes than is the case with us.

On the whole, I believe that a fair statement of the case as regards rates—leaving questions of accommodation out of consideration—would be somewhat as follows: The average American rate, being charged mainly on wholesale consignments of cheap goods for immense distances, is immeasurably lower than ours. On the trunk lines to the West the whole of the rates are kept down, by the operation of the "long and short haul" clause, and the public feeling which gave rise to it, to a level which, though by no means so low as that of the through rates, is yet much lower than that prevailing in this country. But when it comes to the traffic on branch lines, in what may be called local distributive service, or to the traffic in perishables, which can hardly be brought into comparison with wheat and tinned meats, or to parts of the country where the influence of the wholesale through traffic is but little felt, the rates are at least up to the English standard; while for traffic of the more valuable descriptions they are without question very considerably higher.

NOTE ON THE "EXPRESS" SYSTEM

A word or two as to the American "express" business may not be out of place, as the position of affairs is sometimes misunderstood in this country. Professor Hunter, M.P., for instance, after enlarging on the advantages of any system which "restricts the evils of monopoly within the narrowest bounds," writes ("Railway and Canal Traffic Act of 1888," p. 10): "The traffic in light goods requiring rapid transit has fallen into the hands of the parcels express companies. No feature in the American railway system gives such universal satisfaction. It is found more profitable by the railway companies to leave this branch of business entirely in the hands of the express companies. Only recently the Erie Railway Company gave up their attempt to do 'express' business, and contracted with one of the companies to take over their stock at a fair valuation, and pay 40 per cent. of the gross earnings. This figure compares favourably with the sum of 55 per cent. paid by the British Post Office to the railways in this country." Now, in the first place, it is impossible to compare the 40 per cent. of gross receipts handed over by the express company to the Erie with the 55 per cent. paid by our Post Office to the English railways. The express companies furnish their own cars, send their own servants in charge of their freight, do their own loading and unloading, and, in the large towns at least, provide their own station accommodation. If our Post Office gets all this supplied to it for a mere 15 per cent., it surely cannot have made such a very bad bargain. One might add a hesitating doubt whether the argument, that 45 per cent. of the gross receipts is insufficient to pay for a portion of the terminal accommodation and services, is very appropriate in the mouth of one who sometimes appears to consider them as such small trifles that the railway companies ought to be able to throw them in gratis, in return for a rate that was fixed originally as the payment for the mere mileage services.

Further, the bargain made by the Erie Company is only one among many hundreds, and a company with a route to the West, whose inferiority is acknowledged, could scarcely expect to make as good terms as would naturally be obtained by the Pennsylvania or the New York Central. In fact, some of the companies do not make a percentage division at all. The Chicago, Burlington, and Quincy, for instance, receives from the express company operating over its lines a gross sum equal to the estimated receipts for the total weight carried if charged at the highest class rate. Other companies either do their express business themselves or employ a mere paper organisation—themselves under another name—to do it.

"But," says Professor Hunter, "no feature in the American system gives such universal satisfaction." This statement, too, is questioned by those who should know. According to the Inter-State Commerce Commission's first annual report, published and reprinted in England as a Parliamentary paper only a few months before the date of Professor Hunter's book, and freely quoted by Professor Hunter himself on other points, "the complaint of excessive charges upon express traffic has been common." Certainly not without reason, if, as I am informed by the senior partner of one of the largest international forwarding agencies in the States, the express rates may be taken to be on the average something more than double the highest rates of the ordinary freight tariff. For it must be remembered that the express business has reached in America enormous dimensions, and deals with much more than mere parcels. According to the Statistical Report for 1889, the railway share of the business reached 4,000,000*l.* sterling, which would imply that the public paid, if the Erie bargain be a representative one, not less than 10,000,000*l.* Now, the whole of this vast business is quite uncontrolled by law. The express companies are under no obligation to publish their tariffs. They may, and apparently do, charge different customers different prices for the same services. They may practically refuse to give any service at all to a small place where they see no prospect of making a profit. In fact, if a man at a wayside station in Massachusetts wishes to send a present to a friend, say, in Georgia, he will probably find it absolutely impossible to know beforehand what will have to be paid for carriage, or perhaps even to book his parcel through to its destination at all.

There is another and more serious objection—an objection which it must be admitted could hardly apply in this country, where the personal honesty of railway officials is not usually called in question. It is commonly believed in America that the railway companies have in some cases made corrupt bargains, giving the express companies the cream of the business which should properly belong to their own shareholders. The Inter-State Commerce Commission has pressed this point with great earnestness on the attention of Congress. In its first report occurs this passage: "No clear line of distinction exists between the express business and some branches of what is exclusively railroad service; and the express business may easily be enlarged at the expense of the other. Those roads which now do their express business through a nominal corporation might hand over to this shadow of their corporate existence the dressed meat or live stock business, or the fruit transportation, or any other business in respect to which speed was specially important; and they might continue this process of paring off their proper functions as carriers until they should be little more than the owners of the lines of road over which other organizations should be the carriers of freight, and on terms by themselves arbitrarily determined."

Now, it is evident that a system which encourages the management of a railway to give inferior accommodation to traffic in perishable commodities, in order to compel the consignor, as in an instance quoted by the Commission, to pay the express rates, which are four times as high, is not a system conceived in the interest of the public. Accordingly the Commission looks forward to the abolition of this "side-show system," as the Americans call it—a system which, it is worth noting, has been deliberately refused admission on the Canadian Pacific—and in its third report it declares that the law under which it acts "contemplates that the carriers [*i.e.* the railway companies] shall free themselves from burdens that diminish their capacity for cheaper and better service to the public. An enumeration of these includes . . . . . adjunct properties of doubtful value, owned or invested in by managers, service for express companies, and others that might be named."

However, the whirligig of time brings its revenges, and should this system, spite of the universal satisfaction which it has given, be abolished in America, Professor Hunter may console himself with the prospect of its re-introduction here. Only let the English companies be a little more squeezed, and it is quite possible that, as has been said already, they may try experiments in the desired direction—may retire, that is, from their present position as carriers for the public, and reverting to their original position as toll-takers for the use of their road, and job-masters letting out locomotive engines on hire, may leave the private firms to exact from the public for terminal services such charges as they think proper. And if those firms, as in the instance at Bristol quoted by Mr. Grierson to the Committee of 1881, make to persons in trade a charge of 10*d.*, and to private customers charges for the same service varying between 2*s.* and 2*s.* 6*d.*, as compared with a railway rate of 1*s.* 2*d.* charged equally to all, no doubt the trader will be abundantly content. Whether the public at large, who after all are more numerous and more important than the traders, will have an equally good reason to be so, is another matter.

CHAPTER X

WHY ENGLISH RATES ARE HIGH

WHY English rates are high—why, that is, the steady increase in the volume of traffic over English lines has not been accompanied by any corresponding decrease in the amount charged for conveyance, such as has unquestionably taken place in the United States—has practically been explained in the preceding chapters. At this stage, however, it is perhaps worth while to gather up all these loose ends of argument into a connected story. And, in the first place, we may point out that a considerable proportion of the statements made as to the high charges in England, in comparison with those customary in other countries, simply rest on a misapprehension of the actual facts. For instance, an English rate which includes collection and delivery is compared on all fours with a Continental or American rate which includes neither. Or, if the fact is noticed, some absurdly inadequate allowance of two or three shillings for cartage at both ends is deducted, and then the comparison is made with the figures so obtained. Then, again, Continental rates, where the railway obligation to pay for damage or loss is very stringently limited, are compared, not, as they ought to be, with

English Owners' Risk rates, but with rates which include the insurance of goods to their full value. Or, once more, the English special rates are ignored. To take an instance. Iron for ship-building from Lanarkshire to Barrow is set down, not at 10*s.* 10*d.* per ton, the price at which it is really carried, but at 20*s.*, the price which, according to its classification, it would pay for the distance in question, supposing that there were no special rate in force.

When all the misunderstandings under these various heads are put right, the comparison with foreign countries comes out by no means so unfavourably for our railways, as it is usual for the traders' advocates to assert. But, though this may be true enough as far as it goes, an Englishman who has been proud to think that the railways of his own country, instead of humbly following the lead, could be held up as an example to the rest of the world, and has been satisfied to know that, in the opinion of competent foreign observers, this claim on their behalf was not unfounded, can hardly be contented with excuses and apologies. What he demands, and rightly demands, is, not that they should do almost as well, but that they should do a good deal better. Such a critic therefore will naturally enquire, How is it that the English companies are not able to point to reductions throughout the entire range of their business, "plain for all folks to see," such as those which have distinguished the American railways? To this very reasonable question an answer must be attempted in the pages which follow.

It is common to speak as though the high range

of charges on the English railways were due directly to their enormous capital expenditure. This, however, as was suggested in an earlier chapter, cannot be admitted to be correct. As has been pointed out, no manager in fixing a rate ever takes into consideration what his line has cost. The question with him is—ignoring for the present the relation between the rates for one place and another, and confining ourselves solely to an individual rate looked at *per se*—how shall he obtain the largest amount of net revenue. At 4*d*. per mile, let us say, he is carrying 100 tons of merchandise. Supposing he reduces the rate to 2*d*., and in consequence gets 200 tons to carry, evidently he has made a bad bargain for himself. Supposing the traffic rises to 400 tons, we should be safe in assuming that he has increased his net profit. Say, however, that it only increases to 300, whether 300 tons at 2*d*. pay him better than 100 tons at 4*d*. is a question which cannot be answered till we know how much it costs him to do his new business.

If, as is the case over the greater part of the United States railroads, there is plenty of room on the line, and the actual cost for haulage represents almost the whole of the additional expenditure, the bargain is without question a good one. If, on the other hand, the line is so full already that new business can only be taken by increasing the accommodation—that is, by expending fresh capital, as is very largely the case in England—then it is quite possible that the reduction of rate was from the railway point of view a mistaken policy.

But whether the manager reduces his rate, or

whether he maintains it at the old figure, in either case the governing consideration in his mind is, not what his line cost to build per mile, but how best net receipts can be made to increase in a greater ratio than expenditure. Once this principle is firmly fixed in our minds, we shall see why it is that special rates exist; why pigs of lead and ingots of copper are charged a much higher rate than pigs of iron; or why, again, one rate is charged from Manchester to Southampton on cotton goods for export, and another and very different one on the identical wares for home consumption. There is, let us say, a limestone quarry in the village of A, and its output is carried by train to the farmers within a radius of 20 miles at a rate of something like 1½*d.* per mile. One day the pit is bought by an ironmaster, 20 miles off, for the use of his blast furnaces. He applies to the railway for a special rate, and gets one of, say, 1*s.* 6*d.* a ton. Now, why? For this reason: the demand of the farmers for limestone was strictly limited; had they been given it gratis they would only have used a certain number of tons to the acre. In other words, no possible reduction of rate, as long as the limestone was used merely for agricultural purposes, could possibly have stimulated consumption to such an extent as to recoup the railway for the loss it incurred. For blast-furnaces, on the other hand, the demand is practically unlimited. At 2*s.* a ton it is possible that the ironmaster would use 3,000 tons a week; at 1*s.* 6*d.* 6,000; while a reduction to 1*s.* 3*d.* might increase the consumption to 10,000, or even 12,000 tons. It is for the goods manager to judge, in view of all the circumstances of the case, whether the best bargain for him is to carry 3,000 tons at 2s., or 6,000 at 1s. 6d., or 10,000 at 1s. 3d. But, except in the case where he would have to spend additional capital to accommodate the larger traffic, we may take it for granted that he will come to the same decision, whether his line has cost him 10,000l., or 20,000l., or 50,000l. per mile.

Take, again, the case of iron and copper. There is no doubt a possibility of copper being stolen in transit, which scarcely exists in the case of pig-iron, and to this extent the working expenses in the case of copper are fractionally higher. But, broadly speaking, the difference between the rates for the two articles rests on the fact that the possible expansion of the iron trade, owing to a reduction in the charge for carriage—which is a considerable item of the whole cost of so cheap an article—is very large, while possible increase in the copper trade, in consequence of a similar reduction, is very small. We have seen already one instance of this. The Great Western reduces the rate for fish from Cornwall 15 per cent. The reduction is absolutely dead loss, for the reason that, being too small, as compared with the retail price of the article, to produce any impression on that price, it fails to stimulate production and consumption one iota.

Now take the third of the instances we have given. The Manchester warehousman has absolute command of the local calico trade of Southampton already. A reduction of rate which should enable a 5s. dress to be sold for 4s. $11\frac{3}{4}d.$—or, perhaps, in view of the fondness of the female mind for farthings, it would be better to say, enable a 4s. 11¾d. dress to be sold for 4s. 11½d.—would not lead to the consumption of a single additional yard. But with the export trade it is not so. A difference of 20s. per ton may just turn the scale in favour of Lancashire against Bombay, or enable our manufacturers to face the new duty in some foreign market. It is a choice for the railway companies between taking the export trade at 25s. or losing it altogether at 45s., and of the two they prefer the former alternative. But the cost per mile of line travelled over has nothing to do with either the one rate or the other.

There is, however, one sense, and that a most important one, in which the cost of line affects the rates charged for the use of it. The North Western route from London to Birmingham and Manchester and Liverpool is very nearly half a century old. But the line, as Locke and Stephenson left it, is a very different thing from the line as it exists to-day. Millions upon millions have been spent in the interval upon terminal accommodation in the different towns, millions more upon the railway itself, which then consisted of two, but now practically of four lines throughout the entire length, with sufficient accommodation in sidings to form at least one other pair of lines for the whole distance. Now, this new accommodation was not provided till the company had carefully counted the cost. Among the many obligations imposed, both by legislation and public opinion, upon English railway companies, that of providing new capital gratis has not yet been included. We may therefore assume that, in adding to its accommodation—and the same thing of course applies to the other companies that have gone into the London-Liverpool business since the Grand Junction days—the London and North Western balanced against one another its new capital outlay and its probable new receipts. Now, for reasons given in the last chapter—of which cost of land and the expensive standard of construction demanded by English public opinion are the chief—no English main line is likely to be doubled under 50,000*l.* a mile. In other words, no English main line can earn a 5 per cent. dividend unless it can secure a gross revenue of 5,000*l.* a mile per annum and retain one-half of that sum as its net profit.

Further, as we saw at some length in reference to Sir Alfred Hickman's claim that a halfpenny per mile should be taken as a normal standard for traffic in coal and minerals, no line can hold beyond a certain quantity of traffic. What that quantity is, depends on the conditions under which it is carried. In America, for instance, with enormously heavy loads moving continuously for long distances at a slow speed, it is probably, reckoned in tons per mile, several times as great as in England, with small miscellaneous loads moving at the utmost possible speed between a considerable number of local points. But whether it be large or small, the limit always exists. Now, in America it is an admitted fact that no company can live which has nothing to depend on but the farthing-a-mile through traffic. The profit is so fractional that the line cannot hold enough of it to pay interest on the capital required for construction. In England, with lines, say, three times as costly, new construction, whether by the old-established companies or by their younger rivals, must have come to an end long ere this, unless the companies had been able to count on obtaining a generally high average of rate; and if the railway companies were to hold their hand for a single twelvemonth, to cease their habitual expenditure of 15,000,000*l.* to 20,000,000*l. per annum* in adding to their existing accommodation, the trade of the country would receive a blow whose effect all the patent medicines of reduced maxima and improved classifications would scarcely avail to alleviate, much less to cure.

It is worth notice, however, that, even in this country, there may be circumstances under which a company, charging rates practically on a level with the American average, can be exuberantly prosperous. Within the last two years a new route, some 26 miles in length, has been opened from the Rhondda Valley coalfield to the Bristol Channel at Barry Island. The money spent on the line does not appear to be separated from the money spent on the dock, but we should probably be safe to say that the railway has not cost less than 40,000*l.* a mile. The passenger traffic is a bagatelle; the goods chiefly pit-wood on its way to the collieries. The coal is carried—short though the distance be—at a fraction over $\frac{1}{2}d.$ per ton per mile, a price which has to cover the cost of returning the waggons empty. Yet the Barry Company has just declared a dividend of 10 per cent., and its shares stand at over 100 per cent. premium. But here, be it observed, we have practically the American condition of affairs. There are no 50-mile an hour expresses, no fish specials, no fast goods trains to interfere with the steady rhythmical motion of the coal-trains, as they glide from midnight to midnight, week in week out, down from the head of the Rhondda Valley to the level of the sea.

But, it may be said, agricultural branches do not cost anything like 50,000*l.* per mile. True, no doubt; but, on the other hand, an agricultural branch can never be filled to anything like its full capacity. It could accommodate comfortably, say, 200 trains a day. The traffic can only half fill some ten or a dozen. Nor can any reduction of rates create new traffic. You may carry wheat for nothing, you may even pay the farmers to send it, but that will not enable them to grow six quarters to the acre instead of five. Then, again, the trade of an agricultural branch must always be retail. A train at the best of times consists perhaps of only thirty trucks with only two tons apiece, but in the agricultural districts the thirty trucks come down to eight, and the two tons per waggon to 12 or 15 cwt. Putting together, therefore, the two facts, that the capital expenditure has to be charged against a comparatively small turnover, and that the working expenses are exceptionally heavy in proportion to the gross receipts, we arrive at the result that, high as the charges may be on the main line, they need to be still higher on a local branch.

It is of course fairly arguable that the local lines in England ought never to have cost the money they have. They have been built double when single lines might have sufficed, and in every way their construc-

S

tion has been on an unnecessarily expensive scale. This is no doubt strictly true, but the public, not the railway companies, must take the responsibility for the fact. No one, for example, could recommend that a railway company should buy only sufficient land for a single line, and run the risk of being obliged ten years later again to face the verdict of the British jury, as to the proper sum which it ought to pay the adjacent landowner for land required for widening, once its value had been enhanced three or four-fold by its proximity to the railway. Or, again, no one can say that a bridge, every quarter of a mile or so, is essential for the accommodation of the sheep and cows that inhabit the district; but if it is cheaper to build a bridge than to pay the preposterous price demanded as compensation for severance, it surely cannot be extravagant of the railway company to build it.

So, too, in the matter of working expenses. A railway man in any other country would consider it reckless extravagance to put down our elaborate English apparatus for signalling and interlocking, or to pay the wages of a signalman to look after a dozen trains in twenty-four hours. But here the public have thought proper to insist on block-working, and they cannot in reason expect to insure their lives without being prepared to pay the price of the policy. Or, again, the goods service of these lines could perfectly well be done by a few trucks attached to the ordinary passenger trains. But mixed trains are understood in this country to be dangerous, and the Board of Trade has just finally legislated them out of existence.

Is it fair—or, what is more to the purpose, is it practically possible that, in the long run, in a country where new railway expenditure is wanted at the rate of 50,000*l.* every working day, the cost of the change should come entirely out of the pockets of existing shareholders? Parliament, we all know, is omnipotent; and Parliament can compel existing lines to reduce their charges, and to increase their working expenses simultaneously. But what Parliament cannot do, is to compel the investment of fresh capital in British railways; and till it can do the latter, it would perhaps be wise, in the public interest, not to attempt the former.

But to leave the agricultural lines, which after all carry but a fraction of the total traffic—which, moreover, only get their service at existing rates, because the great companies, to which they mainly belong, can afford to look upon them as feeders of the main line traffic, and so to credit them with a considerable amount of revenue which is never actually earned over their rails—and to come to the important traffic of the great cities and the manufacturing districts. We here find collected together all the conditions which tend to make railway service expensive. There is a congestion of traffic of a most miscellaneous character, the distances are short, the service is required to be performed at the most frequent possible intervals, and at the utmost possible speed. It is all very well to talk about waiting to make up a full train-load; but theoretical calculations of the indisputable economies to be thereby effected will not avail to turn aside the reproaches of the customers whose goods are delayed a couple of hours beyond their accustomed time. It is all very well to talk about the extravagance of working coal up to London in trains of thirty trucks at 16 miles an hour, when, if the speed were cut down to 10 or 12 miles, it might be possible to take forty-five trucks. The appreciation of elementary principles of railway working contained in the criticism is deserving of all praise; but the practical railway man must be allowed to recollect that, if he adopts the advice of his academical adviser, either the goods trains and the passenger trains must mark time behind the economically conducted coal train all along the line, or else that this latter will need to spend a still larger proportion of its working day in refuge sidings than it devotes to that unremunerative occupation already.

Another point may perhaps here be noticed. Railway service must, as has been insisted on already, be looked upon as a whole. Admitting, for the sake of argument, that goods rates are what they were twenty years back, abandoning the attempt to prove, what could only be proved by elaborate and detailed comparisons, that consignors get a much better service for the same money than they got twenty years ago, let us see what has happened during the same period in the case of passenger traffic. No human being will surely compare the purchasing power of a shilling in passenger transportation at the earlier and at the later period. The Royal Commission of 1867 drew special attention to the neglect of the third-class passenger of England as compared with his liberal treatment in Belgium and

Holland, in France and Germany. First and second-class accommodation, they admitted, left little to complain of; but nothing, or almost nothing, had been done for the third-class passenger. "It is obvious that the working classes do not obtain that benefit from railway communication by the ordinary trains of the companies which a railway is so well calculated to afford."[1] The scene shifts to 1891, and the man who to-day should attempt to argue that, in accommodation, in speed, in frequency of service, the third-class passenger is as well treated on the Continent as he is in England, would only succeed in making himself ridiculous.

Even the oft-repeated assertion that fares have not been reduced is largely inaccurate. As for first and second-class passengers, not only have express fares disappeared, but also throughout almost the whole of England north of the Thames there have been very substantial reductions in the ordinary fares; to say nothing of the millions upon millions of season-ticket journeys, which in ever-increasing numbers are made in first and second-class carriages at less than third-class fares. For the third-class passenger the penny still remains the normal standard. But indirectly that standard has been largely reduced in many ways. In the North, third-class season-tickets are now usually issued. Near London, there are three hundred trains a day conveying workmen at fares ranging downwards to ·09$d.$ per mile. Then again at holiday times—the only time practically when the wage-earners can afford to leave their work—there are

[1] *Report*, p. lxi.

excursion trains at fares averaging certainly not more than ⅓*d*. a mile, while to all the places with a constant holiday traffic there are cheap tickets available the entire summer through. The workman, for instance, who goes down to Brighton from London, spends not 8*s*. 4*d*. on his return ticket, but 3*s*. To Ramsgate his fare is not 13*s*., but 8*s*., or if he goes for the day he can bring it down to 5*s*.; and so on throughout the length and breadth of the country. To Glasgow and back, 800 miles, a man can book every week for 25*s*., for three-eighths of a penny per mile, that is. He can book to Inverness and back, 1,200 miles, for 60*s*.—his ticket being available by every train, and giving him the right to break his journey at every point of interest on the way.

In face of facts like these, it is nonsense to say that English third-class fares have not been reduced; and to say that they have been reduced is, in other words, to admit that the railway companies have been ready to share their increased profits, whenever obtained, with their customers. For it should be remembered that, vastly as the passenger traffic has increased, it has steadily become less and less profitable to the companies themselves. A train, which twenty years ago earned on the average 5*s*. and cost 2*s*. 4*d*., nowadays is probably earning only 4*s*. 6*d*., while the cost in the interval has risen to 2*s*. 6*d*. Year by year, in fact, a railway company, like every other capitalist, has to subsist on a narrower margin of profit.[2]

[2] Mr. Grierson gave the Committee of 1881 some remarkable figures on this point in reference to the Great Western. Below are

It is not a little remarkable, in looking back over the series of reports of committees and commissions on railway questions, to observe that while the recommendations which told against the railways have largely been carried into effect, those which would have enured to their benefit have been almost absolutely ignored. In his minority report, as a member of the Royal Commission of 1867, Sir Rowland Hill points out that, "while, in common with the owners of other public vehicles, railway companies are taxed by the State, their lines, unlike the old roads, are heavily rated by every parish they traverse ; so that in some rural districts a railway company, though perhaps on the one hand relieving the parish of much pauperism by giving profitable employment to the peasantry, and on the other hand lightening the rates by increasing the value of the property on which they are levied, is yet made to defray in a direct form half the parochial expenditure. In fine, railway companies have been made to feel, in the severest manner, that the justice which society observes towards individuals is seldom main-

reproduced the most important of them.

These figures, by the way, furnish an awkward commentary on the oft-repeated assertion that rates have not appreciably fallen since the first beginning of railways. Will any human being seriously assert that the engines of forty years ago took nearly three times the paying load that is hauled nowadays ? And, if not, how explain the reduction in train-mile earnings, except by admitting that the rates have been reduced ?

Percentage of working expenses to gross receipts.

Year	Per cent.
1844	33
1850	38
1860	44
1870	46
1880	52

Receipts per train-mile.

	Passengers, &c.		Goods, &c.	
	s.	d.	s.	d.
1850	7	5·94	14	11·32
1860	4	7·23	8	2
1870	4	6·20	5	5·68
1880	4	10·14	5	4·45

tained towards a corporation—a loss distributed amongst many being too often regarded as, in effect, no loss at all." And again elsewhere he declares that the tax on railway travelling is an impost so obviously objectionable that it is scarcely needful to say that it should be removed as soon as the public revenue can afford to forego it.

It is also scarcely needful to say that Sir Rowland Hill's recommendation has not been followed. Horse taxes have been abolished, carriage taxes lightened, the proposed van-tax has, amidst the execration of the traders—for even the most crushed of worms will turn at last—vanished into limbo. But the Government tax on railways lives on and shows every sign of continuing to live. As for local rates, in the great towns at least, they are likely to increase, for omnibuses are becoming increasingly popular, and, though omnibus companies pay nothing towards repairing the roads, they can do a good deal towards wearing them out. Last year, according to the Board of Trade Returns, the total sum paid by one company, the South Eastern, for rates, taxes, and Government duty, amounted to one-eighth of its total expenditure. In the case of the London and Brighton Railway it was one-ninth. For all the railways of the United Kingdom it averaged one-fifteenth.

Again, Sir Rowland Hill points out that "it is notorious that under the present system exorbitant prices often have to be paid through fear either of Parliamentary opposition or of partial awards of juries. ... In the purchase of land for railway purposes the amount actually paid is often several times the antecedent value." After recommending that a general law should be enacted giving railways power to construct new lines, subject to proper Government control, without obtaining a special Act, he goes on to say: "It would be for the Legislature to consider whether in respect of lines constructed by authority of Government solely for the general welfare, it would not be just, while carefully respecting all legal rights, to consider in the assessment of compensation what set-off against the value of the land required should be allowed for increased value given by the line to the rest of the estate." Needless to say, once more, that the principle of "betterment" has not yet found its way into English law. If, and when, it does come, it is not likely that it will be applied for the benefit of railway companies.

There was another recommendation in the Report of the Commission, this time signed by all but two of their number. It ran as follows: "We recommend that the liability of the railway companies be limited within a maximum amount of compensation for each class of fares.... Further, that claims for compensation should not be permitted unless within a certain period." Needless to say, this recommendation too is not yet carried out, though some restriction of this nature is practically given effect to in every other country. In America, for example, it is coming to be almost settled law that $5,000 is the maximum amount recoverable in case of fatal injury. Here, on the other hand, a London physician in a well-known case obtained a verdict for 7,000*l*., which being set aside on the ground that the damages were illusory, in a second action he secured 15,000*l.* as compensation.

What this means, at least to the smaller and weaker companies, may be judged by two instances. The Great Northern of Ireland is still carrying over money from revenue to meet claims arising out of the Armagh accident in the early summer of 1889, though its shareholders ever since have had to forego one-third of the income which they would otherwise have received. But even this is as nothing to what has happened to a much smaller company—the Cork and Macroom—which met with a bad accident some eight years back, and has never been able to resume the payment of dividends since. Once more, it may be right that the British juryman should give full scope to his feelings of compassion for everyone who has been injured, as well as for a certain number who have not been injured, in a railway accident, under the impression that the impersonal company can afford to pay; but reasoning men will not forget that, in the long run and over a series of years, the whole of the compensation, *plus* probably a certain percentage for additional risk, has to come out of the pockets of the customers of the line.

But enough probably has been said to show why it is true in a sense that English rates are high. It is worth while to notice very briefly whether they are, as it is often asserted, too high. Of this various tests might be taken. It might be said—it was said three or four years back—that English trade was slowly, very slowly, bleeding to death. In face of the remarkable expansion of business which began in the early autumn of 1889, such a statement will scarcely be repeated to-day. Of course one may be told that, though English trade is still growing, that of Germany, of the States, is growing much faster. True, doubtless; but the fact that a child of a year old grows faster than a lad of twenty, is scarcely evidence to prove that the latter is ill-fed.

There is another barometer which might be used. We hear much about the way railway companies have strangled canals, and it is in consequence, we are told, of this strangulation process that the railways have been able to maintain their rates at the present figure. There are, however, not a few canals still left unstrangled. There is one, for instance, between the not unimportant points of Liverpool and Manchester. It is known as the Bridgewater Canal, and is now the property of the Manchester Ship Canal Company. It carries a great deal of traffic, and pays a good dividend. Yet so far is it from attempting or desiring to reduce the rates which are killing the Manchester merchant, that it actually joins hands with the railway companies in an agreement to maintain the existing rates. Is it not obvious that, if the Bridgewater Canal could carry Lancashire traffic under Lancashire conditions at any important reduction in price, its own interest would lead it to desert the railway alliance and to cut rates to a point at which the railways would be forced to abandon the competition? There is another canal between the not less important points of Birmingham and London. Does the canal compete seriously for Birmingham traffic? —and, if not, why not? Can it really be that the

Birmingham traders are not quite inclined to take themselves seriously ; that they are not quite sure whether they care to have their goods on the road a fortnight, and then delivered, not in the heart of London, but somewhere up near the Highgate Archway, even though they should save a few shillings per ton over the business ? It surely cannot be that the railway rates have drained South Staffordshire so dry, that all the capitalists in the Black Country together cannot raise among them the few paltry millions which are necessary to buy up the Grand Junction Canal and its tributaries, and put the system into something like a reasonable state of efficiency.[3]

Though canals may not be able to hold their own with railways on equal terms, it is yet quite conceivable that, leaving considerations of abstract justice aside, it might be worth while—if not for private commercial companies, then for the State or for local authorities, to run canals, even though not at a profit, in competition with the railways, with the deliberate object of reducing the charges on the latter. This is practically what is done by the French Government, and also by the Government of the State of New York, both of which maintain their canals free of toll at the expense of the public revenue. In France, where the State also guarantees the dividends of the

---

[3] Of course the Manchester Ship Canal stands on a different footing altogether. If ocean vessels can be brought to Manchester almost as easily and as cheaply as into the docks of Liverpool, unquestionably carriage from New York or Savannah to Manchester will be cheaper then than it is now. The point in the text is merely that, under normal English conditions, barge-canals cannot hold their own with railways, not because they are strangled, but for the simple reason that the sacrifice of efficiency is greater than the gain in economy.

companies, the Government is therefore in the unfortunate position of competing with itself; but in America the Erie Canal was deliberately freed from tolls a few years back, because, as long as tolls were charged, it could not compete for traffic with the private railway companies. The "Railroad Gazette," the other day, had some elaborate calculations which appeared to show that, if to the charge for water-carriage from Chicago to New York there was added a proportionate share of the cost of maintenance of the Erie Canal, the total would amount to quite as much, if not something more than the railway rate. In other words, an American railway can hold its own, even in matter of cost, with any water-carriage short of that in full-sized steamers. Germany, too, has spent of late, and is still spending, a vast amount of money on inland water-communications. According to a recent statement of Professor Hadley's, there is no need to spend the money at all, for the German railways could afford to give the accommodation at the same price, were they not hide-bound by the restrictions of their mileage tariff.

All three countries, however, are alike in this, that they are spending and have spent large sums of public money in order to reduce the cost of transportation. When the British public begin to do the same, they will occupy a position logically more tenable than that which they are in at present. "In England," said M. Waddington's Committee in their famous report to the French Chamber, "where this system of liberty and commercial competition is largely in vogue, it is right that the railway companies, who have received nothing, and from whom nothing is demanded by the State "—" *mais nous avons changé tout cela*," M. Waddington wrote in 1880— " and who may be considered only as belonging to the category of private merchants and manufacturers, should have greater freedom in dealing with their traffic and tariffs than is enjoyed in this country."

There is another form of competition which ought, one would think, to temper the rigours of English railway tariffs, that, namely, of traffic by sea. Now, it is not a little remarkable how small a portion of the places with potential sea competition actually have it in reality. In numerous instances it has been tried and failed. Take once more those extortionate fish-rates. Steamers have been tried from Penzance, both for fish and for new potatoes and early vegetables; but not, it is understood, with over much success. They have been tried in competition with Oban and Strome Ferry during the season of the West Highland herring fishery. It is not the railways which have come off worse out of the fray. Again, Mr. Taylor, a Swansea grocer, who was greatly distressed that the prohibitive railway charge for blacking imposed too heavy a burden on his customers, told the Committee of 1881 that there had been a steamer from London to Swansea, but that it had ceased to run. Presumably its owners found the traffic unremunerative. In other words, the railway rates between London and Swansea, taking into account the quality of the service rendered, were lower than a steamer could afford permanently to take in return for traffic of a miscellaneous and fluctuating character. It is necessary to lay stress on this latter point, because the trader so frequently ignores the fact that the expenses connected with a retail distributive traffic are very different from those belonging to the handling of what the Americans would term "straight" car-loads or ship-loads. Another instance may perhaps be quoted to show that the railway rates are not too high, in the sense that they do not strangle trade. During the recent Scotch strike, it was reported more than once that the steamers had taken away from Edinburgh to London cargoes that would naturally have gone by rail. But, if anywhere, surely between the Forth and the Thames steamers ought to be able to beat out of the field the competition of the railway companies, their rates being what we are told they are. But, in fact, vastly as the introduction of triple-expansion engines has reduced the cost of steam-ship working—an economy which has as yet no parallel in railway practice—it is not asserted that steam-ship communication is gaining on the railways throughout the United Kingdom. If it does not do so, if at most of the ports where competition might exist, it is in fact at the present moment non-existent, where is the evidence that the railway rates are too high?

A word more about Lancashire. When the Ship Canal scheme was first seriously mooted, Liverpool started in opposition a fantastic project for a system of plateways along the roads radiating from Liverpool to the manufacturing centres, over whose smooth iron surface vans were to be hauled with the minimum of friction. The plateways have not yet been constructed, have not indeed been so much as commenced. "Why not?" one is fain to ask, if it be true that the railway charges are kept up to their present level, not because the service is enormously costly, but simply by the fact that the existing companies have a monopoly of the only means of communication. Again, it has been brought forward as an argument against the railways that in the immediate neighbourhood of Manchester, from points such as Stockport and Oldham, traders often cart direct, instead of entrusting their goods to the railway company. The point, in fact, tells exactly the other way. It confirms what the railway managers are always saying, that the increased cost of terminal handling and terminal accommodation more than counterbalances any economies which have been effected in actual haulage. Where the distance is short, and where the article carried is such that a considerable amount of handling is required, cartage throughout, which saves two handlings, must always remain cheaper. Coal, say, can be transferred at 2*d.* a ton; it may cost 2*s.* to deal with cotton. Add another 6*d.* for actual conveyance, and we get to an actual out-of-pocket cost of 4*s.* 6*d.*, which is evidently more than the carter need charge for adding six miles to a journey already undertaken.

The moral of our story should then be plain. That English rates are high because the service given is an expensive one, and one which can only be provided over a line constructed at great initial cost. That, whether we look at the return to the shareholders, or at the cost for which similar service is provided elsewhere; whether we have regard to the fact that English trade has steadily grown and increased under them, or to the fact that no serious competition by water-carriage is attempted, there is no evidence to prove that English rates are too high. Before, however, leaving the subject, it is worth while reverting for a moment to the contemporary history of the United States. We shall find, if I mistake not, that the conditions which have made English railway rates what they are, are even now rapidly developing themselves on the other side of the Atlantic.

"Let the country make the railroads, and the railroads will make the country," was the well-known saying of George Stephenson. And true though it may have been in the case of England, it applied with tenfold force to the United States. Here the railways came into towns already rich and prosperous, and had to buy land for their stations and works at building prices. In America the railway men were pioneers, and camped out, one might almost say, at their depôts in the backwoods or on the prairies till the town grew up round them. In this fact, coupled with the remarkable difference of the point of view of the legislation of the two countries in reference to the appropriation of land for railway purposes—the United States looking at the matter from the point of view of the public, whose interest is to get the line as cheaply as possible, England from the point of view of the existing owner, whose rights are to be hedged round with all possible safeguards—is to be found the main cause of the comparatively inexpensive nature of American railways.

This state of things, however, has practically come

T

to an end. In New York, or, to speak more accurately, in Jersey City, on the other bank of the Hudson —for, with the exception of the New York Central, the railway companies do not enter New York City at all—in Philadelphia, in Chicago, in all the great cities, in fact, the railways have outgrown, or at least are now on the point of outgrowing, their original accommodation. They are being forced to face the fact that to enlarge their stations and goods-yards they have got to buy, if not property actually covered with houses, at least building-land at building prices, and the prospect is by no means a cheerful one. As has been pointed out, an expensive line literally cannot hold at $\frac{1}{4}d.$ per ton-mile a sufficient quantity of traffic to pay interest on its capital. And yet the money has to be spent, for unless there is accommodation for receiving and getting rid of the traffic at the terminal points, the line in between those points will remain half empty. More than one of the American railways therefore is in the unfortunate position that it is forced to spend, say, 5,000,000 dollars on two or three miles of line, on which it can never hope to earn interest at more than 1 per cent., because, if it refuses to face the outlay, 200 or 300 other miles, whose total capital amounts perhaps to 30,000,000 dollars, will remain unproductive.

Then, again, the Americans have to confront the problem of bringing their existing accommodation up to the standard, not of course of English, but of Continental lines. The American public have not yet risen to the height of demanding masonry bridges for the use of their sheep and cattle, or even masonry platforms for their own use, but they are very strongly of opinion that it is time trains ceased to run down the middle of crowded streets in town. English readers, perhaps, scarcely realize what the Americans have hitherto had to put up with in this respect. Let me give two instances. The writer happened the other day to time an express on the main-line of the Pennsylvania Railroad, within thirty miles of New York. The speed, in passing through the streets and squares of the not inconsiderable town of Rahway, was between 62 and 63 miles an hour. There was, it is true, a fence to keep the public off the track. It consisted of a single iron rail of about the height and about the strength of a croquet hoop. Or, again, half a dozen of the principal railways of the country have their termini alongside in Jersey City, with their rails running down to the Hudson at right angles to the river's course. There are passenger trains dashing in and out every moment, and shunting engines moving hither and thither, tolling their great bells, in bewildering confusion. And through all this the foot traffic and cart and carriage traffic of Jersey City, with a population of some 200,000 persons, has to find its way as best it can on the level. According to a statement in one of the New York papers, the Pennsylvania Railroad alone has two trains a minute across and through the streets of this unfortunate town; but, by dint of maintaining four flagmen constantly on guard, it succeeded in keeping the fatal accidents during the whole twelve months of 1890 down to only 20.

Now, as has been said, there is a very strong feeling

growing up that it is time this state of things came to an end, and, in fact, at this moment the Pennsylvania Railroad is elevating its passenger tracks at this point. But, to carry out the same process on all the lines in all the towns, will mean an expenditure of enormous magnitude. It is true that in the States the Government, or the municipality, or both, are accustomed to contribute sometimes a half—as was done, for instance, when the New York Central depressed its tracks into the depôt on Forty-second Street—more usually one-third of the expense incurred with this object. But, even so, the railway share of the cost will be a very serious matter.[4] Then again the block system is being adopted in some form or other by most of the leading companies, and what the cost of the block system is, English railway managers know only too well.

Nowhere is the congestion of traffic worse than in New York itself. Goods and passenger accommodation are alike overtaxed even now, and there is both in goods and passengers a steady and rapid increase of local traffic, which requires just as much room at the terminus as through traffic, though it unfortunately

---

[4] Here is one instance. The New York, New Haven, and Hartford Railroad, probably the wealthiest railway company in the States, wants at this moment to quadruple its tracks through the small town of Bridgeport, in Connecticut. It can only get leave to do this on condition of sinking its tracks below the roads. The total cost of the operation is estimated at 1,200,000*l.*, and having a monopoly, which for reasons too long to give here is practically unassailable, the New York and New Haven declines to incur this expense, and proposes to abandon its existing station and go round outside the town. But no competitive company in the States could venture to move to a less convenient station, and no company, whether competitive or not, would dare to make such a suggestion in England.

does not, like the latter, pay large mileage rates by which the terminal cost can be diluted. Passengers, too, are becoming more exacting, and it is thought that tunnels under the Hudson, with termini in New York City itself, will, before many years are out, have to replace the present system of depositing passengers in Jersey City, and leaving them to cross the river in ferry-boats. Then, again, the arrangements for the collection and delivery of goods are very far from satisfactory. As has been said, this work is not undertaken by the railway companies, and the private firms who do the business make enormous charges; three and four shillings for fetching or delivering a single case is something like the usual scale.

Nor can it be denied that the charges are justifiably high, for to deliver a mixed load at a New York freight-shed is often a matter of many hours. A man may wait for a long while before he can get a receipt for the first consignment he hands in, and then be told that the next lot is for a different station and must be taken to a different door; and so the whole weary work of waiting has to be begun over again. One of the great cartage firms declares that not unfrequently the horses are taken out of their carts and sent away to work elsewhere, a watchman being left in charge of the goods till the company is able to take delivery. More than one of the great companies has been seriously considering the propriety of undertaking the work of cartage and delivery itself, not with any idea of making a direct profit out of the business, but simply in order to be able, by better organisation, to utilise more fully the enormously expensive terminal accommodation in New York.

Then again the demand for more rapid transportation of goods is rising on all hands, with consequent serious increase of movement expenses. On the New York Central, for instance, there are now about fourteen fast freight trains *per diem*, which are limited to something like half an ordinary load, and run on the passenger tracks at a speed of 20 miles an hour. This same company reported a year back that it had succeeded in increasing the average load of its freight trains from 186 to 226 tons by paying more attention to securing full loads for each car. On this the "Railroad Gazette"[5] commented as follows: "It would seem as though economy of train-loads had been secured at the sacrifice of considerations of business policy. It is often a short-sighted measure to save money by reducing facilities. It may do for a year or two, but it works badly in the long run."

In the Erie Report for 1890 will be found this passage: "The competition in service has increased the cost of operation largely in excess of the advantages gained. Not many years ago, the average speed of freight trains rarely exceeded 10 miles per hour. Now, upon your road, they run at the average rate of 25 miles per hour. At that time the engines hauling freight trains weighed 30 tons, now they weigh 60 tons. The rails in the track weighed 56 pounds to

---

[5] I have quoted so often from the *Railroad Gazette* that it may as well be said that the *Gazette* is an accepted authority in its own country, being a paper of a kind which unfortunately does not exist here, a journal written by, and for, experts in railway traffic management.

the yard. Now your company puts in steel rails weighing 80 pounds. . . . The tons of freight per train have decreased from 265 tons to 249 tons, or 6·04 per cent. This was brought about by a faster movement of freight trains generally. On account of the more active competition existing among the trunk lines in the movement of merchandise, this fast train movement has reduced the tonnage per mile, and consequently the earnings. The results for the year show a reduction in the net earning per freight train-mile of 14·93 per cent." The same thing is happening in the neighbourhood not only of New York, but of Chicago. " The speed of trains," says the Illinois Central Report, " has been increased consequent on the demands of traffic and competition thereby reducing the size of trains, and making the expense per car heavier." Another of the leading Western roads—the Chicago, Burlington and Quincy—put out for the first time in June last a working time-table for fast freight, both through and local traffic, all over its system.

The truth is that, not only American railway managers, but the American public at large, are beginning to realize to what disastrous results for all interests concerned the adoption of Sir Bernhard Samuelson's advice to compete in rates must lead. Those best qualified to judge evidently believe that rates have practically touched bottom, that the competition of the future—to quote the Illinois Central Report once more—" is coming to be, as in Great Britain, one of adequacy and frequency of service," and that the tendency of rates in the future is more likely than not to be in an upward direction.

It should be added, in conclusion, that even now the competition in facilities has become very keen. A single company, the Erie, delivers to customers at no less than 73 points in New York and its vicinity. The competition in passenger traffic is conducted with a reckless disregard for economy, far beyond anything which this country can show, even in cases such as the oft quoted "25 expresses from London to Manchester." In England, Professor Hunter complains that competition has "led to some practices that are bad for the railway shareholders and of doubtful utility to the trader. . . . It has given rise to an army of touts or agents, whose services are of no value to the trading community, and in other ways it has led to a costly and unprofitable mode of conveying traffic." In this respect unquestionably the Americans are sinners above all who dwell in the United Kingdom. Their army of touts and canvassers would almost suffice to man all the posts in the English railway service. Their houses of call for the sale of passenger tickets and for general information are in every street. The Pennsylvania has four, and the Baltimore and Ohio seven, in Broadway alone. One of the most valuable sites probably in the world—the point where Broadway cuts Fifth Avenue on the south side of Madison Square—is occupied by a ticket agency of the Erie Company. In one sense, no doubt, this competitive system of conducting traffic is costly and unprofitable. The touts and canvassers are not engaged in direct production. But a tree should be known by its fruits, and the competitive system in America, though theoretically it may charge the trading community for services which are of no value to them, has unquestionably rendered to that community services at a price which would be thought impossible under a system such as State-purchase or guaranteed monopoly must naturally produce, where the railway official lies contentedly on his back, and waits until the traffic drops into his mouth.[6]

[6] Londoners have had, within the last few years, an excellent object-lesson as to the so-called wastefulness of competition. Since the London Road Car Company started, there has been an enormous reduction in fares simultaneously with an immense improvement in accommodation. Further, just like the rival companies between London and Manchester, and New York and Chicago, when the Road Car Company establishes a line of omnibuses along a new route, the General Omnibus Company caps it with a second service the following week. Yet the old company still maintains its accustomed 10 per cent., while its younger competitor has just declared a dividend at the rate of $7\frac{1}{2}$. The truth is, that competition within reasonable limits, so far from being wasteful, is a public benefactor. It makes two blades of grass grow where one grew before, and a single blade affords adequate sustenance for either competitor.

PART III

THE PROBLEM FOR PARLIAMENT

CHAPTER XI

THE TRADERS' DEMANDS

HAVING considered the general principles which underlie the fixing of railway rates; having further discussed, as far as limitation of space allowed, the application of those principles, both here and in foreign countries; having seen, too, in outline, the broad features of difference between the railways of the United Kingdom, on the one hand, and those of the Continent and the United States on the other, we are now in a position to pass judgment on the detailed proposals for the reform of our English system, put forward on behalf of the traders of this country. At the outset it is impossible not to express regret at the inaccurate version of the Parliamentary history of this question which is given in the Report published under the authority of the united Lancashire and Cheshire, Devon and Cornwall, and Irish Traders' Conferences. Nothing can be gained in the long run by inaccurate statements of fact. It is, of course, entirely within the rights of an advocate to place his opponent's case in the least favourable light. When, therefore, the Report in question makes the following statement: "It was before this Committee" [that, namely, of the House of Commons in 1853] "that the Great Western Railway first enunciated the doctrine, which they still maintain, that the only limit to their charges should be the amount which the traffic can bear. Their view is that they would allow the merchant or manufacturer to retain a small profit upon the business he is carrying on; anything earned beyond what his capital would give him if invested in Consols should belong to the railway company which undertook the carriage of his materials "—when the Report makes a statement such as this, no one has a right to object. It is merely a rhetorical exaggeration of what is, when stripped of the rhetoric, nothing more than an obvious truism, that the principle of charging what the traffic will bear, if pressed to the point where it becomes practically equivalent to "charging what the traffic will not bear," may be made the excuse for rates which in practice prove to be extortionate or even confiscatory.

But an advocate who, when professing to quote from an affidavit, should omit qualifications here, and soften down inconvenient phrases there, while allowing the Court all the time to believe that he was reading *verbatim et literatim*—such an advocate would rightly be held to have allowed his zeal for his client to get the better of his respect for the obligations which he owed to an honourable profession; and this is really almost what has been done in the Report presented to the Lancashire and Cheshire

Conference. It is emphatically not true that, as stated on page 153 of the Report, "complaints of the abuse of the power entrusted to the companies, and protests against the powers exerted by them . . . . have been endorsed by every Parliamentary Committee which has enquired into them, from 1846 to 1888 inclusive."

On the contrary, the railway companies may fairly claim that, if any impartial person will compare the long series of reports of railway committees with the reports of enquiries into the administration of different departments of the public service, the private companies will be found to come much better out of the comparison than the Government departments. Charges of abuse and extortion have been made by the hundred; but, when sifted in the calm atmosphere of a Parliamentary committee-room, they have usually left behind them what in proportion to their bulk may be considered but a microscopic residuum of fact. The sum and substance of the whole series of Parliamentary Reports might be much more nearly given in a single line from the concluding paragraph of the latest Report of all, that of the House of Commons' Committee of 1882: "Your Committee report that on the whole of the evidence they acquit the railway companies of any grave dereliction of their duty to the public."

If the Lancashire and Cheshire Conference desire to have before them an accurate summary of the Parliamentary history of this question from the earliest period, it is a pity their Report did not go back two years behind 1846. For in the year 1844 there was a very famous Committee, which, under the guidance of Mr. Gladstone, as President of the Board of Trade, and Mr. Samuel Laing, now Chairman of the Brighton Railway, as Secretary of the Railway Department, went very carefully into the whole question of railway legislation. One result of their deliberations was the "Cheap Trains Act" of the same year, which not only gave third-class passengers the right to be carried at a speed of at least 12 miles an hour by one train per diem, but provided that under certain circumstances the State might purchase the railways; and, further, that when railway profits reached 10 per cent., the Treasury might revise the rates so as to reduce the dividend to that figure. Such revision, however, was to be accompanied by a guarantee on the part of the Crown, that the revised rates should produce a dividend to the company of 10 per cent. for the 21 years thereafter succeeding. Perhaps, however, we had better say as little as possible about this legislative precedent, as it might be inconvenient to the Lancashire and Cheshire Conference.

Let us confine ourselves to the Report and recommendations of the Committee. It reported that the complaint of monopoly urged against railways was an indication of the benefits they had conferred on the country, as it was not by force of special privileges granted to them, but by superior accommodation and cheapness, that they had acquired the command of travelling in their district. The Committee went on to say that, as it was desirable enterprise should be encouraged to go on and provide further railway facilities, Parliament should "take no step which would induce so much as a reasonable suspicion of its good faith with regard to the integrity of privileges already granted, because one of the elements of encouragement to future undertakings was just and equitable dealing with those already established." It should be added, as it might possibly be thought to tell in the other direction, that the Committee continued : " At the same time, nothing in the nature of a vested interest (by which the Committee mean an interest and claim over and above positive enactments for some restraint of the general principles in favour of the party) ought to be recognised by Parliament as attaching to existing railways." This passage, however, it is almost needless to point out, refers, not to a revision of existing powers of charge, but to a guarantee against the competition of new lines.

Now let us come to the Report of 1846. According to the Lancashire and Cheshire Conference Report, "the specific suggestion made" [by the Committee in that year] " was that the lowest existing rates then charged should be taken to form the future maximum." Referring, however, to the Report itself, we find that the specific suggestion is in the following words : " That in all instances in which railway companies propose to take powers of amalgamation, the rates and tolls of the amalgamated company should be subjected to revision." The Report, however, goes on to say that competition has hitherto prevented companies from charging their maximum rates and tolls, but that "if a system of amalgamation is to be extensively adopted, the latter inducement to low charges will be materially diminished, if not altogether done away with." The Committee therefore feels that maxima may be required in the future for public protection, and thinks that Select Committees, in passing Amalgamation Bills, ought to "exercise much care in the adjustment and substitution of a maximum rate" for the amalgamated company. "It ought," says the Committee, "always to be borne in mind that the effect of an amalgamation is to diminish the expense of working and managing railways, and thereby to enable the proprietors to secure a greater profit on their existing traffic. And, in this view of the case, it might be taken as a general rule, subject to special exceptions, that the maximum of rates and tolls combined ought not to exceed the lowest rates which have been previously demanded and received by the respective companies."

Now, it is not very easy to put a perfectly satisfactory interpretation on this last clause, the wording of which is by no means free from ambiguity. At first sight the present writer was inclined to believe that the words "demanded and received by the respective companies" meant "demanded and received from Parliament as maximum rates"—not "demanded and received from the public as actual charges." In other words, that the recommendation of the Committee of 1846 was, not that of the Lancashire and Cheshire Conference: "take the lowest competitive rate actually charged and stereotype that as the maximum of the whole line," but "where two companies are amalgamating, take as the standard for the maxima of the new company the lower of the two scales of maxima enacted for the old company "—needless to say, a very different proposition.

Certainly antecedent probability is in favour of such an interpretation. In the words of Mr. Justice Wills's most recent judgment, in the case of Sowerby v. The Great Northern Railway Company: "Although it is very much the fashion in the present day to think that, if any sufficient number of people want the property and services and work of other people without paying for them, they ought to have it, yet I do not think that in 1850 that had become so pronounced a view on the part of the Legislature." But there is more than this. The Report of 1846 was before the Royal Commission of 1867, and this latter body describes its recommendation as being simply: "That in all instances in which the railway companies propose to take powers of amalgamation, the rates and tolls of the amalgamated companies should be subjected to revision." It was again before the Joint Committee of 1872, which summarizes its recommendation in the words: "That in general the new maximum should not exceed the lowest maximum of any of the amalgamating companies." It seemed almost impossible to suppose that 44 years ago a Parliamentary Committee committed itself to what to us in 1891 looks like a policy of simple confiscation, and recommended that "the lowest existing rates then charged should be taken to form the future maximum."

Further consideration, however, has convinced me that the Committee did really mean to recommend that the lowest existing charges should form the basis of the new statutory maxima, but that this was, under the circumstances, a perfectly natural and reasonable proposal. Let us see what these circumstances were. The time was 1846, when the railway mania was at its height, when the great lines were paying dividends of 10 and 12 per cent., and railway shares were looked upon as inexhaustible gold mines. When companies in this condition of exuberant prosperity came to Parliament to ask permission to increase their net revenues by being allowed to secure the economies which amalgamation promised—and when it took three companies to carry a passenger to Brighton, and four to carry him to Dover, those economies were not inconsiderable—it was only right and proper that Parliament on behalf of the public should ask for a *quid pro quo*. And this *quid pro quo* would naturally take the form of a reduction of the maximum powers to the point which, roughly speaking, had been shown by experience to be amply remunerative. There was no question in 1846 of bringing down local rates to the level of competitive through rates, for these latter had hardly begun to come into existence. The classification was still that of the original Acts; special rates, export rates, and the like, were as yet unknown; practically speaking, the charges were still fixed on a simple mileage basis. In fact, the sense of the recommendation of the Committee of 1846 is fairly represented to our modern ideas by the words in which the Joint Committee of 1872 summarises it: "That in general the new maximum should not exceed the lowest maximum of any of the amalgamating companies."

The next Parliamentary Committee referred to in the Lancashire and Cheshire Report is that of 1853. "The Report," so it is summarised on page 11 of the Lancashire and Cheshire document, "estimated that the unnecessary Parliamentary expenses hitherto incurred by the companies in opposing rival schemes amounted to no less than 70,000,000*l*. This was an expenditure barren of results to the public and one not due to be recouped by the imposition of higher rates and fares. As regards the contention that powers are irrevocable, it is to be noted that the Committee considered that (*sic*) the principle heretofore established at law—that an Act of Parliament constitutes an engagement between the promoters on the one side and the public on the other—a principle deserving of more consideration than it had hitherto obtained as a guide to future legislation." It is only necessary to place in juxtaposition to this remarkable paraphrase the precise words of the Parliamentary Committee's Report itself.

They are as follows: "Your Committee consider that the principle heretofore established at law, that an Act of Parliament constitutes an engagement between the promoters on the one side and the public on the other, is a principle deserving of more consideration than it has hitherto obtained as a guide to future legislation. This principle, rightly understood, conveys to the promoters no right that their privileges shall be exclusively maintained when they cease to be consistent with the general advantage; but it does imply that having been authorised by the Legislature to construct expensive works for public use, the resources from which their just remuneration was to spring shall not be taken away upon any other than clear grounds of public policy. The observance of such a principle is valuable to the public as well as to shareholders, since it is of importance to the whole community to develop by every judicious means those communications on which the freedom and facility of trade, and the safety and convenience of personal locomotion, now depend, and therefore to ensure, to a reasonable extent, the stability of the property so invested."

And again : " A most competent witness [1] has estimated the loss of money to the railway shareholders, unnecessarily incurred in obtaining Parliamentary authority for *and in constructing* the railways now in existence, and in opposing rival schemes, at 70,000,000*l.* ; and though it may, perhaps, be considered that this is a high estimate, when taken in regard to the lines actually made, it is no sufficient measure of the loss which has been really sustained, since many are constructed which probably are not laid out in the way best calculated to promote the general convenience, and so to develop the greatest amount of traffic. On the other hand, *it is difficult to estimate the amount of benefit which is derived to the public even from railways which are not remunerative to the shareholders,* by the facilities which are afforded for transit, and by the saving of capital which arises

[1] The witness was Mr. Samuel Laing, now Chairman of the Brighton Railway.

from the shortening of time required for the transmission of goods, and the diminished necessity for holding considerable sums locked up in the stocks of tradesmen."

The Lancashire and Cheshire history proceeds as follows: "In 1863 it was reported to Parliament that the companies were ignoring their duties as trustees of the highways, and making them entirely subservient to their own profit. It was urged that it was the duty of the executive Government to become the guardian of the general interest, and to take measures to compel the railway companies to fulfil faithfully the public duties they have undertaken." Who made this report we are not informed. In the absence of such information, it being impossible to find any other evidence of the existence of a report of 1863 at all, we shall perhaps be right in assuming that 1863 is a misprint for 1853, the more so as a reference to the Fifth Report of the Committee of this latter year seems to furnish sentences on which the Lancashire and Cheshire paraphrase might conceivably be founded. These passages are as follows: "In some cases this union of railways and canals has been effected at the instance of the railway companies, for the obvious purpose of removing a competitor, and obtaining a monopoly of the means of transit. . . . In other cases the union appears to have been effected in the following manner: When a railway company has proposed to construct a railway in a district heretofore served by water-carriage, the shareholders of the canal have possessed sufficient influence to compel the railway company to buy off their opposition by amalgamating them on favourable terms with the railway. In cases of this kind the difficulty of providing a remedy against abuse is greatly increased by the hardship which the railway company will allege to be inflicted upon them, if Parliament, having first compelled them to enter into a losing partnership with the canal, afterwards prohibits them from turning the two schemes conjointly to the utmost advantage in their power. . . . There is another class of cases in which the railway companies appear sometimes to exercise arbitrary and illegal powers to the prejudice of persons engaged in trade, namely, where they evade that provision of the law which requires them to exact no more than equal charges under the same circumstances. Complaints from persons engaged in coal and other mineral traffic have been urged before your Committee, to the effect that special favour is shown to particular classes of traffic to the prejudice of others, and in such cases, as some difference of circumstances can, of course, always be alleged, it is often a difficult question to decide whether that allegation can or cannot be sustained."

It is, perhaps, hardly necessary to add that the Lancashire and Cheshire Conference, and not the Parliamentary Committee of 1853, is responsible for the remarkable simile of "trustees of the public highways," as applied to railway companies. Trustees, the legal horn-books tell us, are permitted under no circumstances to make a profit out of their trust, and whatever may be the opinion of Lancashire and Cheshire traders in the year 1891, it is certain that a Parliamentary Committee in 1853 had no idea of calling upon a commercial undertaking to render its services to the public gratuitously. On the other point of the interference of the Executive Government, the words of the Report are as follows: "Your Committee think it would be possible in certain cases, where the general convenience of a district was in question, to raise the dispute between the public and the companies in such a shape as that the interposition of the Railway Department" [of the Board of Trade] "might be effectually exercised.... Since, however, this control, when actually applied, must be arbitrary in its nature and free from all technical fetters, and since the exercise of it will always affect the pecuniary interest of the company against which it is directed, your Committee feel that the occasion on which it should be exercised must be carefully defined. The constitution of the Executive Government, affording no means of enquiry in presence of the Bar or of the public, is unfavourable for the determination of such questions, and your Committee recommend that the fact of wrong having been done by the company should first be substantiated before a public tribunal."

The Report to the Lancashire and Cheshire Conference further proceeds: "In 1867 the Committee reports strongly on the undefined additional charges, levied under the head of terminals, and advise that the charges made to a trader should be based upon the cost of the services actually rendered to him. Another recommendation was that, whenever a railway company sought additional powers, the Board of Trade should be careful to obtain an equivalent in the reduction of the Company's maximum rate powers."

In this paragraph the word "Committee" is an obvious mistake. The Report of 1867 is that of the famous Royal Commission appointed in 1865, of which the Duke of Devonshire was chairman, which made a most exhaustive enquiry, not into petty details such as those with which the time of the Committees of 1881 and 1882 was so largely occupied, but into the great principles underlying all railway management, and whose opinions have been deservedly treated as of the utmost weight from that day to this. What the Commission said on the question of terminals we shall see presently. Let us here notice only the other two clauses of the Lancashire and Cheshire summary of its Report. The Commission advised nothing so ridiculous as "that the charges made to the trader should be based upon the cost of the services actually rendered to him." On the contrary, it devotes a large amount of space to exposing the foolishness of those who believe in the possibility of basing rates simply on cost of service. It is worth while quoting two or three passages to show what the Commission really did think on this matter:

"The power of granting special rates permits a development of trade which would not otherwise exist, and it is abundantly evident that a large portion of the trade of the country at the present time has been created by, and is continued on the faith of special rates. The conditions under which such rates are granted are so numerous that no special law could be framed to regulate them. It has indeed been suggested that it should be left to a Government board or other tribunal to arbitrate in cases where the traders asked for reduced rates and the railway companies refused them; but it must be recollected that the companies are entitled to derive a benefit from the rates assured to them by Parliament, and the course suggested would be tantamount to transferring this benefit from the companies themselves to individual traders, in order to add to the profits of their business, established with a full knowledge of the system of railway rates. . . . It is worthy of notice that under the Traffic Act the Court of Common Pleas has distinctly recognised the right of a company to charge unequal rates. . . .

"It has further been alleged against the system which permits of unequal rates that, in cases of traffic of the same nature carried on from two districts to a common market, the rates have been so favourable to one district as to shut out the other. Without entering into the question whether a uniform rate over the whole country would not operate effectually to shut out all the traffic now carried to distant markets, it is evident that there can be no mean course between allowing the railway companies to charge what rates they think expedient within a maximum limit, and requiring that a rate proportioned to distance, or at least an equal rate for equal distances, shall be adopted. . . . It is clear that the interest of the railway companies is intimately wrapped up in the prosperity of the districts which they serve. It is possible that railway companies may not always take enlightened views in managing their traffic; but even in this case the public obtains the fulfilment of the conditions upon which it has deemed it proper to concede the right of constructing the railway for the conveyance of passengers and goods, within the prescribed limit as to tolls and charges. . . .

"An important complaint has been made that the system of special rates opens the door to injustice between traders in the same district, if not to favouritism of individuals. It is, however, due to the railway companies to state that, whatever may have been the transactions of the companies at the commencement of railway enterprise, it is now generally regarded by them as impolitic to grant any preference tending to favour individual traders, and some managers disapprove of the transmission of large quantities of goods on more favourable terms than smaller quantities. The witnesses examined before us concur in the expression of their belief that there is no disposition on the part of the railway companies to afford personal preference for the special profit of individual traders; but that the distinctions in rates made by the railway companies are based upon considerations affecting the profit and interest of the railway companies themselves. . . . For the several reasons we have stated, we do not consider that it would be expedient, even if it were practicable, to adopt any legislation which would abolish the freedom railway companies enjoy, of charging what sum they deem expedient, within their maximum rates when properly defined, limited as that freedom is by the conditions of the Traffic Act."

Possibly, however, the phrase in the Lancashire and Cheshire Report, as to the "charges made to a trader," may be intended only to refer to charges made under the head of terminal expenses. There is a recommendation on this point in the Commission's report. The exact words are: "Each trader should be entitled to have a rate fixed according to the service to be rendered to him"—a very different thing, be it noted, from, "based upon the cost of the services actually rendered," as the Commission goes on to point out that the rate they propose to have fixed for each portion of the terminal accommodation and service is to be, not necessarily an actual charging rate, but only a maximum. The third recommendation was, according to the Lancashire and Cheshire version, that, "whenever a railway company sought additional powers the Board of Trade should be careful to obtain an equivalent in a reduction of the company's maximum rates powers." The exact words of the Committee, however, are: "When a railway company comes forward for additional powers, Parliament should take that opportunity of revising the maximum rates of conveyance, as it may appear reasonable." That in the year 1867 revision of a reasonable kind was not necessarily considered the same thing as reduction, may be proved—if it need proof—from a later paragraph, in which, after recommending that the Clearing House classification should be enacted by Parliament in substitution for the imperfect classifications of the old Acts, the Commission goes on to say that, "existing railway companies, in whose Acts of Parliament the classification is essentially different to the Clearing House classification, should apply for short Acts of Parliament to arrange their existing maximum tolls as nearly as possible to meet the new classification. It would still be competent for companies to vary their charges within the limits of the maximum prescribed by the special Acts."

The Joint Committee of 1872, according to the Lancashire and Cheshire history, "was heavily weighted with railway interest, and reported on the whole rather in favour of the railway companies." It is perhaps worth while to mention the names of these unjust judges; they are as follows: For the Lords: Lord Salisbury, Lord Ripon, Lord Cowper, Lord Derby, Lord Redesdale, Lord Belper. For the Commons: Lord Carlingford, then Mr. Chichester Fortescue, who acted as chairman, Mr., now Lord, Cross, Mr. Childers, Mr. Cave, Mr. Dodson, now Lord Monk Bretton, Mr. Ward Hunt. It must, however, be acknowledged that, as far as this Committee is concerned, the accuracy of the Lancashire and Cheshire version of its Report is, by comparison at least, remarkable. A trifling correction must still be made. According to the Lancashire and Cheshire document, "The Committee are not surprised that the conduct of the company should have given rise to discontent and suspicion. . . . And they warn them that a continuance of their policy of concealment and favouritism may become dangerous to them." The words of the Committee's report, after pointing out that the companies have declined to give the public information as to rates and charges which it has a right to obtain, are as follows: "It is not surprising that there should be discontent and suspicion, even *though there may be no real ground for it,* and if the companies should become rich and prosperous this discontent and suspicion may well be aggravated to such an extent as to become dangerous to them."

The last paragraph of the Lancashire and Cheshire Report with which we need deal is as follows: "The Committee of 1881-2 found that many complaints of excessive and unfair charges were well founded, and the Committee of 1888 advised the Irish railways that the high rates charged by them constituted an injury to themselves as well as to the public." Now with the Irish Report of 1888—the Report, once more, not of a Committee, but of a Royal Commission—the present writer does not propose to deal here; and this for two reasons. In the first place, this refutation is already over-long, though it was perhaps worth while to deal thoroughly with the statements on a single page of the Conference Report, in order to show how much reliance can be placed on the other statements of apparent fact, scattered over the 158 folio pages of a document which must be taken as the authoritative version of the traders' case; and, secondly, though the Irish railways could doubtless say a good deal in their own defence—though in particular they could urge, as everyone with any personal familiarity with them knows, that they have done much in the last two or three years to meet the public requirements—the present writer, for one, is half inclined to think that it was a mistake from the outset to imagine that the competitive commercial system of railway management, which was suitable for Great Britain, was naturally adapted for transplantation across the Channel. It may quite well be that the Irish public have failed to make their weight felt in the management of Irish railways; but from that fact, if it be a fact, surely no one will argue that the traders of Great Britain have had any difficulty in making their voices heard with quite sufficient loudness.

But as to the Committee of 1882, we must once more cite the precise words they used: "It is obvious that some of the present difficulties arise from want of knowledge. Some charges which appear *primâ facie* to be unequal and unjust turn out on explanation to be fair and reasonable. . . . Your Committee think that many of these differential charges afford substantial ground for complaint. But they do not consider it necessary to express an opinion as to how far these differential charges constitute undue preferences, because that is a point which the proper tribunal has full power to determine, and each case must be considered on its merits. . . . It may be assumed that some of the inequalities of charges complained of are to the advantage rather than to the disadvantage of the public. Where there is an undue preference the law now gives a remedy. A preference to be illegal and to furnish a reasonable course of complaint must be unjust. It is not unjust so long as it is the natural result of fair competition, and so long as equal rates are given for like services under like circumstances and for like quantities of merchandise. . . . No witnesses have appeared to complain of preferences given to individuals by railway companies as acts of private favour or partiality. . . . Your Committee, in conclusion, report that, on the whole of the evidence, they acquit the railway companies of any grave dereliction of their duty to the public."

Here, then, we may be content to leave ancient history and to come to modern facts. Of the points which were raised before the Board of Trade tribunal last year, and are likely to be contested once more ere many weeks are out, before a Parliamentary Committee at Westminster, there are four of sufficient importance to be dealt with separately. They are as follows: terminals, classification, maximum rates, and exceptional rates for full train-loads. On the first two of these four subjects it may be said that, in principle at least, the Board of Trade decision has been in favour of the railways; on the two latter points it has adopted the views put forward by their opponents.

The history of terminal charges is a striking instance how long a disputed question may remain open in this country before it is finally disposed of by legislative authority. At least as long ago as 1861 the matter was definitely brought to the attention of Parliament. The railway companies pointed out that their maxima had been fixed to cover the rates for conveyance from station to station only, as the early legislation had contemplated a state of things in which trucks would be loaded and unloaded, in premises not belonging to the railway company, and by persons not in their employ. With the full approval of the authorities of both Houses of Parliament, a model clause was drafted, enacting that "it shall be lawful for the company, acting as carriers, to make a reasonable terminal charge for the accommodation afforded, and service rendered by them in respect to any goods or minerals, other than the actual conveyance thereof along the railways."

This clause found its way into a single Act, an unimportant Irish one, and then there arose a violent agitation in the coal-trade, whose members were afraid that, if the companies got power, as it was proposed they should, to charge 9d. as a terminal at each end on coal, they would certainly exercise it. The clause was withdrawn by the promoters, but from that day to this Parliament and the public have been "affected with notice," as the equity lawyers put it, that the railways did not consider that anything more than conveyance of goods from point to point was required to be given by them in return for their maximum rate.

The Commission of 1867 considered the matter at great length. After going through the history it sums up as follows: "It would thus appear that, although there is great diversity in the clauses of this nature, Parliament now considers that the maximum rate should as a rule cover all the cost of conveyance and use of railways and sidings for receipt of trucks ready laden, but not the cost of loading, covering, or unloading. Thus, if a railway company provides special means for facilitating loading, covering, and unloading, or allow goods to remain in the station beyond a reasonable time, they would apparently, under their powers, and the intent of Parliament, be enabled to charge for such services. But, whatever Parliament may have intended, railway companies seem to have generally interpreted their Acts of Parliament as authorising them to make additional charges for the expense of constructing sidings as well as of working them."

The Commissioners were practical men, and they realised the disadvantage of this anomalous state of things, under which the legal right of the company to make charges, of whose practical propriety they were fully satisfied, depended upon the interpretation which might happen to be put upon the clause of an obsolete Act referring to a bygone condition of affairs. They thought, like the Chairmen of Committees in 1861, that it was time Parliament put the whole matter on a clear and unmistakable basis. "If," they say, "the company had to provide conveniences for the carts coming to the station to load or unload the trucks, and some service had to be performed or expense incurred by the companies in addition to the transit of the goods, we see no reason why the trader who requires this additional service should not pay an additional charge. . . . We therefore recommend that terminal charges should be defined to be charges for all services rendered by the railway company beyond conveyance from station to station."

The Joint Committee of 1872 took the conclusions and recommendations of the Royal Commission for granted. The only recommendation they made on their own account under this head was that the companies should be bound on demand to dissect their total rate so as to distinguish between mileage charge and terminals. The Committee of 1881 and 1882 went once more at enormous length into the whole question. After hearing evidence on the subject from the railway managers on the one side and from representatives of the traders on the other, they called in Sir Thomas Farrer, as the representative of the views of the Board of Trade, and this is what he told them: "I give no opinion upon the legal question; it is clear that the Acts of Parliament differ in their terms; but as a matter of equity and practice and of decisions by committees and commissions, and looking at the whole history of the case, I cannot doubt that it is an equitable thing that the railway companies should charge for what we call 'station terminals,' that is, for the use of stations and fixed appliances at stations.... My opinion is, that the railway companies ought distinctly to have the power to charge something which would compensate them for the enormous expense which they have been at in their stations.... Act upon Act has been passed with either a common clause or a special clause in it under which the companies have taken terminals, and on no occasion has Parliament put into an Act anything refusing to the companies, power of taking those terminals. Now, if there had been a very strong feeling against them, if it had been the intention that they should not charge terminals, I think Parliament would not have been content with a vague clause, but would have said distinctly that the company should do these station services for their mileage rates; but that has never been said, that I am aware." And once again: "The fact that these terminal charges have never during the whole of this period been decided to be illegal, is a very strong argument in favour of their legality."

As the result of all the evidence, the Committee appear to have thought that, while it was very evident that the companies had a statutory right to charge for services rendered in loading and unloading, it was questionable whether a charge for the use of stations could be justified except under a few special Acts. They appreciated, however, the fact that all the companies were really, from a practical point of view, in a similar position. They saw, too, the absurdity of the situation, in which a railway company, which loaded its trucks by hand at the cost of 1$s.$ a ton, could charge that shilling, while another company, which had provided hydraulic machinery, and so enabled the work to be done for 6$d.$, might have to pay the 6$d.$ out of its own pocket ; and accordingly they once more recommended that "the right of the railway companies to charge for station terminals should be recognised by Parliament." And now at length the Railway and Canal Traffic Act of 1888 may be considered to have definitely sanctioned them in the following words, referring to the manner in which new schedules of rates are to be drawn up by the company and settled by the Board of Trade : "In the determination of the terminal charges of any railway company, regard shall be had only to the expenditure reasonably necessary to provide the accommodation in respect of which such charges are made."

The legal history of the question need not detain

us for many moments. Fully to appreciate it, it would be necessary to go into intricate questions of decisions, now by the Court of Common Pleas, and again by the Railway Commission, and of appeals from the decision of this latter court, now by way of statement of a special case, and again by way of application for a writ of prohibition to the Queen's Bench Division of the High Court. But this labour would evidently be profitless, for more than one reason. In the first place, we may expect that, in the course of the current session, a new Act of Parliament will finally be passed making the whole of the legal learning on the question obsolete. And in the second place, the legal decisions could only turn on the construction of special Acts of Parliament; and though the position is in all cases identical in practice, the Acts of the different companies vary widely. This much alone need be stated here. The Railway Commission took a somewhat restricted view of the rights of the companies to charge for station accommodation. At length, in the year 1885, the well-known case of Hall *v.* The London, Brighton and South Coast Railway, which had been decided by the Railway Commission in favour of the plaintiff, was reviewed before the Queen's Bench Division of the High Court.

Under its Act the Company had the power to make an extra charge for "services incidental to the duty or business of a carrier." The question practically was what that phrase included. The judgment of the Court was to the following effect: "Our answer is, that the providing of station accommodation and work of the general nature indicated to us by the Railway Commissioners" [*i.e.* weighing, packing, cartage, watching, labelling, and use of sidings] "appear to us to be capable of falling under the definition of 'services incidental to the duty or business of a carrier,' and *primâ facie* to do so." Since the decision in Hall's case, the question has again been raised more than once. According to the traders, the railway companies were so surprised at their success that they have not ventured to contest the matter again, and have settled two County Court actions on terms of paying back with costs the sum alleged to be overcharged. The railway lawyers, on the other hand, say that the traders had an opportunity, which for technical reasons was not available to them in Hall's case, of obtaining the decision, not only of the Queen's Bench Division but of the Court of Appeal and the House of Lords, in the contemporary case of Kempson *v.* The Great Western Railway, and that they did not dare to do so.

What is more to the point, however, is the fact that in February last the whole question was raised once more before the Railway Commission, now presided over by Mr. Justice Wills, the judge who in the case of Hall *v.* The Brighton Railway delivered the leading judgment of the Queen's Bench. The terminal clause under discussion was identical with that in Hall's case, and it is only necessary to quote half a dozen lines from Mr. Justice Wills's judgment: "I think that this case on this point is practically governed by the case of Hall *v.* The Brighton Railway Company, and I go further and say that, if I had heard of it for the first time to-day, I should myself have arrived without hesitation at the conclusion which I have now indicated."

It should, however, be added that Mr. Price—the Commissioner who is, in the words of the Act of 1873, " of experience in railway business "—delivered judgment to the following effect: "With respect to the point of the allowance made to railway companies in consideration of their performing the duty of carriers, I am decidedly of opinion now that they are fairly entitled to receive remuneration for station accommodation. That may seem to be inconsistent with the fact that I concurred in the judgment in Hall's case, which refused remuneration for station accommodation; but my difficulty was not at all as to what was the intention of Parliament, but the language of the proviso itself did not seem to me to be capable of being so construed as to let in the station itself. . . . It seemed to me that this charge could only be authorised in respect to some particular service performed, but not in respect of providing the place, yard, warehouse, siding, or whatever it may be. . . . I always have believed that Parliament did intend to grant something for the use of stations at the time it gave the right and power to railway companies to become carriers themselves." Mr. Price went on to say that the Superior Court having decided that the provision of station accommodation might be included under the phrase, " performing services," he had " no further difficulty in coming to the conclusion that additional remuneration should be given to railway companies in consideration of their performing duties which they have only been called upon to perform since they became carriers."

On this, Mr. Justice Wills added the following: "I may say with regard to the matter that Mr. Commissioner Price has just referred to, namely, as to whether the words 'services performed' would include the provision of station accommodation, I do not think that in the Queen's Bench Division, when that matter was under consideration, any of us had any doubt that those words were quite capable of extending to that. To give a man a roof over his head is as much performing him a service as giving him a dinner." Here, then, the law now stands. Sowerby's case is, it is understood, to be taken to the Court of Appeal;[2] provided, that is, it can be got there in time to influence the decision of Parliament on the Provisional Orders which the Board of Trade have drawn up, in which a charge for station terminals is definitely fixed.

But it is high time to inquire what the Board of Trade's Provisional Order proposes. Broadly, it authorises a station terminal of 3*d.* per ton at each end for coal, ironstone, and manure; 6*d.* or 1*s.*, as the case may be, for other consignments which go in truck-loads; and 1*s.* 6*d.* in the case of ordinary merchandise traffic. In addition it sanctions service terminals, rising according to class, from 8*d.* to 4*s.*, and divided under four heads of loading, unloading, covering, and uncovering, with a maximum fixed for each of the four. Beyond this, once more, come extra services, of which the collection and

[2] Unanimously decided by the Court of Appeal in favour of the Railway Company, March 20, 1891.

delivery of goods is much the most important, for which the companies are still left to make "such charge as is reasonable," with a provision that in case of dispute the Board of Trade may arbitrate.

The principle, therefore, of terminal charges in addition to the maximum mileage rate is fully admitted. The only question is as to the amount. Now at the outset one fact is obvious. If a maximum for each individual service is to be fixed separately, the total of all these maxima is bound in common justice to be higher than where a single maximum is fixed for the whole of the services lumped together. If words have any meaning, a maximum charge means, not the average, but the highest possible charge. In other words, the maximum must be so placed as to leave, above the average standard, room for exceptionally high charges under certain circumstances, to balance exceptionally low charges under certain others. Maximum powers are not actual charges. The charges as a whole must be made up by averaging each individual charge from the highest to the lowest; and if the new maximum line is so drawn as to cut off the tops of the highest charges, these latter must of course henceforward be reduced. Now there is no question that if a company, for example, loads a ton of furniture in London, and unloads it again, say, at Hatfield, its actual costs out of pocket for the terminal services amount to more than 4*s.* This, however, is the maximum which the Board of Trade proposes to allow for the service. It is impossible to suppose that the Board of Trade consider heads of families changing their residences to have a claim on railway shareholders for charitable contributions towards the expenses of removal. We must therefore assume that the railway company is expected to make up its loss on the furniture by an extra profit on goods which are less expensive to handle. Is this reasonable? Are not the high-class goods—those whose weight is small in proportion to their bulk and value—precisely those which are best able to pay their own expenses in full? Is it fair that they should call upon bales of cotton, or carpets and other easily handled goods for a grant-in-aid? But this is what must in effect be done, if maxima, such as have been fixed by the Board of Trade, are in fact enacted by Parliament.

The truth is, as we shall see more fully when we come to consider the new maximum schedules of rates themselves, the attempt to make maxima into actual charging schedules must always break down. The only logical position of a maximum is sufficiently above the highest point actually and justifiably reached in practice to leave a margin for contingencies that are reasonably possible. Anything short of this means that the public authority, while refusing to accept the responsibility of fixing actual individual rates, asserts in general terms that some of the rates fixed by a railway company are excessive, merely on the ground that other rates, in circumstances which at the first glance seem similar, are lower; and then goes on to call upon the railway company to remove burdens from the shoulders which the company believes best able to bear them on to other shoulders which the company considers less able to do so.

It must of course be frankly admitted that, if terminals were fixed on a scale such as is here advocated, they could be of little or no use in ordinary cases in protecting individual members of the public against possible extortion—whether wilful or only stupid, is here beside the question—on the part of the companies. If maxima were fixed at a point high enough to clear the tops of the highest legitimate rates, unquestionably they would be so high that between the lowest competitive rate and the Parliamentary limit there might be that "margin of 100 per cent." which so offends Sir John Harwood; unquestionably traders would still be compelled—to adopt the words of another of their prominent champions — to "sue for reductions of rate *in formâ pauperis,*" instead of securing them by statutory enactment. That, however, is unfortunately unavoidable in this world. The omnipotence of Parliament does not extend to enabling the British public to secure simultaneously the advantages of freedom and those of State control. The question for decision is, Which of the two inconsistent policies offers the greater prospect of advantage?

The present writer, for one, is convinced that the railway history of this country and the United States on the one hand, and of the Continent on the other, proves that on the whole the advantages of freedom are greater than the advantages of State control. But let us suppose that this opinion is wrong, let us admit that the English railways have so abused their freedom that it is necessary they should be subjected to a more stringent control. Then at least let the public

realise that the result must be, that B will be levelled up to A, not that A will be levelled down to B; that the highest rates, hitherto imposed upon traffic which could bear it best, will in future be reduced, and the reduction spread, here a little and there a little, over a large field of traffic that can bear it less well; that, broadly speaking, the general average of rates will be raised and not reduced. But then, when the public, profoundly disappointed at the result of this new process of State regulation from which so much benefit was expected—benefit which was to be put into one man's pocket without being taken out of the pocket of any of his neighbours—when the public goes one stage farther, and demands, as it in all probability will do before many years are out, that the railways shall be taken over by the State altogether, let it be remembered that the authors of this revolution were really those who, while professing their inability to fix actual rates, have yet in practice insisted on fixing a great many, at the same time washing their hands of all the responsibility for the results.

In truth, if ever there was a time when an attempt to cut down the charges for terminals was inappropriate, that time is the present. If we look to America, we see it admitted that the terminal service in New York rendered to a ton of corn passed through an elevator at the minimum of cost, is worth as much as the haulage over 250 miles of road; we see that for the 90 miles between New York and Philadelphia the rates are two-fifths of those charged for the 900 miles between New York and Chicago;

we find the President of the Pennsylvania Railway asserting that the rate received for a haul of 70 miles out of Philadelphia does no more than cover the cost of handling in that city. We can read the opinion of the leading American professional journal, to the effect that, "with the constant cheapening of movement expenses, charges for terminal handling form every year a larger portion of the whole."

We find, further, that disinterested American critics fully appreciate the force of the English companies' claim. Professor Hadley, writing on the question before the decision in the case of Hall *v.* The Brighton Railway, uses these words: "While the train expenses per ton moved have decreased enormously, the station expenses have on the whole risen; in some cases they have risen enormously. . . . The law, as it stands, seems to favour the shipper; but it also seems likely that the railroads can justify their action" [in charging station terminals] "on equitable business principles. If so, business principles are likely to prove mightier than a half-obsolete regulation in a charter." We know too the position of our English lines at this moment. There is hardly one whose goods stations, in the great towns at least, are not too small already for the work they have to do. What importance the English merchant attaches to speed we have already seen. And if the speed, which has characterised the English goods service in the past, is to be maintained, it means the expenditure ere long of millions of capital on new space and new machinery, and of thousands of pounds of income on the payment of additional hands. Yet this is the time chosen to forbid the companies to charge, in not a few cases, their actual out-of-pocket costs.

It is not as if an Act of Parliament were the only protection which the public enjoyed. They have two other and practically far more efficient protections already. As has been pointed out in an earlier chapter, there is the traffic which cannot, and there is the traffic which will not, pay the full rate, whether that rate be charged under the name of mileage or terminal. From half to three-quarters of the total traffic of the country is carried at special rates already—rates which, as a rule, are far below what the railway companies will still be authorised to charge for mileage alone. To the whole of this traffic maximum terminals can offer no protection. Then, again, there is the short-distance traffic, which, if full terminals were charged, would simply go by road. As we have seen, the German Government, having pledged itself to an unnatural uniformity of terminal charge, was in practice compelled to fix that charge at a point which did not pay expenses, and to recoup itself afterwards by increasing the mileage rate, as on any other terms it would have lost the short distance traffic altogether.

When, therefore, for example, the Lancashire and Cheshire Conference tells a long and doleful tale of a farmer in the outskirts of Manchester, who might conceivably find himself called upon to pay a terminal of 5*s.* on 2 tons of turnips, the answer is simply, that the protection to the farmer is not an Act of Parliament, but an adjacent turnpike. It is conceivable that the accommodation rendered to the farmer, including full interest on capital, and out-of-pocket expenses for labour, may amount to something like the sum of 5*s.*; but the railways cannot possibly attempt to charge it. Their limit upwards is the sum which the service they render is worth to the farmer, and downwards their actual additional expenses for dealing with this additional piece of traffic. The real question for them is whether they can afford to touch the traffic at all at the price which the farmer will consent to pay; and that is a question which turns mainly on the point whether or no they have got a sufficient supply of better-paying traffic to utilise their station accommodation to its full capacity.

There is another point which is strongly pressed in the Lancashire and Cheshire Report, namely, that the companies provide terminal accommodation which is not needed, and then debit the traders with the interest on their wasted capital. To this, once more, the answer is, that the business of a railway must be looked at as a whole. If a railway company, for example, buys the land for its stations on favourable terms, or if, on the other hand, it lays out its money in the most unbusinesslike manner, in each case its income depends upon what the public as a whole is prepared to pay for the accommodation that is provided. If, on the whole, its stations are well placed and the land well bought, it may expect a satisfactory return for its outlay; if not, not. But to claim that A, whose convenience leads him to use a cheap station, is to be given his terminal accommodation at a low rate, and that B, whose station happens to be dear, is to pay five times as much, is simply to say that no new station is ever to be provided in any town. For it is obvious that, till the public learn to use a new station, its working expenses, per ton dealt with, must necessarily be heavy; and then, putting the point the other way round, if the public is to be called on to pay these heavy working expenses in full, it will never begin to patronize the new station.

One can only repeat once more the old hotel simile. A member of the Lancashire and Cheshire Conference, let us say, goes down to Bournemouth for a few days holiday. The landlord of the hotel, whose customers are mainly invalids, has gone to great expense in building a winter-garden as a promenade for his guests in rough weather, and his charges are accordingly on a high scale. Our Lancashire friend, however, is in robust health, and prefers to battle against the east wind on the cliff. The landlord has, he thinks, made a mistake; winter-gardens are not wanted; he must refuse to pay his bill unless a handsome rebate is given him; let those who want the winter-garden pay an extra 10s. every time they enter it. Would such a contention hold water for a moment?[3]

[3] On p. 49 of the Lancashire and Cheshire Report, there is an amusing misunderstanding. At the recent Board of Trade inquiry, the North Western put in figures showing the actual expenditure during the year 1887 for terminal purposes at 18 of their stations, which were described by the company as being typical. The cost worked out to 470,017*l*., being at the average rate of 3*s*. 2¾*d*. per ton. Upon this the Lancashire and Cheshire Report points out that there are about 720 stations on the London and North Western. If therefore these 18 stations are representative, "then the total amount receivable at these 18 stations multiplied by $\frac{720}{18}$ should show the total amount of terminals receivable under the new proposals. ... The annual cost, that is, would amount to 18,800,680*l*.,

But let us leave terminals, and come to another point, which was much pressed before the recent Board of Trade inquiry, that of classification. It would perhaps be kind to say as little as possible about the constructive proposals of the traders under this head. There was a suggestion put forward for a brand-new classification, to contain 40 classes, more

while at present the total revenue of the company from merchandise traffic, conveyance and terminals together, yields less than 4,000,000*l.*" The Report triumphantly adds, "It is obvious therefore that, if these stations are representative at all, they are so only in a small degree." It is surely obvious also that the Conference has discovered a mare's nest. The North Western officials never claimed that Broad Street and Camden were typical of Pinner in reference to the quantity of goods dealt with, nor that Waterloo Street, Liverpool, was typical of Speke or Halebank. What they did claim was that the 18 stations given, including some of the largest, some of the smallest, and some middle-sized, gave a fair idea of the work of the system as a whole, and enabled the average cost per ton to be estimated for the entire line. On this basis it would appear as though interest on the cost of terminal accommodation at 5 per cent., *plus* terminal expenses for wages, &c., would amount on the 8,000,000 tons of merchandise carried to, in round figures, 2,600,000*l.*, or, allowing for the case in which the goods came off or went on to another line, and so only one terminal service was rendered, say, 2,250,000*l.* It may perhaps be said that this is inconceivable, considering that the whole goods revenue was a good deal under 4,000,000*l.* For my own part, I fail to see any impossibility in the matter. No figures, as far as I am aware, have ever been published to show the capital cost of the stations as distinguished from the share of the cost of the running lines fairly attributable to goods, or the expenditure out of income on station work as distinguished from train movement; but, for my own part, I should be surprised if the former were not found to exceed the latter. What these figures do show unquestionably is that the maximum terminal allowances of the Provisional Order are insufficient. But that everyone must have known beforehand. Their only possible justification is the historical one that it has been the custom to attribute the great bulk of the charge to the mileage rate; and that, therefore, in order not to break too violently with the past, and also not to make too sharp a contrast between the treatment of merchandise upon the one hand, and on the other of passengers who have never paid terminals, and minerals, where the terminal is only a small portion of the cost, the mileage rate has been left so far above the actual movement expenses as to afford compensation for the inadequacy of the terminal maximum.

or less. Lord Balfour and Mr. Courtenay Boyle did not take very much notice of the suggestion, and it was not pressed. Its main interest is perhaps as showing that the traders' grievances are not quite as urgent as they are claimed to be. For this much at least is certain, that, whether the plan suggested be a good one or a bad—and if railways were likely to be introduced to compete with the canals in Mars, it is quite possible that it might be a good one—the necessary work of rearranging, not merely the classification itself and the eight classes of goods dependent on it, but the hundred million special rates—which could not be left untouched if the classification were revolutionized—with the subsequent necessity of passing through both Houses of Parliament Acts to reconstruct the maximum scale of rates to fit the new classification, would render it impossible to bring the Railway and Canal Traffic Act of 1888 into practical operation till, at the very earliest, the dawn of the twentieth century.

But the traders had another string to their bow. In flat contradiction to the plain words of the Act of Parliament, they insisted that the new classification, which the Act required to be drawn up in substitution for the rudimentary classifications contained in the original Acts of Parliament, should be permanently binding upon the railways, as fixing a standard which they not only could not advance, but which they were likewise to be forbidden to lower. Their reason was explained to be, that so the power of the companies to make arbitrary rates would be curbed. And so far they were no doubt correct. But, as has been pointed out more than once already, even a trader cannot both eat his cake and have it. Fixed rates mean high rates, and the only possible way to obtain low rates is to leave to somebody an arbitrary power of reduction. This somebody may be a State official, if the State will take possession of the railway. That, if railways are allowed to continue as private commercial enterprises, it cannot be a State official, but must be a servant of the trading corporation, has been accepted either as proved, or as too self-evident to need demonstration, by every Parliamentary Committee which has ever considered the question.

The belief that a fixed and permanent classification—"cast-iron," as it came to be called before the Board of Trade tribunal—is possible, seems to show singular ignorance of the railway experience of other countries. Even in Germany, where, if anywhere, simplicity and fixity are accounted of more importance than cheapness, no attempt has been made to maintain a cast-iron classification. On the contrary, in a recent number of the *Archiv für Eisenbahnwesen*, the official organ of the Prussian Minister of Public Works, it is expressly stated that concessions of lower rates have been generally given by reducing articles from one class of the classification to a lower one. As for America, the Inter-State Commerce Commission speaks out on the subject in no uncertain sound. In its first Report the Commission declares: "Conditions change from month to month; the classification cannot be permanently the same, but must be subject to modification on the same grounds on which it was originally made." Again, in a case usually known as the "Car-loads and

Less-than-Car-loads Case," decided in March 1890, the Commissioners laid down that : " A general rule that shall be equitable to all is exceedingly desirable, but in the conflicts of interests is difficult, if not impossible, to apply, and in the frequently changing conditions of commerce, no rule of classification or rates can have an assurance of permanent or absolute equity. Classification is not yet an applied science founded on correct principles and governed by just and consistent laws. It is still in process of growth and development, and the best traffic experts are required to elaborate a system. . . . Except for the rigid methods of Classification Committees and the lack of lawful authority, more rapid and more numerous improvements would doubtless be made."

So much for the cast-iron classification which the traders wanted. Now for what the Board of Trade Provisional Order proposes to give them. It will be, it is understood, a maximum classification, above which the companies cannot go, but from which they may move downwards as far as they please. It must be confessed that, for some time to come, they are hardly likely to make any great strides in the latter direction. The English Clearing House Classification has long been a very low one. A very small portion of the traffic is in the two highest classes. Mr. Grierson's book points out that common paint, for instance, is placed by three of the great French companies in the highest class. In the English Classification it is in the lowest but one. Four French companies put "china in casks or crates" in the highest class, two more in the highest but one ; the English railways, on the other hand, put it in the lowest but one. The French Classification, in fact, is based on the idea that every article not specially reduced is to be charged in the highest class.

The contrast, however, with America is still more startling. That contrast can be best shown by an illustration. Mr. Grierson worked out for the Committee of 1881 the percentage of traffic in the different classes dealt with in the course of a week at ninety Great Western stations. It was as follows:

| Class 5 | . . 2·52 | Class 3 | . . 14·94 | Class 1 | . . 46·88 |
| ,, 4 | . . 6·76 | ,, 2 | . . 28·94 | | |

Quite recently the Great Northern has worked out some similar figures, giving, however, this time, not only the percentage of tonnage in each class, but also the percentage of earnings attributable to it:

	Percentage of tonnage.	Percentage of earnings in £ sterling.		Percentage of tonnage.	Percentage of earnings in £ sterling.
Class 5 . .	3¾	. . 7½	Class 2 . .	30½	. . 30
,, 4 . .	7¼	. . 12½	,, 1 . .	34¾	. . 21
,, 3 . .	23¾	. . 29			

Now compare this state of things with that in America, it being premised that in America, as on the Continent, the classes run in the opposite way to ours, and that consequently their first class is the highest, corresponding to our fifth. Out of about 4,000 descriptions in the Official Classification, the percentage in the different classes is as follows:

| Class 1 | . . 24·59 | Class 3 | . . 16·94 | Class 5 | . . 22·13 |
| ,, 2 | . . 12·11 | ,, 4 | . . 19·41 | ,, 6 | . . 4·82 |

It should be added that of the 1,000 descriptions set down as in the highest class a considerable number pay not merely first-class rate, but 1½, 2, 3, and even 4 times that rate; so that though the lowest class of article pays only 10*s.* between New York and Philadelphia, which we should consider a fairly low rate for 90 miles for merchandise, the highest class pays 92*s.*, which we should look upon as something absolutely inconceivable. And let it not be supposed that traffic does not really go at these high rates. The following table shows the percentage of tonnage of the different classes passing in one month from New York to Chicago:

| Class 1 . . . 22·2 | Class 3 . . . 12·8 | Class 5 . . . 7·8 |
| ,, 2 . . . 6·9 | ,, 4 . . . 13 | ,, 6 . . . 37·3 |

This being the state of affairs, the Board of Trade intervenes. And what does it do? Taking as a basis for its work the Clearing House Classification, it makes sweeping reductions with no corresponding advances. For example, it brings down the bulk of the heavy iron trade, plates, girders, and so forth, one class, and the light iron manufactures of Birmingham one class also. Broadly speaking, the new statutory classification of the Provisional Orders is markedly below the actual working classification which has been in use hitherto. Once more, that is to say, the statutory maxima are fixed lower than the existing charges.

Assuming, therefore—which, in so many words at least, is not denied—that the railway companies have a right to receive from their undertaking their present not extortionate profit of 4¼ per cent., we are face to face with this position of things, that terminal charges have been reduced—not probably below, or at least much below the average cost, but below the figure which covers the cost of the more expensive traffic. The railways have certainly got no margin there. The classification likewise has been brought down to a point considerably below that at present enforced for charging purposes. Not only is there no margin there, but the new classification of itself will imply a reduction of rates. Surely, if the balance is to be held fairly between the railways, which naturally first consider at what price they can afford to give their services, and the traders, who, equally naturally, are seeking to obtain those services at the lowest possible price, the Board of Trade might be expected at least to give the companies, in return for reductions under the head of terminals and classification, a substantial margin of powers in the shape of mileage charges. What it has actually done we shall see in the next chapter.

CHAPTER XII

THE BOARD OF TRADE PROVISIONAL ORDERS

BEFORE coming to the important question of new maximum rates, it will be well to say a word or two on a principle which the Board of Trade proposes to introduce generally into English railway practice—that, namely, of reduced rates for train-loads of minerals. In one way it may seem a small matter. Traders as a rule do not send a train-load, unless it be, perhaps, of coal for shipment in Durham or South Wales. Still, not only is the principle one of importance, but, in view of the immense advantage the Provisional Order proposes to confer on the man who does send them, it is likely that train-loads will be much more frequent in the future.

At the outset one thing is obvious. Hitherto, except in the few cases where special rebates for large quantities may still be in force as the result of agreements made in the early days of railways, the company has obtained any advantage of economy which there may be in dealing with full loads, and *pro tanto* it has been in a position to give better terms to the small man. If in the future the economy is to enure to the benefit, not of the railway company, but of the wholesale dealer himself, it is evidently only fair that the company should be allowed to raise proportionately the price for the retail business; otherwise it is simply a case of "heads you win, tails we lose."[1]

This, however, the Board of Trade has by no means done. They have reduced the coal rates in various parts of the country, for lots under 10 tons, to a point below the charges which are being made at present, and have provided a further reduction for lots of 10 tons, and yet another for train-loads of 250 tons. Let us see how the new departure is likely to work out in a particular instance. The rate in force

---

[1] An amusing instance of how it is possible to misunderstand this somewhat obvious fact will be found in Professor Hunter's book on railway rates (p. 97): "It would appear as if, excluding the mineral class, the average load of an 8- or 10-ton waggon did not exceed 2 tons. Such a margin affords an opportunity of giving a rate not less remunerative to the company than the rates now charged, but which, measured by the ton, would only be a fraction of the present rates. Thus, if the average rate of the goods is $2d.$ per ton per mile, and only two tons are carried, the earnings are $4d.$ per truck. If $4d.$ were fixed for the truck-rate, a trader who could load up to 8 tons would have the rate reduced from $2d.$ to $\tfrac{1}{2}d.$ per ton per mile. Even if the truck-rate were made $6d.$ per mile, the trader would still then get his goods carried at $\tfrac{3}{4}d.$ per ton per mile instead of $2d.$" Surely one moment's consideration will show Mr. Hunter that the existing average of 2 tons is made up of one waggon at $3\tfrac{1}{2}$ tons, and another waggon at 10 cwt. If the $3\tfrac{1}{2}$ tons are to be got into a truck at a truck-load rate, independently of weight, the railway company must either go into bankruptcy, or increase very largely the charges which it at present levies on the small consignments. In one word, *ex nihilo nihil fit.* The concession to the larger trader cannot fall from heaven, and therefore must come either out of the pocket of the railway company or out of that of his small competitor. There is no third alternative; for if the railway companies could load their trucks heavier while maintaining their existing standard of service, we may be sure that they would have done so in their own interest ere now. The point is one of such importance, and of so elementary a nature, that it is constantly present to the mind, not only of railway managers, but of every foreman of a goods-shed all over the country.

at this moment for coal from Wigan to London is 7s. 2d. per ton. The Provisional Order prescribes 7s. 9d. as the maximum for 10-ton consignments, and 6s. 8d. for train-loads. No one, therefore, can fairly blame the North Western if it increases the 10-ton rate in order to balance its loss on the train-loads. Even supposing it does not do so, there is a difference of sixpence per ton in the cost of carriage to the big man as compared with his smaller rival.

Now here, as it seems to me, the Board of Trade is in a dilemma. Either the profits of the coal trade are so enormous that in spite of this sixpence-a-ton handicap the little man can still continue to hold his own—in which case, surely, the trader has small right to sue *in formâ pauperis* for compulsory contributions out of the pocket of the 4¼ per cent. railway shareholder—or else—which is much more probably the case—the difference in rate, which amounts to something like 7 or 8 per cent. of the average value of the coal at the pit's mouth, will enable the big man who can deal in train-loads to drive the small master out of the trade altogether. That the London public will get even the most fractional share of the sixpence is a doctrine doubtless very full of comfort, but one which, in face of their recent experience as to the abolition of the coal-dues, not of 6d. but of 1s. 1d., they can hardly be expected to treat seriously.

The small men having been successfully put out of the way, the next stage, obviously, is an agreement among the few big traders left to keep up prices. For is it not an axiom—it is certainly quoted against the railway companies as though it were—that where combination is possible competition is impossible? Moreover, precedents have been set very recently, not only elsewhere but in this country, by the Salt Union, the Steel Rail Union, and numbers more. And salt-rings and their like, be it remembered, have no maximum rates fixed for them by Act of Parliament, and are not subject to be taken before the Railway Commission if they treat any one of their customers a shade better or a fraction worse than his neighbours. Had the author of the disastrous train-load clause [2]—disastrous for the public interest at least, for it is very questionable whether in the long run it will injure the railways, who will get a good deal of their "marshalling" done gratis—known what train-load rates have led to in America, it is tolerably certain no attempt would have been made to introduce them here.

The exact case of what were practically train-load rates for coal came before the United States Inter-State Commerce Commission shortly after its appointment. A railway company had given a customer, in consideration of a guarantee to consign not less than 30,000 tons *per annum*—which, be it observed, is only 5 train-loads of 250 tons per fortnight—a rebate of 5*d*. per ton; and this is what the Commission said in its judgment: "A discrimination, such as the offer and its acceptance by one or more dealers would create, must have a necessary tendency to destroy the business of small dealers. Under the evidence in the case, it appears almost

[2] Sir Bernhard Samuelson appears to be entitled to claim this distinction.

certain that this destruction must result, the margin for profit on wholesale dealings in coal being very small. The discrimination is therefore necessarily unjust within the meaning of the law. It cannot be supported by the circumstance that the offer is open to all; although made to all it is not possible that all should accept. . . . A railroad company has no right by any discrimination not grounded in reason to put any single dealer, whether a large dealer or a small dealer, to any such destructive disadvantage."

In speaking like this, an American speaks from practical experience. Most Englishmen have heard of the Standard Oil Company, probably the largest and best-organised monopoly in the world, which dictates the price of petroleum not only in the United States but throughout the length and breadth of the habitable globe from Hammerfest to Sydney. But the Americans know how the Standard Oil Company attained its present position. It began by obtaining rebates from the railway companies on the ground of the magnitude of the traffic it consigned. But it ended before very long in compelling the railway companies to pay it a rebate, not only on all the traffic which they carried for the Standard, but also on all the traffic which they carried for its competitors. The exact same thing happened in the cattle trade from Chicago to the Atlantic Coast. It was proved before the Hepburn Committee of New York State that a single firm received from the railways, not only an advantage in freight equal to an ordinary business profit on all the live-stock that it could ship, but an income from all the business that its rivals could transact.

No doubt it may be answered that these rebates were secret, and not, as is here proposed, public and statutory. This is of course true, and it is true also that the honesty of railway management is not so far above suspicion in America as is fortunately the case here. But for all that, if anyone wishes to see personal discriminations introduced into this country, the best possible way of effecting his object is to persuade the Legislature itself to introduce the thin edge of the wedge. If a railway company of its own motion were to propose to give advantages to its big customers in consideration of the wholesale character of their dealings, there might be something to be said, though even then the State would be abundantly justified in interfering as the guardian of the public interest; but for the State deliberately to throw in its weight as a providence on the side of the big battalions, in order to help a great capitalist stamp out the opposition of his smaller rivals, who even now are competing at quite sufficient disadvantages—this is surely a proposal which needs only to be understood by the House of Commons in order to ensure its prompt and definite rejection.

But after all, as was said above, the question of train-load rates is but a small matter by the side of the new schedules of maximum rates. As this is a question of vital importance to the entire country, involving as it does not only the interests of the railway companies, with their 870,000,000*l.* of capital, and their 400,000 shareholders, who, to quote George Stephenson once more, have made the railways which have made the country, but the interests of every customer—in other words, of every inhabitant of the British Isles—it will be necessary for us to deal with the subject at some length.

"Every careful student of the question," says Professor Hadley in the book from which we have already so often quoted,[3] "from Morrison in 1836 down to the Committees of 1872 and 1882, has come to the conclusion that fixed maxima are of next to no use in preventing extortion." In an earlier chapter of his work, dealing with railroad legislation in the United States, Professor Hadley tells the story of the attempts which have been made to fix maximum rates *ab extra* in America. Commissions appointed by the Legislatures have, he says, "been fairly successful in fixing rates in some of the Southern States." "It is a little hard," he writes, "to say just what has enabled them to succeed. One thing is, that the rates in general are so high as to leave them a wide margin above operating expenses in which to make their changes. . . . The South Carolina legistion of 1883 was fully as stringent as that of Georgia; but some of its strictest provisions were repealed after one year's trial. The legislation of Alabama has never gone quite so far as that of Georgia. In Tennessee a recent adverse decision of the courts has deprived the enactment of much of its force. In Georgia itself a reaction against excessive regulation seems to be in progress."

But more interesting and more instructive is the

[3] *Railroad Transportation*, chap ix., on "English Railroad Legislation," p. 178.

history of the Western States and the Granger Laws. The Legislature of Wisconsin "fixed, by the so-called 'Potter Law,' the rates on different classes of roads at figures which proved quite unremunerative. The railroads made vain attempts to contest these regulations in the courts. They were defeated again and again, and finally, in 1877, the Supreme Court of the United States sustained the constitutionality of the Granger Laws. But a more powerful force than the authority of the courts was working against the Granger system of regulation. The laws of trade could not be violated with impunity. The law reducing railroad rates to the basis which competitive points enjoyed left nothing to pay fixed charges. In the second year of its operation, no Wisconsin road paid a dividend, only four paid interest on their bonds. Railroad construction had come to a standstill. Even the facilities on existing roads could not be kept up. Foreign capital refused to invest in Wisconsin; the development of the State was sharply checked; the very men who had most favoured the law found themselves heavy losers. These points were plain to everyone. They formed the theme of the Governor's message at the beginning of 1876. The very men who passed the law in 1874 hurriedly repealed it after two years' trial. In other States, the laws either were repealed, as in Iowa, or were sparingly and cautiously enforced. By the time the Supreme Court published the Granger decisions the fight had been settled, not by constitutional limitations but by industrial ones."

The reason why maxima fixed for railway companies *ab extra* can escape being largely injurious, only on condition of being so high as to be practically inoperative, is fully explained by Professor Hadley, and has been dealt with also in the earlier chapters of the present work. Briefly, it may be put as follows: No rate, practically speaking, is high *per se*. The Liverpool bullion rate, for instance, of which we have already spoken, is immeasurably lower than the rate at which the Bank of England could send bullion to Liverpool by any other means than railway carriage. Extortion, where it exists, is not absolute but merely relative. The new Provisional Order, let us say, fixes 5*s*. 6*d*. as the maximum for coal to London from Derbyshire, and 7*s*. 6*d*. as the maximum from Lancashire or the West Riding. But supposing the railway companies were to reduce the actual rate from Lancashire to 6*s*. 6*d*., and bring down the Derbyshire rate to 3*s*. 6*d*., they would simply put an absolute stop to the entire trade from Lancashire to London. Relatively to the Derbyshire rate, the Wigan rate would have become extortionate, yet the railway companies would have actually made a reduction of 1*s*. below their powers. Obviously, in a case like this, the protection of fixed maxima is utterly illusory.

But there is more than this. There are, as we have seen, two classes of traffic. There is the traffic which only may, and there is the traffic which must, use the railways. Three-fifths of the traffic of the United Kingdom has, according to the Report of 1872, its maximum fixed, not by Act of Parliament, but by the laws of nature and the fact that Great Britain is an island. This portion not only needs no protection, but is actually in most cases paying less than what in the abstract might be called its fair rates already. Yet the companies cannot raise these rates. To do so would be only to drive the traffic to the alternative route, and to sacrifice the half-loaf, which they at present obtain. As for the remaining two-fifths, a great deal of it is low-class traffic, which, once more, would stop at home altogether, if it were called upon to pay full rates, and a good deal of the rest is local distributive traffic on small branch lines, which, as we have seen already, is never asked even now to pay at the rate which it would have to pay, if the companies tried to make the earnings of the branch compensate for its expenses.

We are shut down therefore to this dilemma: either the maximum must be fixed so high as to be practically protective to almost nobody, for the railway companies find it in their own interest in nine cases out of ten to go below it, or else it is brought down to the point where it cuts off the tops of charges actually made for services which not unfrequently, even on cost-of-service principles, are worth more than is charged for them. In other words, a railway company estimates that a service to A costs it—allowing for movement expenses, fixed charges, and a full share of interest on capital—say, 1*l*. It calculates, however, that, as A cannot afford to pay the whole 1*l*., everybody's interest will be served by reducing the charge to 15*s*. Then the State steps in and says, "No. You perform what looks like the same service to other people for 7*s*. 6*d*. The charge shall, therefore, be only 12*s*. 6*d*. You may either go without the 2*s*. 6*d*. altogether, or get it out of the pockets of B, C, and D."

Professor Hadley's view as to the impracticability of statutory maxima is, it may be broadly said, universally held by all competent railway authorities in America. Here is what Mr. Hudson, the author of "The Railways and the Republic," an able book, by one who has carefully studied the subject, writes:[4] "The first crude step towards legislative regulation took the form of fixing by law a maximum limit for rates. It was imagined that the railways, if restricted to a moderate maximum, must adjust all their rates with substantial equity, and that thus both extortion and discrimination would be held in check. Experience fully refutes this idea. Effective discriminations are always possible within the limits of any maximum rates that would allow the railway to earn its interest and dividend charges. Not only will a legal maximum of freight rates fail to prevent discriminations, but no legislative ability can frame a tariff of rates without inequality and injustice to the railways, especially in inter-State" [*i.e.* practically long-distance] "commerce.

"Any rate which would be just to the trunk lines of the Central States would be destructive to expensive railways reaching the mines of Colorado or California. Rates which the mines in the Rocky Mountains or Sierra Nevada can pay, and must pay if railroads are

[4] *The Railways and the Republic.* By James F. Hudson. 3rd edition. Harper Bros., New York, 1889. P. 339. Mr. Hudson is, it may be said, no advocate of *laisser faire*, like Professor Hadley. On the contrary, he is so fiercely opposed to the present state of railway management in America, and so hopeless of seeing any real reforms introduced under present conditions, that he proposes that the railway companies shall be forbidden by law to act as carriers, and compelled to revert to their original position as mere tolltakers, owning lines which any member of the public or any transportation agency can use on payment of a fixed toll.

to be built for them, would amount to confiscation if applied to the coal mines in Pennsylvania, or the grain of Iowa and Nebraska. The schedule which would be just for a railway at one time would be unjust at another. The branch line through a new country must collect higher rates at first, than when it has developed the productive powers of the region. The varying conditions which may properly influence rates are innumerable. It is a hopeless task to adjust the schedules to suit all circumstances, and it is futile to expect an adequate reform of railway abuses by such means.

"The uselessness of attempts to establish equitable rates by law appears in the fact that every such schedule which has been in existence for ten years is now obsolete, being far above the rates now fixed by the railways. This progressive reduction of the cost of transportation has been cited as showing that all regulation of the railways is unnecessary. It is far from proving this; but it does prove that attempts to prescribe rates by law are unnecessary and futile. The laws of trade can bring about whatever cheapening of the cost of transportation competition and economy will produce. The province of legislation is to ensure the free, universal and regular operation of these laws, so that the benefit shall be equitably distributed among all interests and localities, and not monopolised by a few, while others bear the burden. When this aim is secured, and artificial interference with these laws is removed, the question whether rates are low enough or not can safely be left to them."

But Professor Hadley's assertion was not referring

to American, but to English, opinion. Let us see what the careful students of the question have said in this country, and for convenience sake, let us keep separate the two points, whether fixed maxima are likely to afford protection to the public, and how far they may be considered fair to the railway. In 1872 Mr. Rawcliffe testified before the Joint Committee that "a railway company can perpetrate almost any kind of injustice under and within the limits of what are called maximum rates." In the report of Sir Henry Tyler—then Captain Tyler, and Inspecting Officer of the Board of Trade—which is printed in the Appendix to the Committee's Proceedings, there is this passage: "The attempt to limit rates and fares by the principle of fixing maxima has almost always failed in practice, and is almost always likely to fail, for the simple reason that the Parliamentary Committees, and authorities by whom such limits are decided, cannot do otherwise than allow some margin between the actual probable rate, as far as they can forecast it, and the maximum rate, and cannot foresee the contingencies of competition, of increasing quantities, of facilities or economy of working, or of alteration of commercial conditions which may occur in the course of years, after such limits have been arranged by them." "I attach," said Sir Thomas Farrer, "very little value to the maximum rates fixed by Parliament."

The Committee's decision on the question is this: "Independently of the question of vested interest in the companies, it is to be observed that legal maximum rates afford little real protection to the public, since they are always fixed so high that it is, or becomes sooner or later, the interest of the companies to carry at lower rates." The Committee goes on to point out that the chief complaints refer not to the class rates for the retail traffic, but to the special rates for the wholesale trade between great centres, and that these rates could not possibly be affected by any revision of maxima, and then, dealing with a proposal for periodical revision, goes on to say:

"The companies will, if experience is any guide, constantly for their own sakes charge less than their legal maxima. Is this revision to take effect on their legal maxima, or on the actual rates as they voluntarily reduce them? If the former, its results will be small. If the latter, it would be difficult to effect, and may bear hardly on the companies in stereotyping a temporary or experimental reduction." Then, after just noticing that an effectual revision of rates could only be made, if there were, which the Committee has shown there is not, a standard of cost-of-service on which rates could be based, the Report goes on to say: "A still more serious question with respect to periodical revision is the question, On what principle is it to be performed, and by whom? If it is to be purely arbitrary, if no rule is to be laid down to guide the revisers, the power of revision will amount to a power to confiscate the property of the companies. It is not likely that Parliament would attempt to exercise any such power itself, still less that it would confer such a power on any subordinate authority."

Nine years elapsed, and then the question was

taken into consideration once more. Before the Committee of 1881, Mr. Baxter, who was not only a great railway lawyer and Parliamentary agent, but a colliery proprietor, was asked, "Do you think that with the present rates it would be safe for Parliament to cut out the maximum rates altogether, and let the railway companies charge what they like?" Mr. Baxter replied, "I think it would be quite safe to abolish all statutory rates whatever on railways and let them charge what they can. The competition is so perfect throughout the country, and the pressure on the part of the traders is so great, and the system so mature, that I think you might safely supersede all rates in Acts of Parliament, and give to the railway companies an absolute power of charging."

Mr. Baxter's point as to the maturity of the system making superfluous precautions on which so much stress was laid in the early days of railways, receives confirmation from a somewhat unexpected quarter. On page 19 of his book on railway rates, Professor Hunter writes: "If there had existed in the infancy of our railway system a tribunal of experts, capable from time to time of forming a sound opinion on the reasonableness of the charges of the railway company, much might be said against establishing the hard and fast line of a maximum rate and in favour of permitting railway companies to fix their own charges. A maximum toll for the use of a canal was a not inadequate measure of the value of the service for which it was paid. The toll was in fact an aliquot part of a true rent, based on the assumption that a given tonnage would in the course of a year pass over the canal; but the circumstances that determine the cost of carrying goods, and influence the remuneration of the carrier, are so varied and complicated that it is impossible to avoid making the maximum toll too high or too low, or indeed frequently both at the same time."

After pointing out that the United States Congress had made no attempt to fix maximum rates but "simply enacted the common law," providing, however, "a commission of experts," to apply the doctrines of reasonable charges and unjust preferences to any state of facts as it might arise, the Professor goes on to say, not, as might perhaps have been expected, that now that we have got a commission of experts also, we shall do well to follow the example of the United States, but, on the other hand, to make the following observation: "The Traffic Act, 1888, contains an important section providing for the revision, under the superintendence of the Board of Trade, of the classification of goods and of all maximum rates. The traders, if they do not watch closely the proceedings about to be initiated, may find out that they will lose much and gain little by the symmetry and uniformity which are to take the place of the chaos of the old special Acts."

But we are getting on too fast. Let us go back and see what the recent Parliamentary Committees have said on the other branch of the subject, namely, the rights of the companies. No one questions that maximum rates may, for a time at least, if only they are fixed low enough, afford a most efficient protection to the pockets of the railway customers. If, for example, Parliament were to enact that every existing fare and rate charged at the present moment throughout the British Isles should be cut down by one-half, unquestionably passengers and freighters would save money in the interval which elapsed before the companies went into bankruptcy, and a special session of Parliament was summoned to repeal the Act. The question rather is whether any limit can be fixed which shall be simultaneously fair to the companies—that is, be, broadly speaking and in the long run, in the public interest—and also be of practical utility as affording a protection to the public in general against the possibility of extortionate charges. By "extortionate" charges we must understand charges such as a commission of experts, with all the facts of the case before them, and acting as arbiters between the public and the railways, would have no hesitation in disallowing.

On this point we may call two witnesses, neither of whom will be suspected of any undue partiality for the railway companies. Before the Committee of 1881, Sir Bernhard Samuelson put to Professor Hunter the following question: "You stated that there would be some difficulty in obtaining uniformity of classification on account of the differences of classification existing in the Acts of different railway companies, and you stated that that might be an objection to the adoption of the Railway Clearing House Classification as a universal rule." The answer was: "Yes, I consider that the existing classification is to be looked upon in the light of a contract. Uniformity would be a very desirable thing, but you can hardly ask for uniformity at the expense of the terms of the contract you have made." "With whom?" asked Sir Edward Watkin; to which Professor Hunter replied: "I consider the rate clauses are a contract between the public and the railways, and that we cannot, for the sake of uniformity, ask the railway companies to suffer by any change that will be made in the classification." Professor Hunter went on to say that of course it was true that every private Act contained a clause subjecting the company to all future Acts dealing with railways, but that still he was of opinion "that it would require an extremely strong case to justify interference."

To the same effect was the testimony of Mr. Balfour Browne, who at that time had only recently resigned his office as Registrar of the Railway Commission, before the Committee of 1882. "I think," he said, "that the railway companies took their Acts upon the condition of being allowed to charge those rates, whatever they are, and that nobody ought to be allowed to say, We will resile from that Parliamentary contract. Therefore I would allow the railway companies to go on charging their authorised rates."

What were the conclusions of the Committee of 1872 we have already seen. But Professor Hadley is scarcely as accurate as usual in asserting that the Committee of 1882 acknowledged that fixed maxima were of next to no use. On the contrary, the Committee declares itself "of opinion that it is essential to the protection of the public that a maximum rate should be fixed in all cases," and that in "all cases of bills for authorising new lines of railway, or extending the powers of existing companies, the attention of the Committees on such bills should be specially directed by some public authority to the rates and fares, either authorised by such bills, or in the case of existing companies in previous Acts, and that such Committees should have power to alter, modify, and regulate such rates and fares in the interest of the public, and with due regard to the interests of existing companies." That the Committee, however, never contemplated any such revision of maxima as is contained in the new Board of Trade Provisional Orders, is obvious. Its two recommendations are, "Your Committee cannot recommend any new legislative interference for the purpose of enforcing upon railway companies equality of charge;" and again, "Your Committee are further of opinion that the multiplicity of special Acts dealing with rates or charges on the same railway is a great evil, and that railway companies should be required to consolidate their special Acts in so far as they affect rates or charges imposed upon the traders."

It may be added, that in Mr. Barclay's draft Report there was this clause: "Your Committee do not offer any definite recommendation for improving the classifition of traffic or for readjustment of rates, but if there existed any department of State whose duty it was to care for the interests of trade and agriculture, that department might consider and develop the suggestions indicated, and, with the co-operation of the railway companies, would doubtless succeed in producing a much simpler and more equitable system of rating than now. exists." Mr. Barclay, needless to say, was the leader on that Committee of the opposition to the principles professed and the practice pursued by the English railway management. If any member on that Committee had ever dreamed of using a revision of maximum rates as machinery for the reduction of existing charges, of which no word of complaint has ever been heard, that member would probably have been Mr. Barclay. But he made no such suggestion ; and when he proposed that the existing railway companies should co-operate with the Board of Trade in the revision of their own rates, it is safe to say that he did not contemplate placing them in the position of sheep, and honouring them with an invitation to participate in a shearers' festival.

The world, however, has moved rapidly since 1882. Public opinion has gone some distance in the direction of compulsory socialism, and some shrewd observers think that they can already see the pendulum beginning to turn for a backward swing. But be that as it may. Meanwhile we will go on with our history. In 1885, acting upon the suggestion of the Committee's Report, the railway companies introduced bills to codify their existing powers. Whether they really proposed nothing more than this, or whether they surreptitiously seized the opportunity to endeavour to increase their powers, no man can tell. Some people may think that a power to charge 8$d.$ per ton per mile for coal or iron-stone for any distance is not a power of any great practical value, and that its surrender would be dearly bought by the concession of a right to increase the charges upon short distance merchandise traffic by a single farthing per mile. The present writer has no wish to discuss the question, being firmly persuaded that an equitable exchange of powers for powers is a practical impossibility. What the bills of 1885 might have done, would have been to show, in a simple and summary form, the total charging powers of the companies, and so to secure, as a defence against exorbitant charges, in some degree at least, what is probably on the whole the best protection—publicity, with its natural consequence of potential competition. But whatever the abortive bills of 1885 did, they assuredly did not offer, and were not intended to offer, any prospect of an immediate reduction of actual rates; and, as might not unnaturally have been expected at a period of unexampled depression of trade, they disappeared in face of the outcry raised by the traders' representatives.

Then the successive Governments took the matter up. Finally, in 1888, the Railway and Canal Traffic Bill came down from the Lords to the Commons, containing the following clause: "The Board of Trade shall determine . . . the schedule of maximum rates and charges . . . which it would in the opinion of the Board of Trade be just and reasonable to substitute for the existing maximum rates and charges of the railway company, as upon the whole equivalent to such maximum rates and charges," &c. The Commons refused to accept this basis of revision, and left it to the Board of Trade to fix such charges as it might think just and reasonable. *Tabula rasa* was to be made of the past, and the Board was to act at its own discretion, unguided by precedent and unfettered by instructions. If ever a public department was placed in an unjust and unreasonable position, that department was the Board of Trade by the Act of 1888. Parliament had done that which a Parliamentary Committee of sixteen years before had pronounced inconceivable, and had conferred on a subordinate authority, with no "rule laid down to guide the revisers," a power of revision "purely arbitrary," and "amounting to a power to confiscate the property of the companies."

Why any Minister ever permitted his department to be placed in so absolutely impossible a situation, it is difficult to conceive. Of course the Board of Trade decision, as announced in the Reports of Lord Balfour and Mr. Courtenay Boyle, and as subsequently amended in the Provisional Orders, as the result of a number of *ex parte* statements, which the other side has practically had no opportunity to challenge or to controvert—of course the Board of Trade decision has pleased nobody. Under ordinary circumstances, the fact that neither litigant is satisfied with the decision may be taken as fair evidence both of the wisdom and impartiality of the judge. But here, when a cause is tried in which every inhabitant of the country has an interest, both on the side of the railways and on that of their opponents—though with some the interest is larger on the one side, and with others on the other—if no one is satisfied, one is apt to think that the task had been better declined at the beginning.

There is no need to devote a single moment to the wearisome inquiry before the Board of Trade tribunal last year. It sufficed to add two cubic feet of printed matter to the literature of the subject, and to demonstrate to all who attended it the impartiality and the ability of the officers who presided. If it were a case of arbitrating as to the reasonableness or unreasonableness of a particular rate, the railway company and the complainant concerned might both be well satisfied to leave the question to the arbitration of Lord Balfour and Mr. Courtenay Boyle. But when it was a question of fixing maximum rates over the entire kingdom; of drawing a line, which should be a protection to the public, and yet not trench on the just rights of the railway companies; of regulating, not merely the few hundreds of rates which were brought to the cognisance of the tribunal but the scores of millions of other rates of which no word was said—the arbitrators failed for the simple reason that success was impossible at the outset. That they failed so little is a sufficient title to the admiration of any one who can appreciate the difficulty of the task that was laid upon them.

At the outset they were confronted with the difficulty that absolutely no principle had been laid down by Parliament for their guidance. They were told to assume that the whole series of schedules laid down by the wisdom of Parliament, in the long series of special Railway Acts from 1824 to 1888, were worthless, and that was all. The litigants, on the other hand, knew what they wanted. The railway companies claimed that their present not excessive income should be preserved intact. That income, they said, could best be raised under the existing system of rates, each of which practically had been fixed by half a century's experience of the higgling of the market. Let the Board of Trade draw its new maximum lines sufficiently far above the tops of existing rates to leave a margin of, say, 15 per cent. for possible rise in the price of materials and labour,[5] they would be content.

The traders' view, on the other hand, is given in the Lancashire and Cheshire Report in the following terms: "The actual rates for cotton, when averaged, worked out to a mean of 1·69*d.* per ton per mile, and the maximum rate proposed by the traders was 2*d.* Now, the amount of loss which the company would have to endure, if called upon to submit to this rate of 2*d.*, depends entirely upon the amount of variation in the existing rates. If the limits of variation are very wide apart, doubtless the adoption of a mean, even with a substantial margin added, might result in some loss. If the existing limits of variation are not excessive, a reasonable margin should cover them. Putting the argument into the shape of figures, the two cases might perhaps be taken to be clearly represented as follows: On the supposition that actual conveyance charges for a given distance had been found to vary between 80 pence and 120 pence, the mean would be 100 pence, and if the maximum were then fixed at 120 pence, such an adjustment need involve no alteration in existing practice. This is the case of reasonable variation of existing charges.

"Suppose, however, that the mean of 100 pence,

---

[5] Within the last year this possible rise has become a very obvious certainty. Nor is there any reasonable ground to doubt that, as far as wages are concerned, the rise is —we may be glad to think—permanent.

with its maximum of 120 pence, were deduced from rates varying from 60 pence to 140 pence: in this instance certainly all rates over 120 pence would be liable to reduction. So far from having any hesitation in proposing this, the traders say that their main object in demanding revised rates is to obtain this very reduction. They claim that the Act of 1888 gives it them; and they say that, if it does not, it is indeed the nullity which the railway companies represent it to be; and if so, they propose to renew their exertions, and not to cease until Parliament has granted them the protection they ask, and has found means of drafting an Act which shall clearly express their (*sic*) intention so to do." The railway reply was in the first place to ask for the reference to the section of the Act which meant reduction, and secondly to point out that, so far from a variation from 60 pence to 140 pence being excessive, the fact was that in all probability the lower rate was, under the circumstances in which it was charged, the more profitable of the two.

The Report of the Board of Trade tribunal bears traces of the difficulty of reconciling these two diametrically opposite positions. Here is a clause giving to the railways absolutely everything they ought to ask: "The railway companies have built up a traffic remunerative to themselves at rates generally speaking much lower than those at present authorised by Parliament, and consequently we believe that it is equitable to make a reduction in their present powers, and to fix rates, based to a great extent on existing rates, but with a reasonable margin of profit for possible changes of circumstances injuriously affecting the cost of, or the returns from, the carriage of merchandise by railway." Such is the Report, but when we come to the schedules by which it is accompanied, we find that the best calculation the railways can make is to the effect that not only has the margin disappeared, but that in very many instances the existing revenue is markedly diminished.

Of course there are nominal margins in all directions. For example, there is nothing to prevent the companies charging the full local rate of 40$s.$ on cotton goods sent from Manchester for shipment in London. But then the Board of Trade certainly does not need to be told that, if the railway companies tried in practice to charge this 40$s.$, some of the London vessels would be sent round to Liverpool to complete their loading there, while in other cases the cottons would come, not from Lancashire at all, but through Havre or Antwerp from Continental factories.

The explanation of the schedules is perhaps to be found rather in what we may call the traders' section of the Report. Two pages after the passage already cited we read as follows : " The railway companies have urged persistently and strongly that the future maxima ought to be so fixed as to result in no loss of revenue to the company. If by this is meant that the future maxima should be such as to cover all existing rates, we are unable to agree with the proposition. To what extent there is justification for the very wide differences which exist in actual rates, we are not called upon to pronounce. But it is material to a just settlement of powers of charge that it suits the companies, in a large number of instances, to conduct traffic at rates much lower than those authorised in their present Acts, or in the schedules attached hereto.[6]

"If maxima were to be fixed at rates high enough to cover present non-competitive charges, the traders who rely solely on a particular railway would be without the Parliamentary protection which they claim, and as we believe reasonably claim. In

---

[6] One would have fancied that, if there was one question more than another on which the Board of Trade tribunal was bound to make up its mind, it was, whether there is, or is not, justification of the very wide differences which exist in actual rates. Not, of course, in detail in each individual case, but broadly, as shown in typical illustrations. If, for example, the railway companies can prove, as they claim to be able to prove, that, say, 6d. per ton per mile is only a tolerably remunerative rate in hilly and sparsely populated districts, it is surely not only unreasonable, but also unjust, to fix the maximum rate at 5d., because it suits the company elsewhere to charge only 2d. In fact, the Board of Trade arbitrators would have done well to have studied Mr. Fink's figures. His conclusions will bear repetition: "Under ordinary conditions the cost per ton-mile in some cases may not exceed one-seventh of a cent, and in others may be as high as 73 cents per ton-mile on the same road. A mere knowledge of the average cost per ton-mile of all the expenditure during a whole year's operations is of no value whatever in determining the cost of transporting any particular class of freight, as no freight is ever transported under the average condition under which the whole year's business is transacted." Surely the Board of Trade have no right to say broadly that Cornwall, for instance, is to have all its business done at less than average margin above cost, and may call upon Bristol and Birmingham and Cardiff to make up the Great Western dividend. If the railway company thinks it can get more net profit out of Cornwall by lowering the rates, by all means let it do so. But consideration of what the traffic will or will not bear is no business of a State official, who is merely called upon to fix, not actual charges, but maximum rates. Or, rather, it may of course be his business, but only on one condition—that the State, namely, is prepared, as the guardian of the general interest, to make up to the private company the difference, if any, between what the traffic can bear and what the company can reasonably afford to take for carrying it.

determining the figures in the schedule, we have had regard to the highness of the present non-competitive rates, and on the other hand to the fact that the companies will probably have to rely more on increase in traffic than on the raising of their non-competitive rates to recoup themselves from any loss they may sustain by deprivation of the right to charge such specially high rates as are now in some instances enforced." The diplomatic ambiguity of this passage suffices to protect it from detailed criticism, but it would hardly be an unfair paraphrase to say that it comes to this : " We do not know whether the highest existing charges are too high or not. There are certainly some others much lower, so we think they must be. Anyway, we propose to cut them down, as otherwise the traders will declare that we have done nothing for them. We ought to add that we know that the argument that the companies can recoup themselves elsewhere is fallacious, because the traffic elsewhere will not bear an increase. No doubt, however, a reduction of the rate on tea of 10s. per ton, or say one-twentieth of a penny per pound, will so largely stimulate the consumption of that article in Cornwall as to recoup the Great Western before the half-year is out for any momentary loss of revenue. No doubt also, the companies, whose existing lines are all quite full already, will be able, once the traffic is charged at lower rates, to find room for more of it."

But it is ungracious to insist too strongly on the fact that a position which was impossible from the outset, has been proved in practice to be untenable.

A A

To have so largely succeeded as in fact they have, is a sufficient testimony to the infinite pains which the Board of Trade arbitrators took in sifting the vast mass of evidence laid before them at the public hearing. Whether, however, as much can be said for the alterations which the Board of Trade has thought proper to introduce since the public inquiry was closed, is another question. The rates, for example, for traffic in the third class, were fixed in August last at a very low point. The reason influencing the decision was understood to be the protection of the hardware interest, whose goods were in that class, and which was not only important, but very ably represented at the public inquiry. The Provisional Orders, however, which have just appeared, have removed hardware from the third class down into the second; but the third-class rates are left as before.

Another point. Articles carried in class B, such as bricks, building-stone, pig iron, &c., have hitherto been required to be sent in minimum quantities of 4 tons, the obvious reason being that, as they are sent loose, and therefore require a waggon to themselves, the railway companies have a right to be guaranteed a reasonable minimum load. The minimum has now been brought down to 2 tons. In other words, the railway earnings per waggon are liable to be divided by two, for it may be presumed that the President of the Board of Trade does not propose that coprolites, creosote, and brewers'-grains —to take three articles which stand next each other in this class of the revised classification—shall travel cheek-by-jowl in the same railway waggon.

One point more. The draft schedules fixed for the use of trucks the following charges:

For distances not exceeding 50 miles	6*d*. per ton.
Between 50 and 150 miles	1*s*. 0*d*. ,,
Over 150 miles	1*s*. 3*d*. ,,

The revised version reads as follows:

For distances not exceeding 25 miles	3*d*. per ton.
25 to 50 miles	6*d*. ,,
50 to 75 miles	9*d*. ,,
75 to 150 miles	1*s*. 0*d*. ,,
Exceeding 150 miles	1*s*. 3*d*. ,,

Now, it is quite safe to say that the modification (which one company calculates means to it a loss of 16,000*l*. a year net revenue) could never have been made except by an official in an office, not in contact with the actual facts of railway working. Assuming 6*d*. to be a reasonable charge for distances from 25 to 50 miles, 3*d*. for distances under 25 miles is on the face of it ridiculous. It is not in travelling that waggons spend their time, but in waiting at their destination to be loaded, or unloaded, or reloaded. A waggon, sent down to the coal-tips at Cardiff or Hartlepool, is hardly likely to do a second trip in the day, however short the distance, and it may quite well take its turn once in the 24 hours, even for distances exceeding 50 miles. In this case 6*d*. per ton might conceivably be an excessive charge. A waggon, on the other hand, sent to a local consumer half a dozen miles away from the colliery, is likely to take a week before it gets back into work again, as the customer is allowed a minimum of four days for unloading.

The Board of Trade proposes to fix 2s. per week, therefore, as the maximum charge for the hire of a waggon, whose value cannot possibly be estimated at less than 10*l. per annum*, that is, 4s. per week. A mileage basis of charge is unscientific enough in any case, and the Americans are at this moment endeavouring to introduce a charge by time in its place, but to cut up a line into lengths of twenty-five miles, and to divide the shilling into silver threepences to correspond, is an act that could only be accomplished by the official intelligence, whose natural instinct is to call upon the facts to square with his *a priori* theories, instead of endeavouring to modify his theories to fit the facts.

These of course are small matters, but when it is a matter of 16,000*l.* here, and 40,000*l.* there, and so on all through the different classes, the cumulative effect is by no means trifling. The main interest, however, of these illustrations is simply as showing whether a Government department can in fact fix rates more equitably from a London office—in other words, whether it can raise the necessary revenue to induce capital to invest in railway enterprises with less friction and less injustice than is caused under the present system, under which rates are fixed by the representatives of the capitalists, who are in constant contact with the practical conduct of their customers' business.

It is as well to make this point quite clear. The present writer has no wish to argue the question from an abstract point of view. Indeed, for his own part, he is quite unable to adopt the high Tory view of Professor Hunter, or to admit that the Railway

Acts of half a century back are a contract between the public and the railway, binding to all time on the former, unless they are released by the consent of the latter. Such a view seems to him absolutely untenable, except on principles which would forbid the Government to interfere with endowments left, say, to the Universities in the fifteenth century. For, in railway matters, 1840 is really as far off as the Middle Ages. Even so, the point is scarcely of practical importance, for no railway company can exist for five years without coming to Parliament for fresh powers, and when Parliament is asked to grant powers, it can surely make what terms it thinks proper, as to the concessions which the railways shall give in return. The only point urged here will be that on mere grounds of expediency it is, not only not in the interests of the railway companies, but also not in the interests of the railway customers, whether they call themselves traders, or whether they be merely members of the consuming public, that the proposed Provisional Orders of the Board of Trade shall be sanctioned.

The case may, I think, be stated as follows: The companies are not making excessive profits. On the contrary, they are earning very much less than investors who simultaneously have put their money into other certainly not more speculative undertakings, such as gas, and water, and tramway, and omnibus companies. It is true that, in an exceptionally prosperous year, 70,000,000*l.* of capital nominally received over 7 per cent. On the other hand, nearly 60,000,000*l.* received no dividend whatever, and the one fact must be fairly written off against the other. Taking it all in all, railway capital returns less than $4\frac{1}{4}$ per cent. of income. It is impossible therefore to argue that railway shareholders are doing better than they can reasonably expect, and that their dividends are so large that a small slice cut off them will never be missed. On the contrary, it may safely be asserted that a compulsory reduction of dividend resulting from a compulsory reduction of net revenue will scare capital out of the business, and produce a fall in the value of railway stocks out of all proportion to the actual money loss incurred.

Now, anyone with any practical knowledge of railway working must know that the growing trade of the country cannot be accommodated without a steady increase in railway capital expenditure. Certainly that is the universal experience of railway managers, who know only too well that the delightful theory about closing capital accounts is likely to remain a theory, at least till the time when English trade becomes stationary, and then begins to decline. The natural effect of the proposed Provisional Orders will be that the railway companies will shrink from new works, for which the capital cannot be raised any longer on the easy terms to which they have hitherto been accustomed. And if the great lines hold their hands for five years to come, the traffic, if it continues to increase at its present rate, will be brought to a standstill, at least under the conditions of accommodation which are at present given; and the loss to the public by the curtailment of the facilities must be immensely greater than anything which they can gain by the cheapening of rates.

But it is said the English railways are extravagantly worked. If pressure is put on the companies, they will learn to economise in working expenses. We have been told this times without number by gentlemen such as Professor Hunter, and Mr. Jeans, and Sir Alfred Hickman, none of whom can claim to be considered as experts on questions of traffic management. We have been told so also by Mr. Jefferds and Mr. Dorsey, who would perhaps make this claim. But their statements are so extravagant as scarcely to need refutation. Certainly, practical railway men in America show no signs of an inclination to treat seriously assertions such as that the introduction of American methods into England would effect an economy of two-thirds of the total English expenditure. Perhaps after we have seen that of the expenditure of an English railway three-fourths goes for charges which are incurred almost on the same scale, whether the traffic is moved over the line or not, and that only one-fourth can properly be allocated to movement charges at all, we may be forgiven if we decline to treat them seriously also.

If Englishmen want to know what competent American critics really do think, they may be referred to the " Railroad Gazette," which, having no axe of its own to grind, and not being " interested in the construction of waggons on the American principle," writes as follows : " It is the relative shortness of the haul—calculated at 111 miles on the average in America as against under 40 in England—which gives English railroads *the appearance of charging such high rates for freight*. . . . This fact, together with the services assumed by English roads in the way of cartage, and the high speed at which many of their freight trains are necessarily run, is *sufficient to explain the high rates prevailing on English railroads.*"

If then the reduction of receipts cannot be compensated for by reduction of expenditure, we are face to face with the fact that the shareholders' pockets must pay the bill. And let it not be supposed that, when we speak of shareholders, the bloated capitalists who own North Western Stock at 180, or North Eastern Consols at 160, are mainly in question. To a considerable extent, the great lines can protect themselves. They are spread over so great an area of country, and have their eggs in so many baskets, that it is probable that, to some extent at least, they will be able sooner or later to recoup themselves for their loss by charging the public more, or accommodating them less, elsewhere. If the lines to the North, for example, were to enter into an agreement to give no fresh passenger facilities, not to put on new trains as the new traffic came to them, but to let their expresses, which now carry perhaps 60 passengers, gradually fill up till each came to have an average of 90 to 100; if they were to adopt the French method of making passengers come when it suits the company to run the train, instead of running the train when it suits the passengers to come, they would steadily improve their net receipts without adding one farthing to their existing outlay. The point is that it is not in the public interest that they should be pressed to do so.

It is not the great companies which most need protection. "It is quite clear," says the Inter-State Commerce Commission, on a somewhat similar question, "that the more powerful corporations of the country, controlling the largest traffic, and operating on the chief lines of trade through the most thickly settled districts, can conform to the statutory rule with much more ease, and with much less apparent danger of loss of income, than can the weaker line whose business is comparatively light and perhaps admits of no dividend, and the pressure of whose fixed charges imposes a constant struggle to avoid bankruptcy."

But we are told that the companies will be compensated by the increase of traffic consequent on the reduction of charges. Indeed, there are words in the Report of Lord Balfour and Mr. Courtenay Boyle which might almost lead one to suppose them to be lending their authority to this view. To refute it, it is really almost sufficient to state that the reduction amounts to something like $1\frac{1}{2}$ per cent., spread over an enormous number of items, many of them of considerable value, and carried only for short distances. One-and-a-half per cent. is of course a serious matter enough when it is taken out of the 15 per cent. of gross revenue which alone is available for the payment of dividend on ordinary shares. But, frittered away in driblets of a few pence here and a few shillings there, it is absolutely inconceivable that any customer will feel the benefit of it. Had the companies been left to reduce rates to an equivalent amount, by taking substantial percentages off such portions of their traffic as they thought could bear the charges least, no doubt some effect might have been produced, and of course, in so far as the Board of Trade reductions are on the rates for coal and iron-stone and the like, this criticism does not apply. But in any case the reduction is immediate and certain, the compensating increase remote and problematical, and in the interval the ordinary shareholders may whistle for their money.

A still more remarkable justification for the Provisional Orders has been heard from the mouth of the President of the Board of Trade himself. The railway managers pressed upon him that he was reducing their existing revenue, and he replied by asking whether they could not recoup themselves by imposing higher charges elsewhere. Was ever a reasoning being placed by force of circumstances in a more unfortunate position of amusing illogicality? Put into plain English, the President's position is this: "You have exercised your powers of charging so unsatisfactorily, that I propose to interfere at certain points and do the work for you. At the same time I leave your hands unfettered at the points where I have not interfered. Work your wicked will there. Of course any increase of charge you may place on the shoulders of these latter must be an imposition, because you acknowledged them to be less able to bear a high charge than other places whose charges I have already reduced as excessive; but that cannot be helped. I cannot take the responsibility of fixing your rates. So I must continue to leave the matter in your hands, being content to think that, on paper at any rate, your charges will look more reasonable, as my action has tended to narrow somewhat the gap between the lowest charges and the highest."

In truth, it is no reflection on the ability of the Board of Trade officials to say that their position is absolutely indefensible. They have reduced rates, nobody knows why. It might have been thought that a rate of which no human being had ever complained, a rate at which the traffic had grown and prospered, had proved itself a fair rate by the best of all possible evidence, that of experience, and yet the Board of Trade has reduced such rates in hundreds of instances. When we ask why, we get no answer. It is not because the rate is too far in excess of the cost of the service, for we are told expressly that the Board of Trade does not know, and does not care to know, what that cost is. Can it really be simply in order that the figures may move in symmetrical procession across the columns of a printed table? Is it once more the official mind, which has always been persuaded that, if facts refuse to square with theories, so much the worse for the facts.

But if the Board of Trade does not know why the new rates are fixed, at least the railway officials do know why they maintained their old ones. Ask a goods-manager the explanation of some apparently anomalous rate, and he will not unfrequently go into a history almost as voluminous as that of some great international negotiation. He will tell you how there were deputations from traders, followed by report from the local goods agent, then by references to agents in other districts in order to gauge the effect on their relative position, and then to the solicitor to know the legal bearings of the question; how then once more the matter was taken up with the traders complaining, and finally how a compromise was agreed upon, which, though it did not concede everything that was asked, at least left the customers of the company substantially satisfied. But all this process of reasoning, of negotiation, of attention to individual interests, of adaptation, as far as may be, of means to ends, is to be set aside in favour of a system by which a Government department is to fix rates in an office with a sheet of paper and a ruler, and yet at the same time be free to disclaim all responsibility for its handiwork.

One word more. The fiercest advocate of the traders' claims will scarcely deny that rates have steadily, even if slowly, moved downwards; that over a series of years, that is, the public get more and more accommodation all round for the same money. With the *régime* inaugurated by the Provisional Orders, this era may be taken to have definitely closed. The companies have been solemnly warned. "Never reduce rates. Each reduction that you make will be taken as a precedent against you in the future." On the Joint Committee of 1872, Lord Salisbury put to Sir Thomas Farrer a question *à propos* of this very proposal to reduce maximum rates: "Would there not be a danger arising from giving companies the impression that, if in practice they reduce their rates, Parliament will soon make it the practice to reduce the maximum rates allowed to them?" Sir Thomas replied: "Of course it might have the effect of frightening them, and preventing them from reducing, but I rather think that they only reduce when it is to their interest to do so. On the whole, I attach very little value to the maximum rates fixed by Parliament."

Lord Salisbury and the Secretary of the Board of Trade were of course discussing a proposal to reduce margins. A proposal to fix maxima at a point where not only the margin but a portion of the existing rate disappears, is a very different matter. Had that been within the range of practical politics in 1872, we may be very sure what Sir Thomas Farrer's answer would have been. Of course a company only reduces a rate when it is its interest to do so, but if an interested reduction to A is made a precedent for compulsory reduction to B, because on paper the circumstances of the two places or trades are identical, the interest of the company will be in the opposite direction. But the mention of Lord Salisbury naturally suggests a reference to the company which he was the first to drag out of the slough of despond of its early years. That the Great Eastern of late years has deserved well of the public, few will be found to deny. Even the very Fish Traders' Association declared that they had nothing to say against the Great Eastern rates. It is matter of common knowledge that they have been cut down by wholesale all over the line. Nor has the company given to the traders of its superfluity. On the contrary, only last year for the first time did it attain to the magnificent dividend of 3 per cent.

The Great Eastern management, however, was

perfectly frank. It made its reductions in its own interest. "Our district," said its representatives, "is hard hit by the agricultural depression. We will reduce our rates, and do what we can to lighten the burdens on our customers, the farmers. When agriculture recovers, they will not object if we put the rates up again, and claim a share of their gains as we shall have shared their losses." But what has in fact happened? The Board of Trade ruler has drawn its line across the tops of the existing charges, cutting off not a few of them at a point which implies to a struggling company a loss which it can ill afford, and making any serious increase in charge impossible in the future. With this object-lesson before its eyes, is any railway company likely hereafter to be so short-sighted as to go in for a policy of reduction in view of its own immediate interests? Will not rates be kept up all over the country with far more uniformity than has ever existed in the past? Hitherto the companies have agreed as a rule to maintain rates; have agreed every now and then to reduce them. Henceforward, in all agreements there will be a blank uniformity.

Whether the existing competition in facilities will continue in full force as at present, remains to be seen. It is more probable that facilities, too, will be gradually but steadily diminished, and a policy of cheese-paring and stagnation take the place of one of expansion and encouragement to trade. If this be so, the traders and the public will have lost tenfold more than they can ever dream of gaining by petty and nagging reductions of existing rates. No one who knows what a hindrance to real business this long protracted duel between the companies and the traders has been—for it has lasted now almost without intermission for a decade—can doubt that it is in the public interest that the question should be settled. But the present writer is so firmly persuaded that the present settlement can settle nothing, that the traders who have gained trifling reductions will still be dissatisfied, and that the other traders, on to whose shoulders the companies will attempt to transfer some portion of their loss, will be tenfold more so, that for his own part, if Parliament cannot satisfactorily amend the Provisional Orders, he would be thankful to see them rejected altogether, and the question left open for settlement hereafter, and possibly under more favourable auspices.

APPENDICES

APPENDIX A (see p. 140).

RAILWAY RATES FOR PROVISIONS TO BIRMINGHAM.

Description of provisions	Three places from which principally received at Birmingham	Rate per ton s. d.	Condition of rate
Apples	Coventry	10 0	Collected and delivered
	Leamington	10 0	,, ,,
	Ludlow	15 0	,, ,,
Apples	Liverpool	17 6	Delivered in Birmingham
	London	20 0	Collected and delivered
Bread (Flour)	Not received by railway		
	Liverpool	11 3	4 tons collected and delivered
Carrots	Sandy / Gamlingay	11 8	Station to station, 2 tons packed, 3 tons loose
	Potton	10 0	Station to station, 4-ton lots
Cheese	Derby	13 4	Collected and delivered
	Rugeley	12 6	,, ,,
	Tutbury	13 4	Collected and delivered, owner's risk
Cheese	London	22 6	Collected and delivered
	Liverpool	20 10	Delivered in Birmingham
Cocoa	London	22 6	Collected and delivered
Coffee	London	22 6	,, ,,
	Liverpool	20 10	Delivered in Birmingham
	Market Harboro'	18 4	Collected and delivered
Dripping	Not received by railway		
FISH— Herrings (salt sprinkled or fresh)	Aberdeen	55 0	Collected and delivered, owner's risk
	Lowestoft / Yarmouth	41 8	Station to station, owner's risk, minimum 1 cwt.
Herrings in brine	Hull	25 0	Collected and delivered, owner's risk
Kippers	Lowestoft / Yarmouth	36 8	Station to station, owner's risk, minimum 1 cwt.

B B

RAILWAY RATES FOR PROVISIONS TO BIRMINGHAM—cont.

Description of provisions	Three places from which principally received at Birmingham	Rate per ton s. d.	Condition of rate
Mackerel	Fleetwood	24 2	Collected and delivered
Hominy (grain)	Liverpool	11 3	Collected and delivered, 4 tons
Lentils	London	19 2	Collected and delivered
Meat	London	40 0	,, ,,
	Birkenhead	30 0	Delivered in Birmingham, 10-cwt. lots and upwards
	Liverpool	37 6	Delivered in Birmingham, smaller quantities
Oatmeal	Alford	30 10	4-ton loads, station to station
	Annan	22 6	,, ,, ,,
	Carlisle	27 6	Collected and delivered, small quantities
Onions	Leighton	12 6	Station to station, 1 ton and under 2 tons
		10 0	Station to station, 2 tons packed, 3 tons loose
	Bedford	11 8	Station to station, 2 tons packed, 3 tons loose
		15 0	Station to station, 1 ton and under 2 tons
	Biggleswade	11 8	Station to station, 2 tons packed, 3 tons loose
		10 0	Station to station, 4-ton lots
Onions	Cardiff	10 0	,, ,, 2-ton lots
	Liverpool	14 2	Delivered in Birmingham, 2-ton lots
	Goole	17 6	Station to station, 2-ton lots
	Grimsby	15 0	,, ,, 4-ton lots
Potatoes (old)	Newport Salop	6 8	,, ,, ,,
		7 6	,, ,, 2-ton lots
	Gamlingay Sandy	11 8	,, ,, 2 tons packed, 3 tons loose
	Potton	10 0	Station to station, 4-ton lots
Rice	Liverpool	18 9	Collected and delivered
	London	19 2	,, ,,
		15 6	,, ,, 2-ton lots
Sago	Liverpool	20 10	Delivered in Birmingham
	London	22 6	Collected and delivered
Sugar (in cases, casks, or bags)	London	20 0	,, ,,
	Liverpool	17 6	Delivered in Birmingham
	Greenock	25 0	Collected and delivered
	Hull	20 0	,, ,,
Tinned milk	Goole	25 0	,, ,,
	London	28 4	,, ,,
	Middlewich	18 4	,, ,,
Treacle	London	22 6	,, ,,
	Liverpool	17 6	Delivered in Birmingham

APPENDIX B. (see p. 243).

COMPARISON BETWEEN ENGLISH AND AMERICAN RATES.

[I am indebted for the American rates to the courtesy of the officials of the several lines, and they have been supplemented by the corresponding English rates in the rate-office at Euston.]

RATES IN AMERICA. Anthracite Coal per ton			RATES IN ENGLAND. Anthracite Coal per ton		
	s.	d.		s.	d.
Wilkesbarre to Philadelphia, 105 miles (Company's waggons)	7	0	Pantyffynon to Oakengates, 112 miles (Owner's waggons)	6	4
Wilkesbarre to New York, 150 miles (Company's waggons)	7	0	Pantyffynon to Birkenhead, 153 miles (Owner's waggons). The wagon hire would be 9d. to 1s. per ton, which would bring our rate to the same practically as the American rate. There are also rates for coal as follows:	6	4
			Bedworth to London, 107 miles, (Poplar), (Owner's waggons) Waggon hire 9d.	5	3
			Tamworth to London, 115 miles (Poplar), (Owner's waggons) Waggon hire 9d.	5	7
			[1] Wigan to Birmingham, 90 miles (Owner's waggons)	4	3
			[1] Wigan to Coventry (Counden Road), 106 miles (Owner's waggons)	5	7
			[1] Wigan to London, 201 miles (Poplar), (Owner's waggons)	7	2

[1] We do not find waggons for conveying coal in this district, but the charge would probably be from 9d. to 1s. per ton.

MILK.

On the New York, Ontario and Western Railway, milk is carried into New York, distances of from 56 to 244 miles, at an uniform rate of 32 cents per can of 40 quarts, or 1·60d. per gallon.

On the New York, New Haven, and Hartford, the rate for any distance is 35 cents pe can or 1¾d. per gollon.

The scale of charges generally in operation for milk on the London and North Western Railway gives for distances over 50 miles 1½d. per gallon, at Owner's risk.

Their complete scale is as follows, viz.:

	Per imperial gallon	Minimum charge
Up to 20 miles	¾d.	9d.
20 to 50	1d.	1s.
Above 50	1½d.	1s.

Station to station, Owner's risk.

DRAPERY.

RATES IN AMERICA.

	Per ton s. d.
Chicago, Burlington, and Quincy Railway, 50 miles, 31 cents. per 100 lbs.	28 6

RATES IN ENGLAND.

	Per ton s. d.
Manchester and Lancaster, 51 miles, 20s. per ton, collected and delivered in lots over 500 lbs.	20 0

FRUIT.

By special fast trains, station to station, exclusive of loading and unloading.

	s. d.
Kirkwood to Wilmington, 17 miles. Peaches less than car-loads.	
14 cents per 100 lbs. (Owner's risk)	12 11
21 cents per 100 lbs. (Company's risk)	19 4
Wyoming to Wilmington, 51 miles. Peaches less than car-loads.	
28 cents per 100 lbs. (Owner's risk)	25 9
42 cents per 100 lbs. (Company's risk)	38 8
Wyoming to Philadelphia, 87 miles. Peaches less than car-loads.	
35 cents per 100 lbs. (Owner's risk)	32 2
52½ cents per 100 lbs. (Company's risk)	48 4
Cambridge to Wilmington, 117 miles. Peaches less than car-loads.	
47 cents per 100 lbs. (Owner's risk)	43 3
70½ cents per 100 lbs. (Company's risk)	64 10
Kirkwood to Jersey City, 141 miles. Peaches less than car-loads.	
60 cents per 100 lbs. (Owner's risk)	55 2
90 cents per 100 lbs. (Company's risk)	82 10

By ordinary goods trains including loading and unloading, also collection and delivery, unless otherwise stated.

	s. d.
Rickmansworth to London, 19 miles. Plums, currants, and gooseberries in 10-cwt. lots. (Company's risk)	12 6
Broxton to Manchester, 46 miles. Gooseberries and plums in 10-cwt. lots. Delivered in Manchester (Company's risk)	12 6
Craven Arms to Manchester, 83 miles. Gooseberries and plums in 10-cwt. lots. (Company's risk)	21 8
Hereford to Manchester, 115 miles. Gooseberries and plums in 10-cwt. lots. (Company's risk)	24 2
Evesham to Manchester, 118 miles. Fruit in 10-cwt. lots. (Company's risk)	23 4
Wisbech to Manchester, 142 miles. Raspberries and Strawberries in lots over 500 lbs. (Owner's risk)	40 0
(Company's risk)	47 6
Stanbridgeford to Manchester, 147 miles. Ripe fruit including plums and gooseberries in 10-cwt. lots. (Company's risk)	29 2

APPENDICES

FRUIT—cont.

RATES IN AMERICA.	Per ton s. d.	RATES IN ENGLAND.	Per ton s. d.
Cambridge to Philadelphia, 153 miles. Peaches less than car-loads.		Tring to Manchester, 152 miles. Cherries in lots over 500 lbs. (Company's risk)	40 0
57 cents per 100 lbs. (Owner's risk)	52 5		
85½ cents per 100 lbs. (Company's risk)	78 8		
		By passenger train, including loading and unloading; also delivery.	
Delmar to Jersey City, 221 miles. Peaches less than car-loads.		Swanley to Manchester, 201 miles. Strawberries in 10-cwt. lots. (Owner's risk)	70 0
80 cents per 100 lbs. (Owner's risk)	73 7	Orpington to Manchester, 203 miles. Strawberries in 10-cwt. lots. (Owner's risk)	70 0
		Halstead to Manchester, 206 miles. Strawberries in 10-cwt. lots. (Owner's risk)	70 0
		Sevenoaks to Manchester, 209 miles. Strawberries in 10-cwt. lots. (Owner's risk)	70 0
		Rainham to Manchester, 222 miles. Cherries in 10-cwt. lots. (Owner's risk)	70 0
		Sittingbourne to Manchester, 228 miles. Cherries in 10-cwt. lots. (Owner's risk)	70 0
Cambridge to Jersey City, 241 miles. Peaches less than car-loads.		Faversham to Manchester, 235 miles. Cherries in 10-cwt. lots. (Owner's risk)	70 0
85 cents per 100 lbs. (Owner's risk)	78 2	Selling to Manchester, 239 miles. Cherries in 10-cwt. lots. (Owner's risk)	70 0

FISH.

Elizabeth City to Wilmington, 274 miles. Fish, fresh.		Tynemouth to London, 279 miles. Fresh fish (crabs, fresh cod, ling, haddocks, whiting, halibut, skate, mackerel, plaice, coal fish, gurnets, eels, flounders) and fresh herrings.	
1 dollar 54 cents per box or barrel of 300 lbs.	47 3		
80 cents per ½ box of 160 lbs.	46 0		
50 cents per ¼ box of 80 lbs.	57 6	Station to station, Owner's risk, 3-ton loads, by passenger or special fish train	40 0

FISH—cont.

RATES IN AMERICA.	Per ton s. d.	RATES IN ENGLAND.	Per ton s. d.
Edenton to Philadelphia, 338 miles. Fish, fresh.		Berwick to London, 338 miles. Fresh herrings.	
1 dollar 79 cents per box or barrel of 300 lbs.	54 11	Station to station, Owner's risk, 3-ton loads, by goods train.	40 0
90 cents per ½ box of 160 lbs.	51 9	Fresh herrings and sprats, crabs, fresh cod, ling, haddocks, whiting, halibut, skate, mackerel, plaice, coal fish, gurnets, eels, flounders. Station to station, Owner's risk, 3-ton loads, by passenger or special fish train	45 0
50 cents per ¼ box of 80 lbs.	57 6		
Elizabeth City to Trenton, 342 miles. Fish, fresh.		Burnmouth to London, 343 miles. Fresh herrings and sprats, crabs, fresh cod, ling, haddocks, whiting, halibut, skate, mackerel, plaice, coal fish, gurnets, eels, flounders. Station to station, Owner's risk, 3-ton loads, by passenger or special fish train	45 0
1 dollar 54 cents per box or barrel of 300 lbs.	47 3		
80 cents per ½ box of 160 lbs.	46 0		
50 cents per ¼ box of 80 lbs.	57 6		
Edenton to Trenton, 370 miles. Fish, fresh.		Drem to London, 377 miles. Fresh herrings and sprats, crabs, fresh cod, ling, haddocks, whiting, halibut, skate, mackerel, plaice, coal fish, gurnets, eels, flounders. Station to station, Owner's risk, 3-ton loads, by passenger or special fish train	50 0
1 dollar 79 cents per box or barrel of 300 lbs.	54 11		
90 cents per ½ box of 160 lbs.	51 9		
50 cents per ¼ box of 80 lbs.	57 6		

POTATOES.

Washington and Tarboro, 254 miles.		Potton and Swansea, 260 miles. Valley and London, 259 miles.	
Potatoes, 41 cents per barrel of 180 lbs. (Owner's risk).	20 11	Potatoes, old, 4-ton lots (Company's risk).	19 2
Potatoes, 1 dollar 23 cents per barrel of 180 lbs. (Company's risk).	62 10		
Philadelphia and Morehead City, 526 miles.		London and Aberdeen, 539 miles.	
Potatoes, 65½ cents per barrel of 180 lbs. (Owner's risk).	33 6	Potatoes, old, 4-ton lots (Company's risk).	30 0
Potatoes, 1 dollar 96½ cents per barrel of 180 lbs. (Company's risk)	100 5		

APPENDICES

POTATOES—*cont.*

RATES IN AMERICA.	Per ton s. d.	RATES IN ENGLAND.	Per ton s. d.
Wilmington and Newbern, 454 miles.		London and Perth, 449 miles.	
Potatoes, 55½ cents per barrel of 180 lbs. (Owner's risk)	28 4	Potatoes, old, 4-ton lots (Company's risk)	27 6
Potatoes, 1 dollar 66½ cents per barrel of 180 lbs. (Company's risk)	85 1		

APPLES.

Washington and Tarboro, 254 miles.		Liverpool and Glasgow, 220 miles.	
Apples, 41 cents per barrel of 180 lbs. (Owner's risk)	20 11	Apples in lots over 500 lbs. including cartage in Scotland (Company's risk)	18 4
Apples, 1 dollar 23 cents per barrel of 180 lbs. (Company's risk)	62 10		
		Liverpool and Dundee, 292 miles	
		Apples in lots over 500 lbs. including cartage in Scotland (Company's risk)	23 4

TOMATOES.

Washington and Tarboro, 254 miles.		Liverpool and Glasgow, 220 miles.	
Tomatoes, 41½ cents per barrel of 150 lbs. (Owner's risk)	25 5	Tomatoes in cases in lots over 500 lbs., including cartage in Glasgow (Company's risk)	18 4
Tomatoes, 20½ cents per bushel box of 50 lbs. (Owner's risk)	37 9		
Tomatoes, 1 dollar 24½ cents per barrel of 150 lbs. (Company's risk)	76 4		
Tomatoes, 61½ cents per bushel box of 50 lbs. (Company's risk)	113 2		

ORANGES

Callahan to Washington, 827 miles. 50 cents per box of 80 lbs. (Owner's risk)	57 6	London to Wick, 754 miles Collected and delivered (Company's risk)	60 0

MISCELLANEOUS LOCAL RATES.

RATES IN AMERICA. *New York and Bedford, 40 miles.*			RATES IN ENGLAND. *London and Leighton, 39 miles 28 chains.*		
Description	Class in less than carload quantities	Rate per ton minimum charge 25 cents	Description	Class	Rate per ton in lots over 500 lbs. unless otherwise stated
		s. d.			s. d.
Grain in sacks, 10 cents per 100 lbs.	5	9 2	Grain in sacks, 4-ton lots	Special	5 10
Potatoes (Owner's risk) 12 cents per 100 lbs.	4	11 0	Potatoes, old, 4-ton lots (Company's risk)	do.	5 10
Carrots, parsnips and turnips (Owner's risk) 12 cents per 100 lbs.	4	11 0	Carrots, turnips and parsnips for cattle feeding, 5-ton lots (Company's risk)	do.	5 0
Ale and porter in wood (Owner's risk, fermenting, freezing, or leakage) actual weight 15 cents per 100 lbs.	3	13 10	Ale and porter in casks, 2-ton lots (Company's risk)	1	9 2
Hay pressed in bales (Owner's risk, fire and water) 20 cents per 100 lbs.	1	18 5	Hay, hydraulic or machine pressed, minimum charge as for 2½ tons per waggon (Company's risk)	Special	6 8
			Hay (Owner's risk, minimum) 30 cwt. per waggon	2	10 10
Straw pressed in bales (Owner's risk, fire and water) 20 cents per 100 lbs.	1	18 5	Straw, hydraulic or machine pressed, minimum charge as for 2½ tons per waggon (Company's risk)	Special	6 8
			Straw (Owner's risk, minimum) 20 cwt. per waggon	3	12 6
Fruit green, not otherwise specified (Owner's risk) 20 cents per 100 lbs.	1	18 5	Ripe fruit (Company's risk)	3	[1] 16 8
Paper-hangings in bundles (Owner's risk chafing) 18 cents per 100 lbs.	2	16 7	Paper-hangings (Company's risk)	2	[1] 16 8
Paper-hangings in boxes 20 cents per 100 lbs.	1	18 5			

[1] This rate includes collection and delivery within usual limits.

MISCELLANEOUS LOCAL RATES—cont.

RATES IN AMERICA. *New York and Bedford, 40 miles.*				RATES IN ENGLAND. *London and Leighton, 39 miles 28 chains.*		
Description	Class in less than carload quantities	Rate per ton minimum charge 25 cents		Description	Class	Rate per ton in lots over 500 lbs. unless otherwise stated
		s.	d.			s. d
Meats, dressed fresh, of all kinds at Owner's risk and prepaid, 20 cents per 100 lbs. . .	1	18	5	Meat, fresh (Company's risk)	4	²20 0
Beef, lamb, mutton, venison, pork louis and pork cut in pieces (other than dressed, hogs whole) 20 cents per 100 lbs.	1	18	5			
Hogs, dressed, whole, 18 cents per 100 lbs. .	2	16	7			
Tea (Owner's risk, sifting) 20 cents per 100 lbs.	1	18	5	Tea (Company's risk) .	3	²18 4
Butter in wood, 18 cents per 100 lbs.	2	16	7	Butter in casks or boxes, or in tubs or cools with wooden lids . .	2	²16 8
Butter in cans or pails, packed in cases, 18 cents per 100 lbs. .	2	16	7	Butter in crocks, in wood, or in crocks when packed with straw in baskets . .	3	²18 4
Butter in crocks or jars securely packed in cases (Owner's risk, breakage) 20 cents per 100 lbs.	1	18	5	Butter in crocks . . .	5	²26 8
Butter in crocks and in covered baskets (Owner's risk), 40 cents per 100 lbs. . .	¹D1	36	10	Butter in baskets, flats or hampers, or in tubs or cools without lids (Company's risk) . .	4	²21 8
Chairs, bamboo, rattan, reed or willow, 80 cents per 100 lbs. . .	4t1	73	7	Furniture	5	²26 8
Furniture, bamboo, rattan, reed or willow, 80 cents per 100 lbs. .	4t1	73	7			
Book racks, bamboo, crated or boxed, 80 cents per 100 lbs. . .	4t1	73	7			
Cribs, bamboo, crated or boxed, 80 cents per 100 lbs.	4t1	73	7			

¹ D1 means double first-class rate. 4t1 means four times first-class rate, and so on.

² This rate includes collection and delivery within usual limits.

MISCELLANEOUS LOCAL RATES—*cont.*

RATES IN AMERICA.
New York and Bedford, 40 miles.

Description	Class in less than carload quantities	Rate per ton minimum charge 25 cents s. d.
Music stands, bamboo, crated or boxed, 80 cents per 100 lbs. . .	[1]4t1	73 7
Sofas or tête-à-têtes, bamboo, crated or boxed, 80 cents per 100 lbs.	4t1	73 7
Stands, tables, towel racks, bamboo, crated or boxed, 80 cents per 100 lbs.	4t1	73 7
Baskets in cases, 60 cents per 100 lbs. . .	3t1	55 2
Baskets in bales, crates or hampers, not nested in bundles, 80 cents per 100 lbs.	4t1	73 7
Baskets not otherwise specified, nested in bundles, 40 cents per 100 lbs.	D1	36 10
Baskets over-handled in bundles, with ends placed in each other, 80 cents per 100 lbs. .	4t1	73 7
Baskets over-handled, covers, and handles taken off and packed separately, and the baskets nested in bundles, 40 cents per 100 lbs.	D1	36 10
Stave, splint, rattan or willow nested in bundles, or crates, 30 cents per 100 lbs.	1½	27 7
Animals stuffed in boxes (released) 60 cents per 100 lbs.	3t1	55 2

[1] D1 means double first-class rate. 4t1 means four times first-class rate, and so on.

RATES IN ENGLAND.
London and Leighton, 39 miles 28 chains.

Description	Class	Rate per ton in lots over 500 lbs. unless otherwise stated s. d.
Furniture	5	[2]26 8
	5	[2]26 8 with exceptions at lower rates
Animals stuffed in cases (Company's risk) . .	5	[2]26 8

[2] This rate includes collection and delivery within usual limits.

Spottiswoode & Co. Printers, New-street Square, London.

WORKS BY MR. ACWORTH.

4th Edition, with 50 Illustrations. 8vo. 14s.

THE RAILWAYS OF ENGLAND. By W. M. Acworth.

NORTH WESTERN.	SOUTH WESTERN.
MIDLAND.	GREAT WESTERN.
GREAT NORTHERN.	GREAT EASTERN.
MANCHESTER, SHEFFIELD, & LINCOLN.	BRIGHTON & SOUTH COAST.
	CHATHAM & DOVER.
NORTH EASTERN.	SOUTH EASTERN.

'Really a most readable volume. The writer has seized on the points most likely to interest his readers.'—SPECTATOR.

'For indefatigable search after the truth about our railroad system, for picturesque and interesting statement, for discriminating judgment, and for patient investigation of detail, "The Railways of England" stands unequalled in railway literature. It is a valuable estimate of the work which each of the principal companies has done for itself and for the travelling public.'—GUARDIAN.

With a Map of the Scottish Railway System. Crown 8vo. 5s.

THE RAILWAYS OF SCOTLAND. Their present position, with a glance of their past, and a forecast of their future. By W. M. ACWORTH.

'Mr. Acworth's "Scottish Railways" forms an interesting and valuable supplement to the earlier work on English lines; interesting alike to the general reader, the traveller, and the fortunate or luckless holder of railway stock. In some respects there is a marked difference between railways north and south of the Border. The network of iron rails displayed on the map of England represents the invention, enterprise, and energy of a long generation; the Scotch system, in plan if not in execution, was the project of a single year. Scotland, with three-fifths the area of England, can boast of hardly more than one-fifth of our railway mileage. While England, however, is strewn with the wrecks of wretched little companies, shattered to pieces in a vain attempt to compete with overpowering rivals, in Scotland there is not a single independent company paying no dividend.'—ST. JAMES'S GAZETTE.

THE AMERICAN RAILWAYS.

THE RAILWAYS OF AMERICA. Their Construction, Development, Management, and Appliances. By VARIOUS WRITERS. With an Introduction by THOMAS M. COOLEY. Chairman of the Inter-State Commerce Commission. With 200 Illustrations. Royal 8vo. 31s. 6d.

'A great book may be a great evil, but after this we must at least admit that it s here a necessary one, and that 450 pages, even of the most imperial of octavos, is not too large a space in which to rise to the height of so great an argument. Nor is the impression upon our minds produced by this book one of mere size. On the contrary, as we turn over its pages, or even as we glance through the headings of its different chapters, we are struck with the diversity of the interests involved. In conclusion, we might say to those who are likely to visit the States that they would be wise to read this book, for by so doing they will give a new interest to long railway journeys which might otherwise be monotonous. To those who will stop at home we would say that they are yet more bound to read it, for it would be hard to find another work which gives so good an account of what may fairly be said to be the most important industry of the most important country of the world, or so clear an insight into the customary way of life of a very large section of its people.'—THE TIMES.

JOHN MURRAY, Albemarle Street.

THE GREAT METROPOLIS.

Now ready. 3 vols. Medium 8vo. £3 3s.

LONDON: PAST AND PRESENT.

ITS HISTORY, ASSOCIATIONS, AND TRADITIONS.

By HENRY B. WHEATLEY, F.S.A.

BASED ON CUNNINGHAM'S HANDBOOK.

Library Edition, on Laid Paper.

'Vertue had taken much pains to ascertain the ancient extent of London, and the site of its several large edifices at various periods. Among his papers I find many traces relating to this matter. Such a subject, extended by historic illustrations, would be very amusing.'—HORACE WALPOLE ('ANECDOTES OF PAINTING').

'There is a French book called "Anecdotes des Rues de Paris." I had begun a similar book, "Anecdotes of the Streets of London." I intended, in imitation of the French original, to have pointed out the streets and houses where any remarkable event had happened; but I found the labour would be too great in collecting materials from various sources, and abandoned the design, after having written about ten or twelve pages.'—HORACE WALPOLE ('WALPOLIANA').

* *Critical Opinions on the Original Work.*

'It would be a great mistake to suppose that this work is a mere dry catalogue of streets, squares, and public buildings. That it is such a guide is certain, and the best and most complete of the kind we have seen: but it is a great deal more besides; it is a delightful literary companion, teeming not only with rare and valuable information, often quite new, but with stores of apposite quotation from our elder and modern writers, with quaint saws, anecdotes, and reminiscences of characters celebrated and notorious, and with every kind of illustration, historical, local, and personal.'—MORNING CHRONICLE.

'We can conceive no more welcome companion to an enlightened foreigner than this work with its laborious research, scrupulous exactness, alphabetical arrangement, and authorities from every imaginable source. As a piece of severe, compact, and finished structure, it is not to be surpassed.'—THE TIMES.

'Every spot in this thickly-peopled district has its description and anecdote; and every page conveys some information that is curious, interesting, or valuable—communicated necessarily in the most succinct, but, at the same time, in the most authentic manner. There is nothing merely speculative and fanciful—all is fact and substance. It will remain a lasting record of the past and present condition of our huge metropolis.'—ATHENÆUM.

'This is incomparably the most complete and reliable book that has been published on London, its streets and buildings, its past memories and long associations. It is a well-considered, well-digested, thoroughly well-informed book.'—THE EXAMINER.

'The work is so studded with quotations from the old poets and essayists, and with illustrations of bygone manners and historical events, that it may be taken up at any time for amusement as well as information. It is a sort of distillation from English history, anecdote, and biography, with a sprinkling of ancient gossip and scandal!'—INVERNESS COURIER.

JOHN MURRAY, Albemarle Street.

'The old Lord Treasurer Burleigh, if anyone came to the Lords of the Council for a license to travel, he would first examine him of England; and if he found him ignorant, would bid him stay at home and know his own country first.'—THE COMPLEAT GENTLEMAN, BY HENRY PEACHAM, 1622.

ENGLAND AND WALES.

New and Revised Edition (1890). With Map. Post 8vo. 12s.

MURRAY'S
HANDBOOK FOR TRAVELLERS IN ENGLAND AND WALES.

ALPHABETICALLY ARRANGED.

With Descriptions of Places, Railway Stations, Hotels, &c.

'MURRAY'S HANDBOOKS have always been distinguished for the high quality of their literary and architectural information. In the volume before us under each place-name is given a description of the place, railway stations, hotels, and excursions best deserving of the traveller's attention. It will thus be seen that such information is given as will suffice for all ordinary purposes. The book is likely to be of as much use in the library as a handy Gazetteer of home travel.'—LITERARY WORLD.

'This Handbook is a valuable companion to the traveller by road or rail throughout England. The places are all in alphabetical order as in a Gazetteer; only such names being given as belong to places of interest. This includes most places that anyone will care to learn about, and the book will, therefore, be a useful manual of reference for the library, no less than the pocket or travelling-bag.'—THE BOOKSELLER.

'This Handbook is one of the most useful works of its kind ever issued. There is no better or handier book for foreigners, and very few more instructive or entertaining works for Englishmen who take an interest in the topography and archæology of their own land.'—SCIENCE GOSSIP.

'MURRAY'S GUIDE BOOKS now cover nearly the whole of the Continent, and constitute one of the great powers of Europe. Since Napoleon, no man's empire has been so wide. There is not an innkeeper who does not turn pale at the name of Murray.'—HILLIARD'S 'SIX MONTHS IN ITALY.'

'MR. MURRAY has succeeded in identifying his countrymen all the world over. Into every nook which an Englishman can penetrate he carries his RED HANDBOOK. He trusts to his MURRAY because it is thoroughly English and reliable.'—THE TIMES.

JOHN MURRAY, Albemarle Street.

MR. MURRAY'S LIST.

SIR ROBERT PEEL: his Early Political Life as Secretary for Ireland, 1812-18, and Secretary of State, 1822-27. Published by his Trustees, Viscount Hardinge and Right Hon. Arthur Wellesley Peel. Edited by CHARLES STUART PARKER, M.P. With Portrait. 8vo.

A PUBLISHER AND HIS FRIENDS: Memoir and Correspondence of the late John Murray, with an Account of the Origin and Progress of the House, 1768-1843. By SAMUEL SMILES, LL.D. With Portraits. 2 vols. 8vo. 32s.

A MEMOIR OF JENNY LIND: her Early Art-Life and Dramatic Career, 1820-51. From Original Documents, Letters, Diaries, &c., in the possession of Mr. Goldschmidt. By Canon SCOTT HOLLAND and W. S. ROCKSTRO. With Portraits and Illustrations. 2 vols. 8vo.

THE BARONETAGE OF GREAT BRITAIN: a History, a Criticism, and a Vindication. Including all ascertained facts as to the foundation of the Order, with curious particulars as to the varied fortunes of certain titles and their holders, and thoughts on the Degeneracy of the Order. By ROBERT DENNIS. Crown 8vo.

THE QUEEN'S COMMISSION: how to Obtain, and how to Use it; with practical information on the cost and prospects of a Military Career. Intended for the use of Cadets and Subalterns and their Parents. By Captain G. J. YOUNGHUSBAND, of the Queen's Own Corps of Guides; Author of 'Frays and Forays.' Crown 8vo. 6s.

FERGUSSON'S HISTORY OF THE MODERN STYLES OF ARCHITECTURE. *A New Edition, Revised and Enlarged.* With a special account of Architecture in America. By ROBERT KERR, Professor of Architecture, King's Coll., London. With 400 Illustrations. 2 vols. Medium 8vo. 42s.

FERGUSSON'S HISTORY OF INDIAN AND EASTERN ARCHITECTURE. *New Edition.* With 400 Illustrations. Medium 8vo.

MEMOIRS AND LETTERS OF SIDNEY GILCHRIST THOMAS, Inventor. Edited by R. W. BURNIE, Barrister-at-Law. With Portraits. Crown 8vo.

THE LIVES OF TWELVE GOOD MEN. By J. W. BURGON, B.D., late Dean of Chichester; sometime Fellow of Oriel College. *New Edition.* With Portraits of the Author and of the Twelve. One Volume. 8vo. 16s.

MARTIN JOSEPH ROUTH.	RICHARD GRESWELL.
HUGH JAMES ROSE.	HENRY OCTAVIUS COXE.
CHARLES MARRIOTT.	HENRY LONGUEVILLE MANSEL.
EDWARD HAWKINS.	WILLIAM JACOBSON.
SAMUEL WILBERFORCE.	CHARLES PAGE EDEN.
RICHARD LYNCH COTTON.	CHARLES LONGUET HIGGINS.

JOHN MURRAY, Albemarle Street.

MR. MURRAY'S LIST.

ADVENTURES IN THE LIFE OF COUNT ALBERT OF ERBACH. A True Story. Translated from the German. By H.R.H. Princess Beatrice. *Second Edition.* With Portraits and Woodcuts. Crown 8vo. 10s. 6d.

IMPRESSIONS OF A TENDERFOOT, during a Journey in search of Sport in the Far West. By Lady Seymour (Mrs. Algernon St. Maur). With Illustrations. Crown 8vo. 12s.

A PLEA FOR LIBERTY: an Argument against Socialism and Socialistic Legislation. With an Introduction by Herbert Spencer, and Essays by various writers. Edited by Thomas Mackay, Author of 'The English Poor.' *Second Edition.* 8vo. 12s.

A DICTIONARY OF GREEK AND ROMAN ANTIQUITIES; including the Laws, Institutions, Domestic Usages, Painting, Sculpture, Music, the Drama, &c. Edited by Wm. Smith, LL.D., W. Wayte, M.A., and G. E. Marindin, M.A. *Third Edition, Revised and Enlarged.* Vol. I. (to be completed in 2 vols.). Medium 8vo. 31s. 6d. each.

MARCIA. A New Novel. By W. E. Norris. *Fourth Edition.* 3 vols. Crown 8vo. 31s. 6d.

A RIDE THROUGH ASIA MINOR AND ARMENIA. With Sketches of the Character, Manners, and Customs of both the Mussulman and Christian Inhabitants. By H. C. Barkley, Author of 'Between the Danube and the Black Sea,' &c. Crown 8vo. 10s. 6d.

STUDIES IN EUROPEAN HISTORY; being Academical Addresses. By the late Professor Döllinger, D.D. Translated by Margaret Warre. With Portrait. 8vo. 14s.

ELECTRICITY; the Science of the 19th Century. A Sketch for General Readers. By E. M. Caillard. With Illustrations. Crown 8vo. 7s. 6d.

ESTHER VANHOMRIGH. A New Novel. By Mrs. Woods, Author of 'A Village Tragedy.' Now appearing in 'Murray's Magazine.'

FORTIFICATION; its Past Achievements, Recent Development, and Future Progress. By Major G. Sydenham Clarke, C.M.G., Royal Engineers. With Illustrations. Medium 8vo. 21s.

LUX MUNDI. A Series of Studies in the Religion of the Incarnation. By Various Writers. Edited by Rev. Charles Gore, M.A. *Eleventh Edition.* 8vo. 14s.

LIFE OF ALEXANDER N. SOMERVILLE, D.D., in Scotland, Ireland, India, America, Africa, Australasia, and the Chief Countries of Europe (1813-89). By George Smith, LL.D. Portrait and Map. Post 8vo. 9s.

JOHN MURRAY Albemarle Street.

CABINET EDITIONS OF STANDARD WORKS.

GROTE'S HISTORICAL WORKS. 14 vols. Crown 8vo. 5s. each.
  I. HISTORY OF GREECE.
  II. PLATO AND OTHER COMPANIONS OF SOCRATES. 4 vols.

HALLAM'S HISTORICAL WORKS. 10 vols. Crown 8vo. 4s. each.
  I. HISTORY OF EUROPE DURING THE MIDDLE AGES. 3 vols.
  II. CONSTITUTIONAL HISTORY OF ENGLAND. 3 vols.
  III. LITERARY HISTORY OF EUROPE. 4 vols.

MILMAN'S (DEAN) HISTORICAL WORKS. Post 8vo. 15 vols. 4s. each.
  I. HISTORY OF THE JEWS. 3 vols.
  II. HISTORY OF EARLY CHRISTIANITY. 3 vols.
  III. HISTORY OF LATIN CHRISTIANITY. 9 vols.

MOTLEY'S HISTORICAL WORKS. 6 vols. Crown 8vo. 6s. each.
  I. HISTORY OF THE UNITED NETHERLANDS. 4 vols.
  II. LIFE AND DEATH OF JOHN OF BARNEVELD. 2 vols.

ROBERTSON'S (CANON) HISTORY OF THE CHRISTIAN CHURCH; from the Apostolic Age to the Reformation, 1517. 8 vols. Crown 8vo. 6s. each.

STANHOPE'S (EARL) HISTORY OF ENGLAND; from the Reign of Queen Anne to the Treaty of Versailles, 1783. 9 vols. Crown 8vo. 6s. each.

STANLEY'S (DEAN) WORKS. 9 vols. Crown 8vo. 6s. each.
  I. THE JEWISH CHURCH; from Abraham to the Christian Era. 3 vols.
  II. THE EASTERN CHURCH.
  III. MEMORIALS OF CANTERBURY.
  IV. LIFE OF DR. ARNOLD. 2 vols.
  V. CHRISTIAN INSTITUTIONS.
  VI. CHURCH AND STATE.

CAMPBELL'S (LORD) BIOGRAPHICAL WORKS. 14 vols. Crown 8vo. 6s. each.
  I. THE LORD CHANCELLORS OF ENGLAND. 10 vols.
  II. THE CHIEF JUSTICES OF ENGLAND. 4 vols.

JOHN MURRAY, Albemarle Street.

www.ingramcontent.com/pod-product-compliance
Lightning Source LLC
Chambersburg PA
CBHW032011220426
43664CB00006B/207